SOUTHERN CALIFORNIA
DOG
OWNERS
GUIDE

THE STARTER BOOK

BOB AND LAURA CHRISTIANSEN
CANINE LEARNING CENTER
CARLSBAD, CALIFORNIA

Printed in the United States of America

Published by

Canine Learning Center

Post Office Box 2010
Carlsbad, California 92018
619 931-1820

Library of Congress Catalog Card No. 94-94624
ISBN 1-884421-88-1
Typesetting and design by **Word Wizards**®, Oceanside, California
Cover design and graphics by **Patton Brothers**®, San Diego, California

DISCLAIMER

Every precaution has been taken to avoid errors, mistakes and omissions. No liability is accepted for any errors, mistakes or omissions which may occur, no matter how caused.

CAUTION

Dog Owners Guide is unable to assume any responsibility or liability for any listing. Inclusion in this publication does not constitute an endorsement, recommendation or guarantee by the authors or the publisher for any product, organization, or person. This publication is for general instructive use only. Readers are advised to make their own inquiries and to seek out conscientious service providers who subscribe to high standards. *Dog Owners Guide* reserves the right to refuse publication to anyone not acting in the best interests of dogs.

Books are available at special discounts for bulk purchases to dog-related charitable activities, educational groups, breed clubs or breeders.

TO THE READER

This book is intended to be a helpful all-inclusive local resource guide for dog lovers in Southern California. Every major facet of dog ownership is covered and at your fingertips. In writing this book, we have attempted to put forth useful, accurate information that is readily accessible to all owners, especially those who are contemplating acquiring a dog or who have recently purchased a puppy and are inexperienced in what to expect. Most dog owners have the best intentions when they obtain a cute little puppy, however, frustrations can soon develop and frustration can soon lead to anger, neglect and abandonment. Don't let that happen to you! We sincerely hope and believe the information in this book will help ease your access to dog-related organizations, help you understand dog behavior and help you achieve a successful relationship with your dog.

We would like to thank all those animal lovers who have helped contribute to this book: Ann Wilde, Mary Wamsley of the Los Angeles SPCA / SC Humane Society, Claire Newick, Helen Hamilton, Diane Calkins, Captain Theresa Williams of the San Diego Animal Control, Ellyn Sisser, Dr. Robert Cartin DVM, Mission Animal Hospital, Helen Woodward Animal Center, and all the breeders and breed clubs. Special thanks to All Creatures Hospital, Dr. Michael Mulvany DVM and Jean Hamilton for their input.

We would like to hear what you think. If you have any ways of improving this publication, please write to:

Canine Learning Center
P.O. Box 2010
Carlsbad, CA 92018

Contents

Ten Things A Dog Asks Of Its Family

1. My life is likely to last 10 to 15 years. Any permanent separation from you will be painful for me. Remember that before you buy me.

2. Do not break my spirit with harsh treatment. Your patience and understanding will more quickly teach me the things you would have me learn.

3. Place your trust in me, it's crucial for my well-being.

4. Don't be angry with me for long, and don't lock me up as a punishment. You have your work, your entertainment, and your friends, I have only you and I like being with you.

5. Talk to me. Even if I don't understand your words I understand the tone of your voice when you are speaking to me, especially when you use friendly tones.

6. Be aware that I am normally a social animal; however, I need to make positive associations at a young age to feel confident and well-adjusted around other dogs and humans.

7. Remember that I was bred for activity, both mental and physical, and I enjoy playing games, taking walks and an occasional good run.

8. Before you scold me for being uncooperative, obstinate, or lazy, ask yourself if something may be bothering me. Perhaps I'm not getting the right food. I may need medical attention, or I may just be getting old. But keep in mind I respond very well to praise.

9. Take care of me when I get old; you, too, will grow old.

10. Remember that I only want to love and please you so treat me kindly. No heart is more grateful.

1

Should You Get A Dog?

Things to Consider Before Deciding on a New Dog

1. What breed will you choose? Purebred or mixed breed? Each breed was bred for certain functions and all have different exercise, training, and grooming requirements. Mixed breeds make wonderful pets. The trick is to find the right size, weight, coat and *temperament* to fit your family. Purebred dogs are genetically more predictable.

2. Who will be the one to walk, feed, clean up after, train, play with and groom the dog, get him licensed and provide medical care? Be realistic, it's a job for adults or responsible older children. If you have children, can you teach them to be respectful of the new puppy?

3. Have you considered the costs involved in caring for a dog, like food, equipment, vet bills, a license and insurance? (Min. $300.)

4. Do you have permission from your landlord, preferably in writing?

5. How will you teach him the rules of the house? Chewing, barking, digging, housesoiling, etc., are normal dog behaviors. Dogs usually continue these behaviors until effectively trained. Can your family accept this and be patient, kind and consistent during the teaching process?

6. Do you have enough space to house the dog properly? How will you keep the dog under control? Barking and free-roaming pets are a nuisance to neighbors, endanger the dog, and against the law.

7. Will you mind hair shedding, fleas and odors (varies from dog to dog), or will it annoy and burden you? Do you, your friends or relatives have an allergic reaction to pet hair?

8. Will you be a responsible pet owner by providing vaccinations and spaying or neutering your pet?

9. Do you have enough time and energy for daily activities? Will it be difficult to spend the time to train, exercise and groom? Will the pet blend into your routine or will it become an annoyance or burden?

10. Do you have the emotional stability and staying power to be a responsible owner for the lifetime of your dog?

Dog Facts

There are 52.3 million dogs that live in the US, 37.9% of all households own dogs, 1.5 dogs average per household.

Each year 8.4 million dogs are euthanized, that means one every 3.7 seconds.

Of the estimated 52.3 million dogs, a little less than 27% end-up in shelters.

Of the 13.9 million, 44% or 6.1 million are surrendered by owners.

Over 56% or 7.8 million are picked-up as strays.

Approximately 60% of all dogs entering a shelter are euthanized, 15% reclaimed, 25% adopted.

One out of five dogs born finds a permanent home.

Twenty-five to forty percent of shelter dogs are purebred.

There are approximately 5.7 million dogs in the state of California (35.7% of all households).

Reasons for Surrender

1. Landlord objects to complaints from other tenants — behavior problems
2. Not enough time for the dog
3. Owner moves

What You Can Do to Solve Pet Overpopulation

1. Spay/Neuter your pet at an early age and encourage others to do the same.
2. Don't be an uneducated owner. Take a basic obedience dog class and learn fundamental dog behavior.

3. Safeguard your pets. Don't let your dog roam, especially if your pet is unaltered. Properly secure unspayed bitches (especially while they are in season) from unplanned matings. Most accidental litters are a result of roamers who meet up with bitches who are in season.

4. Make sure identification is in place and secured with an O ring. Dog licenses are the main way lost dogs get found.

5. Acquire your pet from a reputable local breeder or animal shelter.

6. Leave breeding to knowledgeable, experienced professional breeders who are dedicated to improving the standards of the breed.

7. Make a donation to a low-cost spay/neuter non-profit organization like Pet Assistance.

8. Take responsibility for your pet. If, for whatever reason, you need to give up your dog, make every effort to find a good home. Don't kid yourself into thinking someone will come to the shelter and give your dog a home on their farm. Statistics tell us that approximately 60% of all dogs that enter shelters will be euthanized.

9. If you are experiencing behavior problems, get the help of a trained professional. Call your veterinarian or pet store and ask for a referral to a good behaviorist or trainer. Many dog problems are unknowingly caused by minor owner handling errors.

10. If you are going to move, take the pet with you. Talk to your future landlord and explain that you have a well-behaved dog. Take an AKC Good Citizenship Test and show the certificate to your landlord. Offer to make a dog security deposit that will protect the owner from financial loss to his or her property.

11. If you never have bred before and you have the slightest inclination to breed your dog,

don't. Too many stray and unwanted dogs are the product of casual breedings or accidental breedings. When a dog is born from an unplanned litter, chances are it will be condemned to a life of misery, deprivation and death.

Note regarding early-age spaying/neutering: The following organizations endorse early-age (8-16 weeks) spay/neutering to stem the overpopulation of dogs and cats: the Humane Society of the United States (HSUS), the American Kennel Club (AKC) and the American Humane Association (AHA). The American Veterinary Medical Association (AVMA) supports the concept of early-age ovariohysterectomies/gonadectomies in dogs and cats.

Don't be part of the problem —
Be part of the solution!

2

The Breeds

AKC Popularity Ranking 1993

Rank	Breed	Size	Lbs.	Coat
1	Labrador Retriever	Large	55-75	Short
2	Rottweiler	Very Large	80-135	Short
3	German Shepherd Dog	Large	65-85	Medium
4	Cocker Spaniel	Small	25-28	Medium
5	Golden Retriever	Large	60-75	Medium
6	Poodle (Toy)	Miniature	8-10	Medium
6	Poodle (Standard)	Large	45-65	Medium
6	Poodle (Miniature)	Miniature	15-17	Medium
7	Beagle	Small	15-20	Short
8	Dachshund (Short-haired)	Small	16-22	Short
8	Dachshund (Long-haired)	Small	16-22	Medium
8	Dachshund (Wire-haired)	Small	16-22	Short
9	Dalmatian	Large	45-65	Short
10	Shetland Sheepdog	Miniature	16-18	Medium
11	Pomeranian	Miniature	3-7	Medium
12	Yorkshire Terrier	Miniature	5-7	Long
13	Shih Tzu	Miniature	12-15	Long
14	Miniature Schnauzer	Miniature	14-17	Short
15	Chow Chow	Large	60-70	Medium
16	Chihuahua (Long)	Miniature	5-6	Medium
16	Chihuahua (Smooth)	Miniature	5-6	Short
17	Boxer	Large	65-70	Short
18	Siberian Husky	Large	35-60	Medium
19	Doberman Pinscher	Large	60-75	Short
20	English Springer Spaniel	Medium	44-55	Medium
21	Basset Hound	Medium	40-60	Short
22	Chinese Shar-Pei	Medium	40-55	Short
23	Maltese	Miniature	4-6	Long
24	Lhasa Apso	Miniature	13-16	Long

Rank	Breed	Size	Lbs.	Coat
25	Boston Terrier	Small	13-25	Short
26	Pekingese	Miniature	12-14	Long
27	Collie (Rough)	Large	50-75	Long
27	Collie (Smooth)	Large	50-75	Short
28	Pug	Miniature	14-18	Short
29	Miniature Pinscher	Miniature	8-9	Short
30	German Shorthaired Pointer	Large	45-70	Short
31	Brittany	Medium	30-40	Medium
32	Bichon Frise	Small	11-15	Medium
33	Bulldog	Medium	40-50	Short
34	Akita (Japanese)	Very Large	75-100	Medium
35	Great Dane	Giant	120-150	Short
36	W. Highland White Terrier	Miniature	15-18	Medium
37	Scottish Terrier	Small	18-22	Medium
38	Corgi, Pembroke Welsh	Small	26-30	Short
39	Samoyed	Large	40-75	Medium
40	St. Bernard	Giant	145-165	Medium
41	Weimaraner	Large	55-85	Short
42	Alaskan Malamute	Large	75-85	Medium
43	Cairn Terrier	Miniature	13-14	Medium
44	Australian Shepherd	Large	45-65	Medium
45	Chesapeake Bay Retriever	Large	55-75	Short
46	Keeshond	Medium	35-40	Medium
47	Great Pyrenees Mountain Dog	Giant	90-115	Medium
48	Airedale Terrier	Medium	45-60	Short
49	Mastiff	Giant	170-180	Short
50	Schipperke	Miniature	15-17	Short
51	Old English Sheepdog	Very Large	90-100	Long
52	Newfoundland	Giant	120-150	Medium
53	Irish Setter	Large	60-70	Medium
54	Fox Terrier (Wire)	Small	16-18	Short
55	Norwegian Elkhound	Medium	45-55	Medium
56	Papillon	Miniature	7-8	Medium
57	Silky Terrier	Miniature	8-10	Long
58	Vizsla (Hungarian)	Medium	50-60	Short
59	Bullmastiff	Giant	100-130	Short
60	Italian Greyhound	Miniature	6-8	Short
61	Rhodesian Ridgeback	Large	65-75	Short
62	Bouvier des Flandres	Very Large	90-100	Medium
63	Whippet	Small	23-25	Short
64	Australian Cattle Dog	Medium	35-50	Short
65	American Eskimo Dogs (Std)	Small	25-35	Medium
66	Basenji	Small	22-24	Short

Rank	Breed	Size	Lbs.	Coat
67	Bloodhound	Very Large	80-110	Short
68	Soft Coated Wheaten Terrier	Medium	35-40	Long
69	Afghan Hound	Large	50-70	Long
70	German Wirehaired Pointer	Large	50-75	Medium
71	Bernese Mountain Dog	Very Large	75-105	Medium
72	Gordon Setter	Large	40-80	Medium
73	English Cocker Spaniel	Small	26-34	Medium
74	Borzoi	Very Large	60-105	Medium
75	Bull Terrier	Medium	40-59	Short
76	Irish Wolfhound	Giant	105-120	Medium
77	Giant Schnauzer	Large	75-95	Medium
78	Am. Staffordshire Terrier	Medium	40-70	Short
79	Japanese Chin	Miniature	4-9	Medium
80	Fox Terrier (Smooth)	Small	16-18	Short
81	Shiba Inu	Small	15-28	Medium
82	Chinese Crested	Miniature	10	Hairless
83	French Bulldog	Small	19-28	Short
84	English Setter	Large	50-70	Medium
85	Portuguese Water Dog	Medium	40-59	Medium
86	Welsh Terrier	Miniature	19-20	Short
87	Bearded Collie	Medium	40-59	Long
88	Corgi, Cardigan Welsh	Small	28-33	Short
89	Border Terrier	Small	11-15	Medium
90	Tibetan Terrier	Small	22-30	Long
91	Belgian Sheepdog	Large	60-89	Medium
92	Pointers	Large	50-75	Short
93	Brussels Griffon	Miniature	8-10	Medium
94	Standard Schnauzer	Medium	30-50	Medium
95	Kerry Blue Terrier	Medium	30-40	Short
96	Saluki	Large	55-65	Short
97	Belgian Tervuren	Large	60-75	Medium
98	Manchester Terrier, Toy	Miniature	7-12	Short
98	Manchester Terrier, Standard	Small	13-22	Short
99	Australian Terrier	Miniature	12-14	Medium
100	Belgian Malinois	Large	60-89	Short
101	Flat-Coated Retriever	Large	60-70	Long
102	Kuvaszok	Very Large	80-115	Medium
103	Tibetan Spaniel	Miniature	9-15	Medium
104	Staffordshire Bull Terrier	Medium	28-38	Short
105	Norwich Terrier	Miniature	11-12	Short
106	Briard	Large	60-89	Long
107	American Water Spaniel	Small	25-45	Medium
108	Welsh Springer Spaniel	Medium	35-40	Medium

Dog Owners Guide

Rank	Breed	Size	Lbs.	Coat
109	Norfolk Terrier	Miniature	11-12	Short
110	Irish Terrier	Small	25-27	Short
111	Lakeland Terrier	Miniature	10-17	Short
112	Komondor (Hungarian)	Very Large	80-95	Long
113	Pulik (Hungarian)	Small	26-39	Long
114	Scottish Deerhound	Very Large	75-110	Short
115	Bedlington Terrier	Small	17-23	Medium
116	Affenpinscher	Miniature	7-8	Medium
117	Petits Bassets Griffons Vendee	Small	35-45	Medium
118	English Toy Spaniel	Miniature	9-12	Medium
119	Wirehaired Pointing Griffon	Medium	50-60	Medium
119	Black and Tan Coonhound	Large	65-90	Short
121	Finnish Spitz	Small	24-35	Medium
122	Greyhound	Large	60-70	Short
123	Clumber Spaniel	Medium	35-60	Medium
124	Irish Water Spaniel	Large	45-65	Medium
125	Curley-Coated Retriever	Large	60-65	Medium
126	Pharoah Hound	Medium	40-60	Short
127	Miniature Bull Terrier	Small	23-28	Short
128	Skye Terrier	Small	27-28	Long
129	Dandie Dinmont Terrier	Small	18-24	Medium
130	Field Spaniel	Medium	35-50	Medium
131	Ibizan Hound	Medium	42-50	Short
132	Sealyham Terrier	Small	23-24	Medium
132	Otterhound	Very Large	65-115	Long
134	Sussex Spaniel	Medium	35-45	Medium
135	Harrier	Medium	40-59	Short
136	American Foxhound	Large	60-70	Short
137	English Foxhound	Large	70-75	Short
Misc	Jack Russell Terrier	Miniature	12-15	Short
Misc	Border Collies	Medium	35-50	Medium
Misc	Cavalier King Charles Spnl.	Miniature	13-18	Long
Misc	Spinoni Italiano	Large	50-60	Short
Misc	Greater Swiss Mt. Dog	Very Large	120-130	Short
Misc	Canaan Dog	Medium	35-55	Short

Breed Groups

Sporting Breeds— This group consists of the gun dogs used in the field with the hunter. They hunt principally by picking up scents carried in the air. They are separated mainly into three divisions depending upon the purpose for which they were developed. These are:

8

Pointers and Setters are breeds that locate game far ahead of the hunter. These breeds will indicate the position of the game by assuming a peculiarly rigid stance or by pointing their nose toward the scent of the game.

Retrievers were bred for duty in the field. They are experts in "finding and returning" game to the hunter. They are powerful swimmers.

Spaniels were developed to work in rough cover and close to the gun when locating, flushing and retrieving game.

The Hounds— This group consists of the breeds which hunt animals and run down game with their athleticism and speed. Some trail by *scent* like the Bloodhound. Others chase by *sight* like the Greyhound and Afghan, while still others give voice on the trail like the Beagle and the Basset. Also, there is the Dachshund, equipped for digging and fighting when he goes to ground for the badger.

Working Breeds— For the most part these are large dogs bred to assist man in his work. They pull sleds and carts, perform rescue, serve as watchdogs and police dogs and perform many other specialized tasks according to the purpose for which they were bred.

Terriers— The word Terrier derives from the Latin *Terre* which means earth. Thus Terriers are dogs bred to rout out varmints such as badgers, woodchucks, foxes, weasels and rats. The chief characteristics of all Terrier breeds is their gritty tenacity, courage and devotion to home and family.

Toy Breeds— The Toy Group is composed of very small breeds; hence, the word toy. They usually are less than 10 pounds in weight. They have been household pets for centuries. Many are miniatures of other breeds and although the Toys look frail and fragile they are fairly hardy. They require little exercise, space or food and therefore make excellent pets for apartment dwellers.

Non-Sporting Breeds— This is a miscellaneous collection consisting of breeds that did not fit in exactly with other groups. This varied group has been selectively bred either for esthetic effect, or to perform some precise function.

Herding Group— The Herding group consists of 15 breeds of dogs whose talent and claim to fame is their ability to herd sheep and cattle. Man's use of dogs to help him tend livestock dates from ancient times, and a good herding dog is still prized today. Quickness, stamina and an uncanny intelligence are the marks of the herding dog.

3

Acquiring A Puppy

*The most important part of buying any puppy
is an honest and ethical breeder*

Advantages

Puppies are new molds that you can shape into a sound personality and with whom you can develop a close bond. You can teach them right from the start and keep bad habits from developing. You know where they came from and how they were bred. You can watch them grow.

Disadvantages

Puppies require a lot of care and attention and several weeks or months of housebreaking. You can never be 100% sure how a puppy's personality and habits might turn out. Some puppies are like adolescent children and may be extremely active and mischievous. This developmental stage requires patience. Some puppies may challenge for dominance and you may need to be firm, not harsh, to establish control.

Quality Breeders

A great deal of the success you will have with your dog depends on what happened to the dog **before** you acquired him; its socialization, genetic background and early conditioning are the result of the breeders' efforts. There is no organization or registry that can guarantee the quality of a dog. Technically, anyone who breeds dogs can be considered a breeder. With that in mind it is up to you to do your homework and buy quality.

Types of Breeders

Hobby Breeders- The serious and dedicated hobby breeder regards his dogs as a hobby of love. Hobby breeders do not expect a big profit and may only breed once a year, if that. When someone breeds dogs for the enjoyment, pleasure, and thrill of producing the very finest specimens of the breed, the result is superior quality. These breeders acknowledge responsibility for each and every puppy produced and stand behind every dog they breed.

Commercial Kennel- This breeder has progressed from a hobby breeder who plans one or two litters per year to a large operation that produces many litters per year. This type of breeder adheres to high ethical standards and constantly works to improve his or her line.

Backyard Breeder- This is a person who owns a pet and thinks it would be good income to have puppies. This person knows little about the science of breeding for health and sound temperament and cuts corners in order to make the litter pay off. They may use the closest and cheapest mates, may not provide a proper diet, not give preventative vaccinations, and sell the puppies as soon as they are weaned. They usually deal in the more popular breeds because the puppies will sell quickly and easily.

Accidental Breeder- This is a person whose bitch got caught by the neighbor's dog or they have a litter because they want the kids to witness the birthing process or they may want to pick up some quick money. There is no planning and the bitch may not have received proper care or be of sound reproductive quality.

Puppy Mills- These operators may have a number of bitches of popular breeds they keep in cramped cages or stalls, one or two studs (which may be purchased champions of record), and will breed the bitches every heat period. Sometimes the bitch will never leave her small confined area. Her puppies are usually taken from her as soon as they start to eat solid food. This deprives the puppy of lessons they can only learn from their litter mates and may result in a number of serious temperament problems.

Pet Shop Dealers- This source of acquiring a puppy is difficult to appraise because the standards and practices for each business varies. Pet shop puppies usually come from a variety of different breeders with some being thousands of miles away. Unless there is considerable quality control, such as routine inspections of breeders' facilities and breeding practices, it is difficult to ensure quality.

The fact is you will probably pay the same cost wherever you purchase your puppy. It's up to you to ensure that you get quality.

Ten Things Quality Breeders Do

1 Quality Breeders conscientiously plan each litter based on parents' appropriate temperament, freedom from congenital and hereditary defects, and qualities in relation to the breed's AKC approved official standard. Before deciding to produce a litter, breeders consider the possibilities of properly placing puppies they cannot keep for themselves. A quality breeder breeds only the best dogs or "champions" — a champion is a dog who has proven itself to be an outstanding example of the breed in temperament and structure and is worthy to be bred. Most breeders plan breedings well in advance and may have waiting lists of buyers. Don't expect to call and take "immediate delivery." Most will know of other reputable breeders who have litters or are expecting litters.

2 Quality Breeders verify in writing that the parents have been pronounced normal and that congenital health problems in the breed have been cleared by a veterinarian specializing in the field, or through a national registry such as the Orthopedic Foundation for Animals (OFA), Canine Eye Registry Foundation (CERF) and von Willebrand Disease (VWD). Each dog certified clear is given a certification number (preliminary evaluation is given to dogs under two years). The OFA, CERF certification number of the sire and dam appear on the AKC application for individual registration (blue slip). The OFA, CERF numbers (or a copy of the preliminary OFA evaluation) of the parents will be provided by a quality breeder if the problem exists in the breed. See Health Caution section.

3   Quality breeders take care to plan the spacing of litters so that puppies are not consistently available. The average breeder breeds every one to three years. Quality breeders breed only healthy, mature stock over one and one half years of age. Bitches should have no more than two litters in any 18-month period and no bitch should be bred after the age of eight years. All breeder stock is kept under sanitary conditions and given maximum health protection through worming, inoculation, and proper veterinary care at all times.

4   Quality Breeders register their stock with a national registry and keep accurate records of breedings and a four or five generation pedigree. (A pedigree is a list of each dog's ancestors.)

5   Quality Breeders present the puppy to the new owners no sooner than 7 weeks of age. All new owners are provided with written details on feeding, general care, dates of worming and inoculations and a four-generation pedigree.

6   Quality Breeders screen future owners. They will ask many questions to ensure the puppy will go to a proper home. Quality breeders are concerned about the welfare of their puppies and do not want to create a mismatch which could jeopardize the life of their pups and the reputation of their kennel.

7   Quality Breeders require purchasers to spay and neuter those dogs which for any reason will not be used for breeding, and to properly safeguard unspayed bitches from unplanned matings and most of all, to ensure a healthier animal. Some breeders offer an AKC Limited Registration which means the dog is a pure bred AKC registered dog; however, no offspring of the dog may be registered with the AKC. This ensures that only the best stock is bred. Limited Registration dogs may not be shown in conformation but may be shown in obedience.

8   Quality Breeders will make sure you are aware of the pros and cons of their breed as well as the grooming, shedding and trimming requirements, if any.

9   Quality Breeders are always available to help with any questions or problems that may arise and assume responsibility for every puppy they produce throughout the lifetime of the animal. They care about their breed and are actively involved in rescue work.

10 Quality Breeders usually participate in dog clubs. This indicates depth of involvement. The breeder is exposed to other points of view, learns more about their breed, general dog care, modern breeding practices and is kept up to date. Frequently they will be breeding in accordance with a club "code of ethics."

Buyer Beware

Don't be overly impressed by AKC papers. They are only a birth certificate and do nothing to ensure quality of the puppy or the breeder or the seller.

Seek out a breeder with whom you have confidence.

Visit many breeders, see the mother and other relatives, and see the conditions under which the puppy was raised. A surprising amount of behavior is inherited. Also, the puppy's environment has a great deal to do with his personality. The parents may be one of the best indications of the future temperament of your new puppy.

Do not request a less expensive, pet quality animal from the breeder if you have plans to breed or show.

The buyer should not purchase any purebred animal without AKC registration papers or a written sales agreement specifying condition of sale and a time guarantee. The bill of sale should state breed, sex, and color of dog, date of birth, dog's registered sire and dam names and puppy's litter registration number, if available. Have the breeder sign and date the bill of sale information.

Dog ownership requires commitment. Dogs must be cared for daily, receiving a healthy diet and regular exercise, plus grooming and veterinary attention, including regular inoculations against the major infectious canine diseases.

No puppy should be sold unless it receives at least one vaccination which includes distemper, hepatitis, leptospirosis, and parvo virus. Written proof should be provided stating what vaccines it has received, when and by whom.

If the puppy was dewormed, what was the drug used and when was it given? If the puppy was not dewormed, was a fecal exam done?

Beware of illness; signs of runny nose or eyes, skin sores, dirty ears or fleas. A healthy puppy will have clear, shiny eyes that are free from discharge. Its coat will be glossy with a minimum of flaking skin. It should be alert and playful.

Your primary needs should be to find a breed with a good temperament that is suitable to your household and a dog with sound health. The looks, color and sex of the animal should be secondary.

Don't make buying a dog like buying a car. This is not done on impulse but rather a rational, well-thought-out decision that you will have to live with for 12 to 14 years. If you make a mistake, it could cost the life of the dog you choose. Research the temperament and physical requirement of each breed for compatibility **before** you buy. Be prepared to wait until the right puppy becomes available.

Your puppy should be examined by a vet within 48 hours after purchase and should be checked for general health. If the veterinarian deems the animal unsuitable for reasons of health, the dog should be returned for a second animal or a total refund. Put it in writing!

If paying the price of a show potential/breeding quality animal, provisions should be made in the bill of sale for a refund or replacement animal in the event a show quality dog has disqualifying faults or hereditary diseases.

Quality breeders set a reasonable price for their young puppies. They give first class care and cannot afford to sell at a low price.

4

Puppy Care

Puppy's Equipment

Collect these items together before your puppy arrives:

1. A suitable bed — a basket, box, or a thick lambswool pad.
2. An old blanket or a towel that is soft and easy to clean.
3. Two bowls — one for food the other for water. Look for stoneware or solid metal or stainless steel.
4. A buckle collar and leash (Never use a slip collar (choker) until 5-6 months of age).
5. Dog brush, comb, currycomb, shampoo, flea products and nail clippers (Ask your breeder for type).
6. A dog chew, like a good quality rawhide, and a dog toy that is safe.
7. High quality puppy food.

Additionally, look at the advantages of a good dog crate (It can be a big aid in training), baby gate, seat belt or car restraint, carpet stain and odor remover.

Puppy Proofing = Safety

Eliminate all potential dangers before they become problems.

Remove and safeguard anything that the puppy could chew or swallow that may be of danger such as:

Cleaning compounds, bug sprays, rodent poisons, antifreeze drippings, electrical wires, and mothballs.

Dispose of chicken or turkey bones in a safe manner.

Leave toilet lids down.

Keep upper story windows closed.

Avoid flea collars and dips until 15 weeks of age.

Keep your puppy away from toxic plants.

Check to see the fencing is secure.

TIP Ask your veterinarian when it is permissible for your puppy to be around other dogs.

The First Night Your puppy will benefit from sleeping near you for the first few nights and should be provided with comfort during your absence. A hot water bottle and a blanket should give it some physical comfort. If you don't have a crate, use a cardboard box or basket. A crate provides a simulated den that is portable and useful in training and is highly recommended.

During the first few nights you have to be firm; the puppy has to get used to its sleeping place. If it starts crying and yowling, don't coddle it. After a few nights of disrupted sleep acclimatization will take its natural course. If it starts crying in the middle of the night refer to housebreaking suggestions.

Observe your puppy's routine. Try to establish a routine and stick to it.

A dog is a pack animal. Once you remove your dog from its litter, your dog will look to you for its physical and social needs.

Feeding Puppy Puppies are entirely dependent on their owners to provide a balanced diet that meet all of their nutritional requirements. A dog's nutritional needs change as they grow, so there are different foods for puppies, for mature dogs, for extra-active dogs and older dogs.

18

Each dog should have the diet that is formulated for his stage of life. Foods designed for puppies are higher in fat (to meet their high energy needs), higher in protein and fortified with vitamins and minerals to enhance growth and development. Feed a puppy a specially formulated puppy food until it reaches maturity (12 to 18 months of age — the larger the dog the longer they take to mature). Any change in diet should be done gradually over a 3 to 5 day span.

General Rule for puppy is feed smaller portions more often:

Weaning time	
3 weeks to 3 months	4 meals a day
3 months to 6 months	3 meals a day
6 months to 1 year	2 meals a day
1 year and up	1 or 2 meals a day (1/2 daily amt if 2)

TIPS Feed your puppy a high-quality, premium dog food. All dogs are individuals and their needs may vary depending on activity, breed and age. Feed for 30 minutes per feeding then remove. Have regular times of the day for feeding. Try not to feed after 6 or 7 pm. Regarding strenuous exercise, allow one hour before and after feeding. The dog should always have clean water available. For puppies less than three months of age, you may prefer to soften their dry food with a little warm water.

Identification Animal Control officials state one of the main reasons for euthanizing is the fact dogs are turned in with no traceable identification. Any dog has the potential to get out and get lost. It is vitally important for your dog to wear a collar with his license number, rabies vaccination tag, and medallion with dog's name (some people include the word REWARD), your name, address and telephone number. Other methods are available, such as tattoos or microchips. See Identification Suppliers in Service Resource Directory Section.

TIP Don't use an S Ring. Use an O Ring. S rings get caught, are easily opened, and the ID gets lost.

Puppy Vaccinations

It is vitally important that you immunize your puppy against infectious diseases that can seriously harm or kill it. Make arrangements with your veterinarian for a vaccination *series* and follow their recommended schedule based on exposure to diseases in your area.

According to the American Veterinary Medical Association, a general schedule is: a puppy's first vaccinations would ideally take place at six to eight weeks, followed by two more vaccinations three to four weeks apart. Afterward, yearly booster vaccines will provide ongoing protection. The most serious life-threatening diseases are distemper, hepatitis, leptospirosis (known as DHL), parainfluenza, parvovirus (known as PP) and rabies. Rabies vaccinations are usually given around four months, with re-vaccination one year later. Three-year immunity vaccines are available. Bordetella and coronavirus vaccine may also be recommended by your veterinarian depending on exposure. It is the law that all dogs must have rabies vaccinations.

Ten Do's & Don'ts for Children's Safety

1 Don't approach dogs you don't know without the permission of the adult owner.
Not all dogs are friendly and some may bite.

2 If an adult tells you it's ok to pet their dog...
Do not run toward the dog.
Do not hug, poke, grab or pound on the dog's head.
Do approach slowly and quietly.
Do allow the dog to sniff your hand first.
Do pet the dog gently under his chin or on his chest.

3 Do not touch or pet any dog that growls, snarls or runs away from you.

4 Do not play roughly with any dog.

5   Do not put your hands through fences, car windows, or cages where dogs are.

6   Do not attempt to take bones, food or toys from a dog.

7   Do not frighten or startle any dog, especially when it is sleeping.

8   Do not attempt to punish a dog in any way.

9   If a dog you don't know comes up to you...
    Do not run or yell.
    Do not look directly at him.
    Do stand perfectly still.
    Do watch the dog out of the corner of your eye.
    Do walk away slowly after a minute or two.

10 Do treat all dogs, cats and other animals kindly.

5

Puppy Training

Establishing Leadership

If you've ever watched a young litter of pups at play, you'll recall the pups jumped at and nipped one another. Some were pushier than others. What you observed was the forming of a pecking order. Having evolved from the wolf (a pack animal) the pups instinctively know that a hierarchy, for the survival and safety of the pack, must be established. When the new pup is brought into a human household the instinct does not change. You must take over as leader and teach the pup he falls below humans in his new pack. The pup will accept and be comfortable with the lowest position as long as you are a kind, strong, firm and consistent leader.

To establish leadership there are some rules that must be followed:

Nothing in life is free. Anything your pup wants or needs must be earned by obeying a command (sit).

This is difficult because it is natural for us to give our dogs food, petting, attention, etc. without thinking about it. However, this indiscriminate attention sends the dog the message that he is a dominant member of the "pack." A dog that perceives himself as dominant over you is certainly not going to be easily trained and may cause you some serious problems.

Give your dog one 15-minute down/stay per day

Make sure you are always in a position to follow through. When you give your dog a command or correct him for anything you must be able to enforce what you say. If you tell him to sit and he chooses not to, you must immediately place him in a sit. If you do not, you have effectively taught him that your command means nothing.

Leaders eat first. Feed your dog after you eat.

Leaders enter and exit a door first. Use a leash or command to have your dog wait until you invite your dog to follow out the door.

Create an environment for success. Use your voice and body language effectively. The tone of your voice is more important than words. Say it as if you mean it, and then, if necessary, follow through. Avoid whining or pleading with your dog.

Do not hit your dog as a means of control. This teaches the dog to fear and retaliate. Build leadership by nonconfrontational means only.

There will be a great sense of security instilled in your dog knowing that you are firmly in control.

How to Discipline

You must teach your puppy what is, and what is not, acceptable. To make it easy for both you and your dog remember:

1. Prevent negative behaviors from occurring and reinforce positive behaviors.
2. Never use your hands as weapons.
3. Be consistent.
4. Use a drag line while supervising the dog.
5. Use your voice. Low guttural sounds tend to be effective.
6. Never discipline after the fact.
7. Praise is a motivator. Use a happy, high pitched voice when praising.
8. Tone of voice is very important. Commands tones should be given in a happy, high pitched voice when you want your dog to move. Use a firm, low voice when you want your dog to stay.

Puppy Training Classes

The earlier you start working with your dog the better. It is important that positive associations and impressions be made with people, places and things in their environment and with humans and other dogs. Your puppy should receive temperament training that is designed to build its confidence and *prevent* future behavior problems, while inhibiting and channeling the biting instinct into more positive outlets.

The best time for puppy class is between 10 and 18 weeks and after the second vaccination. The class situation should be a sterile environment to guard against infectious disease. Consult with your veterinarian.

TIP Do not use a training collar (choke collar) until after the age of five-and-a-half months.

Canine Learning Centers
San Diego City & North County- 9 Locations
619 931-1834

Training with Food

Food is used as a lure/reward in the early stages of training. Trainers use food to lure the dogs into proper position and direct the dogs movements without unnecessary pulling, tugging, yanking or leash jerking. Food is used to convey to the dog the trainer's pleasure in its behavior and at the same time reward it for performance. The best part of using food as a training aid lies in its ability to reinforce positive behavior, motivate your dog to enjoy working for you and reduce the stress inherent in training. Other reward methods are verbal praise, petting or stroking, attention and play.

TIPS Use small tidbits (about the size of M&M's).

Give the treat at the *exact* moment the desired behavior occurs.

Always couple food rewards with verbal praise and/or petting.

Food rewards work best when the dog is hungry.

Don't overfeed with treats. Figure out your dog's daily caloric needs and use part of that for training.

Eliminating the Food Reward

Make sure your dog has a good understanding of the exercises before phase out. Rewards should be given on a random basis (like a slot machine). Start reducing the frequency of the reward slowly over a period of weeks.

Training Equipment

Medium link steel or nylon slip collar for dogs over the age of 20 weeks, otherwise a buckle collar.

A 4-foot to 6-foot leather or nylon leash.

A 20-foot to 30-foot nylon long line.

Soft food treats cut to the size of an M&M.

Safe toy.

Sit

There are two ways to teach the sit command, either using food as a lure/reward, or physically placing your dog in the sit position.

The food method — start by placing the dog in front of you, holding a piece of food or other lure just above your dog's nose (not too high or this will cause the dog to jump). Slowly bring the food back towards the tail and give the single command "Sit." It may be necessary to place your hand behind the pup to prevent rear movement. At the precise second the pup sits, praise him using a happy, high-pitched voice and give him the small food treat. Release him with your chosen release word. Repeat.

The physical placement method — start by placing your puppy at your left side facing the same direction. Place the puppy in the sit position by pulling up on the collar while gently tucking your hand behind the pup's knees. As the rump hits the ground say, "Sit." Praise your dog then release him using a release word. Repeat!

For adult dogs, give the command "Sit" at the same time gently pull up on the leash with your right hand while gently pushing down on his rear with your left hand. The instant he sits praise using a high, happy voice then release him with your release word. Repeat.

The Release Word

Choose a word such as okay, free, break, up, etc., and use the word consistently to release the dog from commands. Praise should not be used as a release.

Sit/Stay

Place your dog in a sit. As you give the verbal command "Stay." Also, give a hand signal by bringing your left hand, palm open, down towards the dog's face. The command must be in a firm voice. If your dog stays in place for just a few seconds, release him. Gradually lengthen the time and build on success. If the dog attempts to get up, verbally correct "No, Sit" and immediately place the dog back into position. Release and praise. Puppies have short attention spans. Don't demand a long stay from them.

Down

Start with the dog sitting on your left and kneel next to him. Rest your left hand on the dog's shoulder and with your right hand, hold a piece of food or other lure above your dog's nose. As you give the verbal command "Down" slowly bring the lure straight down under the dog's chest to the dog's toes. The instant the dog lies down, praise him and give him the treat.

Stand

Give the verbal command "Stand." Place your left hand just in front of the upper part of your dog's rear legs to stop the forward movement. With your right hand hold a lure at the dog's nose or gently pull outward on the leash keeping the leash level to the dog.

Recall

Attach a long line to the pup's collar. While a helper gently restrains the pup by the chest, show him you have a piece of food and then move about twelve feet away. Call your pup by his name followed by the command "Come." Backpedal or turn and run away from your dog. When your dog reaches you, stop and face him and reward him with lots of praise and a treat.

Make a fun game out of it. Gradually work at a greater distance and around distractions. Avoid at all costs doing anything negative when practicing the recall.

Step on the Leash

This exercise is used as a means of establishing leadership and control. (Do not use on puppies under 12 weeks of age.) With a leash attached to your dog's buckle collar, step on the leash close to the snap. This puts your dog in a position where it is uncomfortable to sit or stand.

If your dog struggles or resists lying down, let him. **DO NOT** discipline, look at, talk to, or touch the dog. As your dog learns to accept the position, slowly move your foot up the leash a few inches from the snap to allow head movement. If your dog attempts to stand, move your foot back close to the snap. To release, simply step off the leash. Do not use a release word, pet or praise. Begin the exercise during quiet times for a few minutes, a few time each day. Gradually increase the time. Use the exercise for control at the veterinary office, during dinner time, etc.

Settle

Your pup must learn to lie still for you when you require it. This serves two purposes:

- Establishes leadership by requiring cooperation.
- Prepares the way for teaching the pup to accept routine handling.

To teach your dog this exercise start by placing the pup gently on his side with his head on the floor. Use the word "Settle" in a firm tone.

Require the pup to lie still for a few seconds then release him with your release word. Most pups will put up at least some resistance to this. Use your voice and hands effectively. At the first signs of resistance, correct in a firm tone and physically place. Follow with praise and *slow* stroking, then release.

Walking on the Leash

A positive association with the leash must be made so that the puppy will not perceive the leash as a shackle.

To accomplish this, let the puppy wear the leash around the home on a *buckle* collar while supervised. Do this in a spirit of play for short intervals. Once the pup accepts the leash dragging along, pick up the end and follow him. Proceed to encourage the pup to follow you. Walk at a fast pace with the least amount of pressure on the leash as possible. Praise the dog for walking along nicely. If the dog pulls or becomes distracted, turn and walk briskly in the opposite direction the dog is going. When he catches up to you, praise him in a happy, high-pitched voice. Another way is to simply stop when your dog pulls on the leash and continue after the leash slackens.

Remember the Four P's

Dogs love to learn. Training your dog helps you gain control and gives you the ability to communicate what is expected so that your dog can live harmoniously in your home. In teaching dogs, leadership and authority is the secret of success. You must establish your authority and leadership and communicate with your dog in a positive manner. Never hit! The four P's of training are Patience, Persistence, Practice and lots of Praise.

TIP If you learn when and how to praise effectively and appropriately correct your dog you will have at your fingertips the primary means of communication with your pet. Praise is the language of dogs — and people.

Basic Obedience Classes

Every dog should know basic commands such as *sit, stay, down, stand, heel* and *come*. Your dog should also learn the meaning of *no* and *ok* and be taught not to pull on the leash. Your dog should be able to do this in any circumstance or situation, not just at home. A training class will provide a place of learning in a distracting environment. Take a class and choose a trainer who emphasizes the use of positive reinforcement such as verbal praise, play or treats. You should look for a class where the instructor teaches not only basic commands but dog behavior as well.

Choosing a Trainer

For the first-time dog owner, there is nothing more important than choosing the right instructor to help you through the training process. You need to decide exactly what you want to train your dog to do. Do you want your dog to be a well-behaved companion or do you want to obtain an obedience or conformation title?

Look for a trainer who specializes in a given area. All dogs and dog owners can improve their relationship with basic dog obedience training. The biggest difference in trainers is the use of corrections. Some trainers teach emphasizing positive reinforcement methods using praise and food while others use various forms of coercion with various intensity. Meaning and relevance should be understood by the dog before anyone ever thinks of force or punishment. Positive training and motivational methods place a minimum amount of *stress* on the dog.

The best method of finding someone is word-of-mouth. A good trainer will have an excellent reputation. Select two or three well-referred trainers and ask them the following questions.

Ten Questions You Should Ask a Potential Trainer

1   How do you correct a dog?

2   What methods do you use?

3   Do you use compulsion? If so, how severe?

4   How would you deal with an aggressive dog?

5   How would you train (your breed)?

Puppy Training

6   Do you use prong collars, shock collars, choke collars, head harnesses, nylon slip collars or buckle collars?

7   Do you use dominance techniques? Explain.

8   How long have you been in business?

9   How many students are in your classes?

10 Ask if you can monitor a class, and if you can, observe how the trainer works with the students.

Does the trainer explain carefully what is going on, what to expect, and how to do it? Does each student get the attention needed? Are the trainer's methods humane?

Remember, trainers train people to train their dogs. A trainer should have good communication skills. There are many trainers who know a lot about dogs but have a hard time communicating their knowledge. Dog training is both an art and a science that requires using the proper technique for a particular dog temperament. The object of training is to establish a better relationship with your dog. Commands are not an end in themselves, but a means to bring about a better companion dog.

Training Tips for Your Puppy...

Reinforce your puppy with praise and a small piece of food when it urinates or defecates outside in the designated area. Make all desirable behaviors rewarding to your dog through the use of praise, petting, food, etc.

Never punish your puppy if it makes a mistake. Don't rub its nose in it or hit it with a newspaper. If it makes a mistake indoors, clean the area thoroughly with a 50/50 solution of vinegar and water. Don't use ammonia. When dogs urinate they establish a "scent post." It is important that your clean-up removes all trace of odor.

Don't give your puppy unsupervised freedom indoors and avoid leaving unattended outdoors for more than a few minutes. This prevents undesirable behaviors from becoming habits. You can not train a dog you are not with.

31

Provide a peaceful "safe place" where your puppy can sleep and relax.

Try to develop a routine for eating, walks, play and bedtime.

Even with the most well-behaved dog, there will be some unpleasant moments. Be patient and work to correct your new pet's bad habits.

Don't use a training collar until the dog is between five and six months of age.

Avoid confrontational games such as tug-of-war and wrestling.

Proper discipline begins with the lowest level necessary to get the message across. Never hit or strike your dog in any way. Physical discipline seldom solves behavior problems and, in fact, frequently causes some very serious problems. For a number of reasons, punishment is an ineffective and often counterproductive method of changing behavior. A far better approach to obtaining good behavior from your dog is to *prevent* inappropriate behavior and train and reward appropriate behavior.

Training Tips for all Dogs...

Dogs must have a clear idea of what it is you want them to do, and the meaning of the command before any correction is administered.

Because everything your dog does is rewarding in some way, allowing undesirable behaviors to occur is the same as training it.

Dogs live in the "here and now." Corrections or positive reinforcement must occur as the behavior is exhibited. A delay of even two seconds reduces effectiveness. After the fact punishments are to be avoided.

Do not give any command that you are not in a position to physically require should the command be ignored. Give the command in a firm voice but do not repeat a command that is not obeyed. Instead, immediately require the behavior. For instance, if a sit command is ignored, place the dog in a sit. Follow with praise even though you physically required the sit.

Consistency is essential. If there is no clearcut rule, the only possible result is confusion and inappropriate behavior.

In order to build reliability, it is necessary to train in multiple locations. Begin with conditions that present very low levels of distraction, like a hallway or room. Once the exercises are successful, proceed to more distractive conditions. (Dogs are excited by movement.)

Dogs learn best by working for a few minutes at a time, several times per day if possible.

Be firm and exacting in your training sessions but keep them lively and fun. Finish each session on a positive note and follow with a brief play period.

Be prepared for occasional "bad days." Dogs have them too!

Dog Behaviorists

Dog Behaviorists are people who study the way dogs act and react to their environment by taking into account the dog's evolutionary development. Behaviorists try to convey in everyday language why dogs behave a certain way in certain situations and how you can use this knowledge to make life with your dog as rewarding as possible.

Preventing Behavior Problems

6

Starting Off "The Right Way"

Fact — Puppies are extremely social animals. The socialization that occurs in a pup's or adolescent dog's life could be the most influential factor in determining how successfully and happily he will relate to his environment. The dog owner holds the key to this important process.

Begin early. The most important socialization period is from 3 to 12 weeks of age. Dogs that are isolated during these critical weeks may become fearful and/or aggressive and are unable, during the entire course of their lives, to handle new people or normal situations. Provide contact with as many different types of people as possible — men, women, children, teenagers, oldsters and quiet or loud people, as soon as your dog has received its vaccinations against disease. Expose him to parks, shopping centers, school yards. Avoid isolating him in yards.

Enroll in a puppy or beginner obedience class. A good program stresses control through positive reinforcement and *nonconfrontational* leadership techniques. These approaches benefit the dog by building confidence and trust as well as controlled exposure to other people and dogs.

Reinforce confident behavior. If your dog shows any concern or aggressive behavior in any circumstance, do not draw attention to the situation by attempting to soothe, calm or console him with sympathetic tones or petting. Doing so rewards him for the behavior. Corrections can be reinforcing or counterproductive. Instead, reward your dog by praising and petting when he shows calm or positive responses to people or noises. Lead your dog into potentially fearful situations with confidence. If you are tentative and nervous, your dog will sense this. Your abilities to successfully send appropriate signals will be enhanced by establishing leadership over your pup. If you see any sign of fearfulness or fear-related aggression, begin working with it immediately. Dogs do not "outgrow" such problems. In fact, if left untreated, they worsen. A fearful animal needs exposure but it must be *carefully controlled* to avoid making the problem worse. A dog's behavior can be complex, and treatment may require the expertise of a behaviorist.

Puppy Socialization & Development

Fact — Less than 30% of family dogs remain with one owner their entire life. A majority are given up because the owner could not deal effectively with problems stemming from puppyhood like chewing, barking, house-soiling, etc.

One of the most important qualities of a pet dog is its temperament. A dog with a good temperament is a joy to own, whereas an aggressive, antisocial, fearful or untrained dog can be a nightmare. A dog's temperament is much more adaptable than is commonly thought and it is greatly affected by the process of training and socialization that occurs during puppyhood. In many ways puppyhood is the most important time of a dog's life, a time when experiences are new and have a longlasting effect on shaping the dog's future personality.

Dog owners should pay heed to this crucial period in the life of their dog, since this is the most important time to influence the proper development of their pet's behavior. It is much, much easier to prevent problems from developing than it is to attempt to cure them once they have become firmly entrenched. In the world of domestic dogs, the puppy is usually removed from its natural sources of information at about eight weeks and in most cases finds itself the only dog in a human "den." At eight weeks the puppy is not prepared to deal with the world at large. It thus becomes a human responsibility to continue the pup's education. Failure to do so results in the puppy's inability to adapt to its environment, or at least to adapt in a harmonious way with its human pack members. Enrolling your dog in puppy class will stimulate the puppy's learning, develop his potential, help socialize him with other people and other dogs and give the dog/owner relationship a chance to fully develop.

Housebreaking
The goal is to teach the puppy to eliminate outdoors and give you a sign that it needs to go out.
The Keys
Establish a Routine
Reward Success
Supervise
Never Correct or Punish after the Fact
Deodorize Mistakes

The normal healthy puppy will want to relieve himself when he wakes up, after each feeding, following strenuous exercise or after any excitement. The objective is regularly scheduled daily feeding and walking. Use a crate or confine your puppy to a safe area when you are unable to supervise. Remember, you cannot train a dog that you are not with. Don't let your dog run unsupervised. Look for signs that the dog has to go, such as sniffing, whining, turning in circles or going to the door. Place your dog on the leash and take him to his spot. Praise him for successful achievement. Teach your puppy to perform on command. Use short words like, "Hurry up." Praise him for successful achievement. Set a time limit of three to five minutes. If a puppy does not do his business by then, put him back in a confined area. Repeat the process in ten minutes.

Any excitement, such as play, may result in floor wetting. When an accident happens, never punish after the fact, especially by striking with a newspaper or rubbing his nose in it. Thoroughly deodorize the entire stained area with an odor neutralizer. The only effective correction is to catch the dog in the act. If you see the dog about to eliminate make a loud noise by banging on a wall or counter; when they stop, say "outside" and immediately take them to their spot outside. You must make it clear to the dog that it is not the act of elimination that you are displeased with, it is the location.

A puppy cannot effectively control its elimination until approximately five to six months. A young pup's bladder is not mature enough to go through the night without relieving itself. Take the pup out before you go to bed and then confine the pup to a small area like a crate where it is comfortable and able to stand up and turn around. When you hear the pup become restless, get up and take it out. If you are a heavy sleeper, you will need to set your alarm for four to six hours after retiring. A puppy should hold it through the night around four to five months.

Note: A crate is strongly recommended.

Crate Training

Crate + Dog = Happy Home

Crates simulate a den. A den to a dog is a place that provides protection from predators and the elements, a place where he or she feels safe and secure. The use of a crate can help prevent housebreaking and chewing problems. Here is how to crate train:

First, form positive associations with the crate by tossing in dog treats or feeding your dog in the crate *without* closing the door.

DON'T FORCE HIM. Let him take it slowly. He may be shy at first.

Once he is accustomed and unafraid, make him stay in the crate by restraining him at the door with your hand for a few minutes. Gradually increase the time. Make sure you praise him!

Once he is comfortable with this, restrain him with the door while using praise. Eventually, the pup will sit quietly and sleep with the door closed.

Do not always leave the house when you place your dog in the crate (you don't want your dog to associate your leaving with being in the crate).

Don't release your dog from the crate when it barks, only when it is quiet.

If you are going to be gone for an extended time, arrange for someone to let your dog out.

Don't use housebreaking pads inside the crate. Never punish your pup by putting him in the crate.

Place the crate in an area where the pup can see family activity.

Keep your pup in the crate during all unsupervised short intervals (not more than 3 to 4 hours except night time sleeping). For longer periods, use a puppy pen.

Most young pups have to go every 2-4 hours. At 5-6 months, a dog can usually "hold-it" longer.

If you can, let a new puppy sleep in your room in a crate.

Puppy Nipping or Biting

Mouthing and nipping at hands and clothing is a natural puppy behavior although it is unacceptable to the family. Puppy teeth are sharp and can hurt human skin and tear clothing. The nipping has absolutely nothing to do with teething. Your pup will nip as a means of controlling you to see where he falls in the hierarchy of his new human pack.

Never use your hands to discipline your pup for mouthing. Avoid slapping, squeezing or holding the mouth shut or shaking the dog and pinning it down. All of these ways may teach the pup your hands are weapons and he needs to defend himself when he sees them. Using your hands negatively towards the pup may also teach fear, confusion and mistrust. A good strong leader never has to use force to get compliance. Remember to praise your pup for all appropriate behavior including *light* mouthing. Use chew toys to redirect the pup's nipping. This will be most successful if you distract and redirect as the pup is *about* to misbehave. If the nipping is too hard a loud firm UUUH! should temporarily stop the pup. Immediately praise if pup stops.

A dog generally will not respect leadership in a child. Your pup will view your children as litter mates. Play between children and dog should be supervised by adults. No roughhousing, chasing or wrestling games. This encourages the pup to be more oral and fight against you. Children may use a sharp yip sound to stop the pup then an adult should take over.

As always, make sure the pup is getting plenty of exercise to expend some of his energy.

Due to the age they were removed from their litter or personality, some puppies are mouthier than others. Positive obedience training is recommended so the pup will learn what is expected. If you're having trouble controlling your pup, seek the help of a professional trainer or behaviorist.

Chewing

Dogs chew for many reasons. In puppies, teething is a factor, along with investigation and curiosity. In older dogs chewing may be a means of relieving monotony and or stress. Our goal should not be to stop the dog from chewing but to channel the behavior to appropriate objects. We believe it is important for a dog to have a wide variety of chew objects differing in size, texture and shape. Dogs learn with more variety and stay interested longer.

Providing safe chew toys is step one. To your dog these objects and your remote control or new pair of shoes are all objects to chew. You must teach the dog what is his. Everything else belongs to us. Praise all appropriate chewing.

Most owners neglect to do this and fail to take advantage of an easy and pleasant way to avoid undesirable chewing.

Prevent undesirable chewing, (See crate training), especially in your absence. Each time your dog engages in inappropriate chewing and you are not there to correct him for it, he has learned to do it. You have actually trained the behavior by default. Even more importantly, you are risking your dog's life. Allowing a chewer to get a hold of inappropriate objects can be deadly. Poisoning, blockages, punctured intestines, electrocution are just a few of the dire possibilities.

Discipline may be used only when you catch the dog in the act. Clap your hands, toss a magazine near the dog, yell "HEY," or attach a length of light cord or rope to a collar so a sharp "pop" may be given. Praise the dog the second he stops and substitute an acceptable item. Praise the dog for any attention given to the appropriate item.

TIP Tug of war games may cause a dog to become more oral and excitable and are to be avoided. Meal times should be on a consistent schedule to eliminate the possibility of hunger stress. Don't make a big fuss when you leave or arrive. If you find your dog has chewed something inappropriate, don't hit the dog or punish the dog. Put the dog out of sight in a safe place, clean up the mess, count to ten and act like nothing happened. At that time it is too late for any meaningful training to take place.

Chewing problems can be exasperating and costly, however, if you can apply good prevention, correction and reinforcement techniques, most chewing problems can be solved. The help of a professional behaviorist may be required for severe problems.

Digging

There are many reasons for a dog to dig. Some dig cooling pits to lie in, others bury things. Some dig after vermin or as a means of escaping the yard. Many dogs dig out of boredom and frustration or because digging is simply an enjoyable pastime.

A number of things can be done to channel and correct your dog's digging — but there is one familiar rule that must be recognized: you can't train a dog you are not with. A key to solving any problem involves preventing and retraining.

One solution is to create a doggie digging pit, a chosen place where a dog is encouraged to dig. The owner may bury some interesting toys in the pit while the dog watches. The dog is then enthusiastically encouraged to dig them up and is praised. The dog should be confined to the well-stocked digging area when the owner is not present.

This will encourage the habit of digging in the right area. Next, the owner must spend some time in the yard with the dog watching it closely. The dog must be immediately verbally corrected for the beginnings of inappropriate digging and instructed back to the digging pit.

Chicken wire buried at an angle or a strong piece of plywood driven vertically two feet into the ground may discourage digging to escape.

Correcting outdoor behaviors can be much more difficult than training a dog to behave acceptably inside the home.

Remember the dog's social and exercise needs. Are they being met? If not, they may contribute to problem digging and misbehavior. Digging is a natural behavior for a dog. Beware of only taking a corrective approach to the problem. If in doubt about what to do, consult a professional trainer or behaviorist.

Possessiveness (Food and Objects) It is not unusual for a dog to growl or even bite when someone approaches his food dish or prized possession. This is natural response which, in the wild, ensures survival, but in our homes is inappropriate and dangerous. Punishment is not an effective approach and may make matters worse. We must teach our pups that people around his food dish is very positive.

Start announcing chow time by shaking the food bag. Ask your pup to sit and put down his empty dish. Drop two or three pieces of kibble in the dish. After the pup eats them repeat the procedure three or four times. Next, drop some kibble into the bowl. While the pup is eating, offer him a small piece of chicken with your hand next to his bowl, repeat. Now, put more kibble in the dish and while the pup is eating pick up the bowl, add a piece of chicken, give it back to him. Now, while the pup is eating, gently pet him and offer more desirable treats. By practicing this exercise your pup will learn that your hands come to give, not to take away. A trust will develop.

Make sure your pup will relinquish objects to you. Start by pressing firmly but gently at the dog's muzzle directly behind the two canine teeth. The pressure will cause the dog to open his mouth. Now, while he is holding a favorite chew toy press at the muzzle and say "Out" or "Give." When the pup relinquishes the article praise and give it back to him. Repeat the procedure several times with many different objects, always ending the session with the pup keeping the article.

Please note: These exercises are to prevent aggression. If you own a dog that is already exhibiting threatening behavior do not attempt a cure on your own. Seek the help of a qualified behaviorist.

Barking

Barking to a dog is like singing to a canary or talking to a human, a natural normal behavior. This normal behavior may occur at inappropriate times or become too excessive if not controlled by the owner. Barking is a way of communicating a message. Some dogs are more prone to excessive barking than others. This may be due to genetics, early learning or personality.

Some of the most common reasons for barking are:

Barking for attention or reward.

Barking out of boredom or barking to seek companionship.

Barking out of stress, fear or frustration, or because of strong territorial instincts.

It is vital we take advantage of and cultivate a dog's social instincts by making him a part of the family.

Provide a proper diet, quality time, training and an exercise schedule that is convenient. Your dog will look forward to being with you while expending excess energy. Provide mental stimulation as well as physical. Teach your dog tricks and work on obedience commands. Avoid keeping the dog in the yard for long periods of time as this may encourage inappropriate barking.

Teach the dog to distinguish between appropriate and inappropriate barking. This may be accomplished by introducing the dog to regular service people, mail person, utility worker, gardener, etc.

Teach your dog the meaning of "quiet." by putting the barking on cue. For example:

Most dogs bark when a doorbell rings. You may take advantage of this by setting up a training situation. You'll need an assistant.

Assistant quietly goes to your front door. You say:

"Rover, speak!" This is the cue for assistant to ring bell. Dog barks, you say "goooood speak, Rover, goood speak!" Repeat several times.

Now while the dog is barking say"Okay now, Rover, quiet. Quiet, quiet."(say this in a hushed tone while gently cupping dog's muzzle closed). Reward for ceased barking. "Gooood quiet, ...Rover!" Repeat process.

Barking is something that can be controlled. Remember, there is a reason and a reward for every behavior your dog exhibits. If barking has become a problem you may want to consult a professional behaviorist.

Jumping Up

Jumping by dogs is a natural instinctive behavior. When dogs jump on people they are trying to greet and get near the face of their pack members.

Jumping, although natural, is unacceptable to humans and can be dangerous. There is nothing more annoying to some people than to be bounded by an enthusiastic pooch, regardless of its size. Whenever we take something natural (jumping) away from our dogs we must teach an acceptable behavior. Jumping is usually exhibited when a dog first meets people. The best way to stop your dog from jumping is to teach him to sit and stay. There are dozens of things a dog cannot do while sitting and staying. Jumping is one of them. Avoid overexciting your dog when a guest arrives. Ask friends to participate in a simulated training session. Have a friend come to the door. Place your dog in a sit/stay. After a period of time your dog should calm down and assume a normal manner. Be consistent and persistent. Anticipate jumping situations. Have a leash available at all times to use for control.

Another method is to turn your back on the dog when he jumps. Pay no attention to him until he settles down. Also, make sure your dog is spayed or neutered.

Excitement/ Submissive Urination

Dogs that urinate when greeting are exhibiting submissive behavior. Punishing or drawing attention to the behavior will make it worse. The way we greet and interact with the dog must be changed. There are several ways in which owners can greet submissive dogs and minimize the probability of eliciting submissive urination. For instance, the owner can squat down while keeping the upper body straight. Avoid direct eye contact, vigorous petting and speaking in a high or excited voice. Redirecting the pup's attention by tossing a toy or piece of food before greeting will also help. The owner may also teach the pup to sit/stay for greetings and practice in easy situations. Handling the problem in the right way should eliminate the problem.

The Home Alone Dog

Provide early morning and after work exercise.

Provide a safe place for your dog when you are gone. Make sure your home is free from hazards. Use a safe room, a fenced yard, a dog run with shade, etc.

Use positive obedience training to build your dog's confidence and provide quality time.

Make your pet feel comfortable by providing a blanket, soft music, safe toys and a bowl of water.

Break up the day by using pet sitters, doggie day care, neighborhood friends or a responsible neighborhood boy or girl you can trust to let the dog out, take it for a walk and play with it.

Don't make a big fuss over your departures and arrivals.

Establish a routine.

Provide the dog with quality time when you are home.

As a general rule crates should not be used for more than 3 to 4 hours except overnight at which time the dog should be let out in the middle of the night until 6 months of age.

Dogs are social animals and could benefit from the company of another pet.

Use a puppy pen, or cordon off an area that is safe and is easy to clean.

Outside Dogs Dogs are pack animals and happiest living inside with their family. But some dogs can live outside when necessary if you provide the proper shelter. Dogs need interaction with their family. Many behavior problems stem from backyard boredom.

Ask your breeder if your breed adjusts to outdoor living. Be prepared to move your pet inside when heat or cold become extreme. Make sure your pet can't escape your yard and has shade, plenty of fresh water and regular exercise. Consider a second dog if you must keep your dog outside.

Note: A good puppy training program can help your dog make the adjustment to living indoors.

7

Animal Shelter Adoptions

Advantages

An older dog is more settled, both in appearance and personality.

An older dog is probably housebroken and may have had some obedience training.

You don't have the hassles of puppyhood and the frustration of the adolescent stage.

It's less costly.

You probably would be saving the dog's life.

Disadvantages

As an adult, it may be more difficult to change bad habits — but it can be done.

Older dogs may be resistant to new leadership.

You never know what experiences the dog has had and how it affected its temperament.

The Pet Adoption Process

Dedicated personnel in adoption agencies work hard to place pets in *permanent* homes. Every effort is made to assure that each pet offered for adoption is the kind of pet you would want for your family. Dogs that have apparent health or behavior problems are not put up for adoption.

You will be asked to fill out a questionnaire at many agencies. This questionnaire will help to determine a good match. Most agencies require that you be 18 and you have the consent of your landlord. The screening process is designed to protect dogs and future owners from untenable situations. Adoptions usually include spay or neuter surgery, vaccinations, and health examinations. You may be required to show verification that the pet is allowed at your residence, proof of residence, and you might be asked to introduce your other family dog (if applicable) to make sure they can get along. Fees are around $50-$75 for dogs. Call your local agency for their fees and requirements.

The Second-Chance Dog

Adopting a dog from a local shelter is an inexpensive way to get a family pet and save a dog's life, but it's not for everyone.

Shelter dogs may have been spayed or neutered, vaccinated and examined by a veterinarian. As a family consider the responsibility of time and care. Too often families get a dog for the children with the understanding that the children will be responsible. What usually happens is the children are not up to the task and the responsibility falls on the parents. Determine who will care for the dog's needs. Consider the kind of dog you want. Have a general idea about size, coat, temperament, sex and breed characteristics.

Be reasonable in your expectations. Most dogs are under stress from their experience in shelters. They are confined and probably lonely, surrounded by strange noises and people. Most of these dogs are the consequence of owners who did not have the time nor the understanding to deal successfully with their needs, some are strays but most are victims of circumstance; an owner who has to move, a landlord who objects, an owner who dies, a divorce. They are separated from the things they know and need your patience.

Don't be too discouraged when a simple behavior problem is the reason the dog was abandoned. What they need most is to have their confidence built. They need owners who are patient and who will take the time to work with them. Bonding won't happen overnight. GIVE IT TIME!

Questions you should ask when you visit a shelter:

1 Find out why the dog is up for adoption.
2 Does it like children?
3 Has it ever bitten anyone?
4 Is it housebroken?
5 Was it an inside or outside dog?
6 Does it require any special care?
7 Does it respond to obedience commands?
8 Is it shy or fearful?
9 Does it bark aggressively, growl or raise its hackles around you or other dogs?

Visit the shelter during the week when shelter personnel have more time. Ask them for their insights. Shelter workers and volunteers are concerned with creating the right match for permanent placements.

Many shelters have quiet areas where you can get to know the pet better. Take a ball and some treats and see how the dog responds to you and the family. Don't be surprised if the dog is frisky, jumps up on you or pulls on the leash. Dogs act out of character in kennel situations. They will probably be excited from being out of the kennel and with people.

TIPS If a dog is affectionate towards you, don't worry too much about why it's there.

Make sure the dog is in good health, with clear eyes, shiny coat, pink gums and tongue. Most veterinarians offer FREE exams for rescued animals.

Homecoming for your Adopted Dog

When you get home, your new family member may be shy, confused and disoriented. He may jump on your furniture, urinate indoors, or show a number of signs of bad manners. Don't worry, with time, patience, persistence and understanding he will soon get the message and know what is expected of him.

Treat your new pet as if it were never house-broken. Go back to basics. Establish a routine. Give your dog 6 to 12 weeks to adjust to its new home. Begin by *preventing* problems from occurring by dog-proofing your home and confining your dog to a safe area (with plenty of water) when you are not able to supervise. At first, do not leave your new dog in the company of children unchaperoned. Children can play rough with a dog and be inconsiderate. Spend as much time as you can with your new companion. Build the dog's confidence with basic obedience that uses positive reinforcement methods (praise, treats, petting, play, etc.). Dogs need to know where they fall in the hierarchy; they need activity, regular exercise, a good balanced diet and the companionship of their owner(s). Give the dog attention, but allow him personal space. Never correct after the fact. Never hit your dog or use your hands as weapons. Never yell at your dog. A kind, firm, patient approach will prove successful in the end. For best results seek the help of a reputable trainer or behaviorist who uses positive methods.

Separation Anxiety — a Common Problem

A lot of rescue dogs exhibit "Separation Anxiety" which means the dogs cannot emotionally cope with the absence of their owners. They manifest their anxiety by vocalization (barking, whining, etc.), destructive behavior, escaping, housesoiling, and, in some severe cases, self-mutilation.

NEVER CORRECT or PUNISH a dog that exhibits separation anxiety. When you come home and punish your dog for something he did earlier, he is likely to associate the punishment with his enthusiastic greeting. Therefore, punishment only increases his anxiety. Focus on the positive and reward using verbal praise, treats, petting, etc.

Don't make a big fuss over your departures and arrivals. No *long* affectionate greetings or goodbyes.

Use obedience commands like *sit/stay* to build the dog's confidence.

Use mock departures of varying duration (from 1 minute to 10 minutes), use different stimuli such as grabbing your keys, starting your car, etc.

Use pet sitters, doggie day care, neighborhood friends or a teenage boy or girl who can be trusted to play, exercise and let the dog out during the day.

Taking on a shelter dog with a past is not easy. Only you know if you have the patience and understanding to work through difficulties. Things may proceed slowly, but, if you are committed, the rewards of reclaiming a life can be immeasurable.

Of the people who adopt shelter animals, 79% take home pets younger than 6 months of age, according to the Humane Society of the United States.

A Second Dog

The main thing to think about when considering a second dog is space and combinations of dominant or submissive personalities. Will there be enough space for each dog to have a retreat?

If the newcomer is a puppy, the adjustment is usually smooth. If the newcomer is fully grown, you have to proceed with more caution. An ideal combination is a neutered male and a spayed female. Trickier are two bitches, because they often don't get along. More difficult is two males, because sooner or later they will try to establish dominance by fighting. Neutered males are easier. Try to determine if the breed profile suggests dog dominance. Avoid the combination of two dominant dogs or dogs whose breed tends to be aggressive toward other dogs.

TIPS Introduce new dogs outside on neutral ground to avoid initial territorial disputes. Use positive reinforcement. Give adult dogs some quiet time away from the new puppy and some individual attention.

Introducing a New Dog to...

Another Family Dog

Introduce dogs on loose leashes in a neutral area. The dogs will use their body language to establish hierarchy. Maintain loose leashes at all times. Some may play bow and romp around together. Give verbal praise to older dogs for positive behavior. If you can, take the dogs for a walk together.

Use a happy, positive tone of voice to show you are pleased with any positive behavior. If you decide to adopt, when you return home let the dogs run around together in your back yard while dragging a leash that is connected to a buckle collar, and let them settle any differences themselves unless they threaten life and limb. When it is time to go inside introduce your new dog to your home while still on leash. Make sure you do not show partiality. Feed both at the same time and in separate food dishes.

An Infant

Most dogs are curious about infants. They should adapt quickly and easily to the presence of a new baby. Since the consequences of a problem can be severe you should observe safety precautions. A baby could be accidently hurt when a dog becomes excited and cannot be controlled. Before your child arrives home, teach your dog obedience commands to control it in exciting situations.

When you bring your baby home, greet the dog without the baby present. Allow the dog to sniff the smell of the baby on you or an article of clothing.

After the excitement has decreased and the dog appears relaxed, gradually introduce the baby. The dog should be on leash, one parent attending to the dog, the other the baby. Place your dog in a sit/stay position approximately 10 to 15 feet from the baby. If the dog appears calm and under control, slowly bring the baby to the dog and allow the dog to sniff (at a safe distance). Reward the dog.

Canine Health & Care

Healthy Signs

Skin should be smooth, flexible and free of scales, scabs, growths or areas of redness.

Coat should be glossy and pliable, without dandruff or areas of baldness. There should be no external parasites or mats.

Eyes should be bright and shiny, free from excessive watering or discharge.

Ears should be light pink, clean with a small trace of wax.

Nose is usually cold and moist.

Temperature is normally 100 to 102.5 degrees (average 101.3).

Gums should appear pink, firm and pigmented.

Teeth should be clean and free of tartar. Breath should be odor free.

Pulse is 70 to 130 beats per minute at rest.

Stools should be firm and free of parasites.

Exercise

One of the most important things you can do for the mental and physical health of your dog is to provide regular exercise.

As a general rule, a twenty- to thirty-minute walk twice a day is sufficient. Dogs are most energetic in the morning. Regularly scheduled walks and runs will help vent a lot of energy that, if pent up for long, can manifest itself in problem behaviors.

TIP Teach your dog to retrieve. If you throw a ball, your dog will search, run after it, and bring it back with great pleasure. Start at an early age and make it exciting. Praise your dog when it successfully retrieves.

Spaying & Neutering

Ten million healthy, friendly dogs and cats will be euthanized in the United States this year simply because they are unwanted. Neutering your dog or cat will not only help control the overpopulation problem but help to prevent health problems, such as tumors and cancer.

Spaying your female dog won't alter her temperament; however, neutering a male dog will make it a better-behaved pet. To prevent unwanted pregnancies, make this decision at an early age (well before the first heat cycle in female dogs). Consult with your veterinarian.

Spay/ Neuter Facts vs. Myths

Myth It is wrong to deprive an animal of the natural right to reproduce.

Fact There is no physical or behavioral benefit for a dog to bear or sire a litter. A neutered dog will feel no sense of denial or lack of fulfillment.

Myth Neutering will change my pet's personality.

Fact You will benefit by any personality change. Neutered pets tend to be calmer, more contented animals. Males are less likely to engage in several undesirable behaviors including mounting, urine marking in the house, roaming and aggression towards other male dogs.

Myth Neutering my pet will make him fat and lazy.

Fact Too much food and too little exercise lead to obesity.

Myth My dog will become a wimp.

Fact Hunting and protective territorial instincts are not diminished by neutering.

Did You Know... Spay/neutering your dog will reduce the likelihood of several serious illness, including testicular or ovarian cancer.

Spay/ neutering is the only effective solution to a serious pet overpopulation problem. Many dogs surrendered to animal shelters are the result of accidental breedings, owners who think they can make a quick buck by breeding, or want to teach their kids about reproduction and find they can't place the puppies.

Please have your dog(s) or cats spayed or neutered.

Grooming Every dog should be groomed thoroughly and regularly. The grooming routine includes attention to the coat, teeth, nails, eyes and ears. The time and effort varies depending on your breed. It's up to you to be your dog's best friend by looking after his physical needs on a regular basis.

Coat All dogs should be brushed once a day. Not only will your dog be neat and clean but it's a great way to bond with your pet. Dogs love it. First, feel your dog all over for any foreign objects and remove them carefully. Using your recommended brush, hold the hair up a small section at a time and brush downward in short, brisk strokes. When you have done the whole body this way, begin again at the head and use long sweeping strokes to brush in the direction the hair grows to smooth the coat. Make sure you don't pull or hurt the skin. "Plucking" to remove the dead hairs is occasionally necessary for breeds like the terriers. Professional grooming should be used periodically. Consult with your breeder or local club for the kind of equipment you will need.

Bathing Frequent baths remove natural oils and are not good for dogs. Use a shampoo especially formulated for dogs.

Pads & Nails This area requires special attention. Always check between the dog's toes for dirt and foreign objects and possible hair mats. Nails should be trimmed every month so they just clear the floor. Purchase a specially designed nail trimmer at your pet store. Don't use scissors. Ask your groomer or veterinarian to show you how. A dog's nails are sensitive, and the nails should not be clipped too far back.

Ears At least once a week, dirt, dust, and ear wax should be removed from the ears using a cotton swab dipped in alcohol. Proceed gently, and do not probe deeply. Clean only the outer ear. The inner ear should be cleaned and ear wax removed by a professional. If your dog scratches behind the ears a lot, or keeps shaking its head violently, or both, it may have an inflammation. Do not try to clean out an infected ear; seek the service of your veterinarian.

Eyes Make sure hairs do not rub against the eyeball, and any discharge is removed. If there is any inflammation, reddening, tearing or excessive blinking, your veterinarian should be consulted.

Teeth Dogs develop plaque and tartar just as people do. You should clean your dog's teeth twice a week. Use a regular toothbrush and toothpaste formulated for dogs, or salt water or a mixture of equal parts of salt and baking soda. Older, hardened deposits should be removed by your veterinarian.

How to Choose a Professional Groomer

In the state of California there are no special government licenses or requirements to become a groomer. It is important that you know as much as possible about the person to whom you are about to entrust your dog. How long have they been grooming? How did they learn to groom? Ask your veterinarian whom they refer.

Visit the grooming shop before you make your first appointment. Is the shop clean and sanitized? How are the other dogs being treated? Will your dog be in contact with other animals? Is your groomer certified? What shampoo is being used on your pet? What flea-killing agent?

What drying techniques? When practiced properly, grooming should be an enjoyable experience. Look for signs of mishandling when you pick up your dog. Is your dog frightened or timid? Notice how your dog reacts toward the groomer. The Southern California Professional Groomers Association states "when you pick up your dog you should expect nails trimmed, ear hair removed, ears swabbed clean, tummy and pads shaved, dog trimmed according to breed standard, correct shampoo for skin type, and a warning to any noticeable problems." The National Dog Groomers Association of America sets standards and service guidelines for its members, as well as conducts certification programs.

TIP: When you pick up your pet make sure your pet is wearing its own ID tag. Give your dog praise and attention when you pick it up. This helps create a positive association with the grooming experience.

Tick Removal

Ticks should be swabbed with alcohol or a special tick solution and then pulled out slowly with tweezers. You must be careful to remove the blood-sucking parasite completely, including the head and biting parts; otherwise sores and infection may develop.

Nutrition

Part of being a responsible pet owner is providing your dog with a nutritious diet. Throughout its life your pet should be fed a nutritionally balanced food specifically formulated for its age (Puppy, Maintenance, Performance and Senior are the most common stages) and life-style.

Examine your dog's physical condition regularly. Are the eyes clear? Is the coat shiny? Is there dandruff? Are the gums and tongue pink? Are the stools watery or abnormal? Does the animal eat and defecate regularly? Is your dog lethargic? If the answer is yes, consult with your veterinarian to determine a diet that is right for your dog.

The following are a few basic rules of nutrition.

Choose a premium quality food found in pet food stores, animal feed stores or veterinary offices. Quality ingredients in the food cost the manufacturer more and therefore cost you more, but the food is easily digested and has a higher percentage of nutrients that are absorbed in the dog's system. The food is more concentrated, so you don't have to feed quite as much as you would a cheaper dog food to meet your dog's daily nutritional requirements. In the long run, it costs you less.

The basic building blocks of canine nutrition, Protein, Fat, Carbohydrates, Vitamins and Minerals, must exist in *"proper balance"* formulated for the life stage and activity level of your dog.

Calcium/phosphorus ratio levels must be maintained within a range of 1.2% calcium to 1% phosphorus, no more, no less. Zinc is an important mineral that must be included in diets. You can do considerable harm by feeding homemade diets that are nutritionally incomplete.

Dogs, unlike people, do not need variety in their diets.

Labels must list the ingredients in descending order, along with a guaranteed analysis of the product's protein, fat, fiber and moisture. You should also find a claim about its nutritional value for a particular life stage. If manufacturers claim high protein on the label, make sure you know the source. The most readily digestible protein for a dog is the white of an egg which is given a Biological Value rating of 1 by nutritionists, followed by: muscle meats-.90; beef-.84; fish-.75; soy-.75; rice-.72; oats-.66; yeast-.63; wheat-.60; and corn-.54. The cost per pound would fall in the same order. Look on the label to determine from what source the protein is derived. Too many vague terms on the labels are still used and allowed by the government which makes it difficult to compare food quality. You need to choose a manufacturer that you can trust.

TIPS Do not feed table scraps, but if you can't resist those pleading eyes, limit table scraps to no more than 10% to 15% of the diet.

Don't give your dog chocolate!

Feed the amount of food necessary to maintain the dog's proper weight and health.

The Association of American Feed Control Officials (AAFCO) has developed protocols for testing dog food based on controlled feedings. To find if your food has met their approval call: 800 851-0769.

Food Formulated for Age

Feed dog food formulated for your dog's age. The following are examples of size and maturity rate.

Toys	up to 15 lbs.	6 months
Small	15-35 lbs.	9 months
Medium	35-55 lbs.	10-15 months
Large	55-100 lbs.	18-20 months
Giant	100-175 lbs.	22 months

Vitamins for Dogs

Never supplement your dog's diet before consulting your veterinarian. Most commercial dog foods are so sound nutritionally that it could be dangerous to supplement them without the advice of a knowledgeable professional who is aware of your pet's individual health status. Excessive amounts of vitamins are toxic, and minerals like calcium and phosphorus must be kept in the correct balance.

Obesity Test

To determine if your dog is obese, place your hands on its rib cage. You should be able to feel the ribs by gentle pressure. If you cannot, your dog is overweight.

Note: Feeding your dog too much is as bad as not feeding your dog enough. Overweight dogs can develop many problems and their lives can be shortened.

6g Owners Guide

Pill Medication The easiest way is to disguise the pill in their food. Otherwise, tilt your dog's head upward slightly, then place the pill deep into the dog's throat. Quickly remove your hand and after your dog closes his mouth keep his head elevated and rub or blow on its nose. Usually a dog will lick his nose when he has swallowed the pill. Repeat until successful.

Medical Supplies You may need these items:
Rectal thermometer (Normal temperature is 100.8 to 102.5; average 101.3)
Petroleum jelly
Hydrogen Peroxide for cuts & wounds and to induce vomiting
Sterile gauze pad and adhesive tape (1 inch wide) and cotton balls
A triple antibiotic ointment such as Neosporin or Bacitracin for surface wounds
Charcoal tablets for poisoning
Use as a stretcher, if needed, a flat board or cardboard box, blanket or towel
Toothbrush and dog tooth paste
Tweezers

First Aid First aid should be practiced in an emergency situation before you can reach a veterinarian. First, call your veterinarian and alert him or her to the situation. If you are uncertain, they can advise you on the phone.

Restraint You may find it necessary to muzzle your dog if it is injured. Place a strong bandage or necktie about 3 feet long over the dog's muzzle, tie a simple knot under the chin, cross the ends, and tie them behind the ears.

Emergency Transportation Place on a large, firm surface like a plywood board. Large towels or blankets are okay if nothing else is available.

Bleeding Stop the bleeding as soon as possible. Use a pressure dressing; a wad of cotton that will normally stop the flow of blood wrapped by gauze to hold it in place. For severe bleeding, a tourniquet may be necessary. Seek a veterinarian immediately. Tourniquets should be loosened every ten minutes and should be used very carefully. Keep him warm and calm, in case of shock. Do not give liquids, in case of internal injuries.

Fractures The affected limb is usually held in an unnatural position. Keep him as still as possible and transport the dog to your veterinarian using a firm surface. Try to keep the limb supported at all times with a cushion.

Poisoning

Symptoms are abdominal pain, trembling and drooling, shallow breathing, convulsions and eventual coma. Seek veterinary care immediately. Try to save any of the substance or packaging that the pet may have eaten.

TIP If a pet is left alone in a garage, make sure all hazardous materials, especially antifreeze is out of reach. Dogs are attracted to the smell and taste of antifreeze.

Keep snail bait and ibuprofen away from dogs.

National Animal Control Poison Center University of Illinois 24 hour Hotline (Fee) 1 800 548-2423

Poison Control Hotline 800 876-4766 San Diego 800 544-4404 LA

Summer Cautions

Hot Days Make sure your dog has plenty of fresh water, shade and air. Your dog may eat a little less than usual.

Hot Cars Make sure you don't leave your pet in a car during the hot summer months. Temperatures can heat up fast to unbearable and dangerous levels. If you have to take your pet, park in the shade and provide a constant air supply. The best advice is to leave him at home.

Heatstroke Dogs are susceptible to heatstroke. Be mindful of shade and water and excessive activity during hot weather. Take long dog walks early in the morning or early evening. If you think your dog has heat exhaustion, immediately apply cool water with a garden hose and proceed to a veterinarian. When a dog's rectal temperature is 104 or more, the dog is in serious trouble.

Swimming Most dogs love to swim but don't assume your dog knows how. Go into the water with a stick or ball and call your dog. Never frighten your dog or throw him in. Don't let him overdo it. Be careful of strong tides and access to the beach. Many dogs have drowned because they cannot climb up the embankment or concrete wall of the swimming pool. If you have a pool, teach the dog how to use the steps.

Snakebite

Symptoms include swelling, labored breathing, glazed eyes and drooling. Proceed to vet while keeping the dog warm, calm and inactive.

Bee Stings

Sting bites produce pain and swelling. A dog that has a severe reaction needs veterinary attention. An ice cube over the sting will ease the pain and swelling.

Disaster Preparedness and your Dog

Be prepared with:
2 weeks supply of canned and dry pet food
2 weeks supply of bottled water
Flashlights, batteries, candles and radio.
Can opener
Heavy blanket
Set of bowls
Crate
2 leashes per dog
First aid kit and medications
Health records & vaccinations
Photo, in case your dog gets lost
Most important, always keep ID tags on your pet, in addition to your name and number, use a contact number for a person that is out of your area.
Secure all bookcases and cabinets to the wall.
Ask a neighbor, in advance, to care for your dog in the event you are away when disaster strikes.

Have a plan for boarding — know hotels that accept pets, line up a reputable kennel. Red Cross shelters do not accept animals inside their buildings.

Dog Fights

Dogs fight mainly over territory, social hierarchy, or a female in heat. The best advice is to prevent fights before they start. Keep dogs separated. Otherwise, you must act quickly and make sure you don't endanger yourself. Try throwing water on the dogs, if available. After the fight flush open wounds with water and hydrogen peroxide and seek veterinary attention.

How You Might Avoid Being Bitten by a Dog

When Dogs Might Bite

When they feel threatened or afraid.
When they are protecting their territory, food, toys, family or pups.
When they get excited — even in play.
When they don't know you.
When their chase response is triggered.
When they have been bred or trained to be aggressive.
When they are in pain or irritated.

How to tell when a dog may bite

The dog will stand stiff and still, with his hair (hackles) up.
The dog may stare at you.
The dog may hold his tail stiff and up in the air and may wag it back and forth very fast.
The dog may growl, snarl, show teeth, or bark strongly.

What To Do

Stand very still and try to be calm. DON'T SCREAM AND RUN.
Don't stare directly at the dog — but be aware of it.
Don't make any sudden moves.
Try to stay until the dog leaves; if it doesn't very slowly back away.
If the dog comes up to sniff you, don't resist.
If you say anything, speak calmly and firmly.
Plan, in case of attack, to buffer a bite with a purse, jacket or other object.
If you fall or are knocked down, curl into a ball with your arms and hands over your head and neck. Try not to scream or roll around.

If you get bitten, report all bites to police or animal control, seek treatment and remember to give a description to the authorities so they can find the animal and determine if the dog has rabies.

Life Expectancy The length and quality of your dog's life will depend on genetics, nutrition and care. You can't control genetics but you can have an influence on nutrition and care.

Small and medium dogs age fifteen human years their first year then nine years the next year and four years every year from two on. A seven-year-old dog would be 44. Large and giant breeds age 12 years the first human year and 7 years thereafter. A 5-year-old-dog would be 40 in human years.

The Older Dog Dogs are considered in their senior years around the age of eight. About 10% of the dog population is over 10. Our special friends need thoughtful care in order to make their remaining time with us comfortable. Your veterinarian should be consulted as to the best care to prolong the quality of life for your dog. Pay close attention to: feeding and nutrition, grooming and preventive care.

Feeding Activity levels and metabolism rates slow, reducing the amount of calories required. Your dog will need a special diet formulated for older dogs. If you don't make the adjustment your dog can become overweight, hastening illness. An ideal diet would be lower in protein and lower in fat than a normal maintenance diet. The source of protein is important to consider. For best direction consult with your veterinarian. Because older dogs eat less, the diet should be of high quality to supply the necessary daily nutrients. Because digestion and absorption takes longer, try feeding smaller portions more often but no more than their daily caloric requirement.

Prevention Dogs, like people, should have periodic physicals for early detection and treatment. Vaccinations should be up-to-date. Ideal weight should be maintained. Moderate exercise helps to fight obesity and keep the joints supple. Older dogs adjust poorly to physical and emotional stress. They love routine. Special care should be exercised to prevent exposure to extremes in weather and to provide a shelter away from rain, cold and drafts. Make sure your dog's teeth are clean and free of tartar to prevent bad breath, gingivitis and periodontal disease.

Grooming The older dog's coat can get dry and brittle. Skin tumors are more common. Frequent brushings, combined with regular bathing with a specially formulated shampoo recommended by your veterinarian is advised. Toe nails need to be trimmed more often. When wet, your dog should be toweled dry thoroughly and kept in a warm room.

Euthanasia

When life becomes difficult and ceases to be enjoyable, when the dog suffers from a painful condition for which there is no hope of betterment, it is perhaps time to say goodbye.

Death of a Family Pet

As an integral part of the family we are emotionally affected by the loss of our dog. Unfortunately, there are no social rituals like funerals and wakes that act to support us during these troubled times. Society does not offer a grieving pet owner a great deal of sympathy. Still, the loss of a pet affects our emotions and usually progress through several stages. Recognizing them can help us cope with the grief we feel:

Denial The initial response many owners exhibit when faced with their pet's terminal condition or sudden death.

Bargaining typically happens when the individual will try to make a deal to spare the life of their pet.

Anger can be exhibited by hostility and aggression or can turn inward, emerging as guilt. You can get mad at your veterinarian or someone else but you are just relieving frustration at the expense of another. You can also go through a number of "if onlys," i.e., if only I had acted earlier.

Grief is the stage of true sadness. The pet is gone and only emptiness remains. It is important to have the support of family and friends and to talk about your feelings. It is helpful to recognize that other pet owners have experienced similar feelings and that you are not alone in this feeling of grief. See below for helpful hotlines.

Resolution All things must pass — even grieving. As time passes, the distress dissolves as the pet owner remembers the good times, not the passing. Many find the answer lies in giving a good home to a dog in need of a good owner.

The pet loss support Hotlines:

University of California
School of Veterinary Medicine
Davis, California
916 752-7418

The Delta Society
206 226-7357

San Diego County Bereavement Program
619 275-0728

9

Veterinarians

Tips on Choosing a Veterinarian

Look for a veterinarian who will take the time to speak with you, will make the effort to explain any problems in layman's terms and is accessible.

The key word is *confidence*. Look for cleanliness and note how the hospital smells. If you don't feel comfortable being there, chances are neither will your pet.

Is the staff friendly and caring? Do they make you feel comfortable?

What are their hours? Is anyone on duty at night, in case of emergency? Most vets are not open around the clock, but make sure you know where you can go after hours.

All certified veterinarians must have credentials. You should know his or her credentials and their reputation.

Can you take a tour of the facilities? Do they have any special equipment? Are the sick animals isolated from the other animals?

The Puppy Exam

Smart puppy buyers make the sale of their new pet contingent on passing a medical exam by a veterinarian. This initial exam consists of a check for detectable birth defects that could cause problems down the road. The vet will also check for skin infections and sores, ear mites, intestinal worms, ticks, fleas, nutrition and general health.

See "Free Puppy Exam" Coupon Offer.

Vaccinations
Don't overlook this. Vaccinations save millions of dogs' lives yearly. It is the best thing you can do to prevent such diseases as distemper, parvovirus, parainfluenza, rabies, bordetella, hepatitis and leptospirosis.

The American Veterinary Medical Association recommends that puppies receive a *series* of vaccinations, beginning at six to eight weeks of age, followed by two more vaccinations three to four weeks apart. Thereafter, renew the dog's protection with booster vaccines each year. The exception to this is the rabies boosters. The State of California requires up-to-date rabies vaccine starting at four months. Your veterinarian is the best source of advice concerning a schedule that is best for your dog.

TIP Don't take your puppy around other dogs until your veterinarian says it is okay.

Sickness & Emergencies
You should call your vet when your pet is behaving in an unusual manner which lasts. Here are a few signs to look for in a dog that signal the time to make an immediate call:
Vomiting and/or diarrhea that persists
Loss of appetite
Labored breathing
Isolation, or wanting to hide
Fever
Persistent cough
Listlessness
Increased urination or straining to urinate
Unusual odor from mouth, skin, ears or rectal area

Less Immediate signs that still need to be checked out:
A lump or bump on the skin
Lameness that persists without improvement for more than 24 hours
Persistent scratching, particularly if it results in hair loss or reddening of the skin.
Watery eyes or glassy appearance of eyes

Runny nose
Increased water intake
Weight loss

Emergency Hospitals

In an after-hour emergency call your veterinarian. If he or she is unavailable, refer to the service directory under Emergency Hospitals.

Internal Parasites

Worms can cause serious damage. Roundworm, hookworm, whipworm and tapeworm are the most common. A dog might have worms even though you don't see them in their stool. Be concerned if you notice your dog run its fanny on the floor. Your veterinarian will consider the best and safest medication for your pet.

TIP Don't give your pet medication for worms without receiving positive test results from your veterinarian.

Heartworm

These parasites are deadly. Every pet owner should be aware of this condition. Heartworm is spread by infected mosquito that bites a dog. Larvae then burrow into the dog and undergo several changes which lead to the development of worms. This large thread-like parasite lives in the right ventricle and major arteries of the heart. Ask your veterinarian to recommend a method of prevention.

External Parasites (Fleas and Ticks)

Fleas and ticks have ruined many dog-owner relationships so it's important to get a handle on this problem before it is out of control. On your initial puppy visit you should ask your veterinarian about a program and products he or she recommends. Because fleas spend most of their life off the dog, treatment of the dog is only partly effective. It is most important to eradicate fleas in the environment (indoors, outdoors, cars, etc.) and do it all at the same time.

How to Fight Fleas

Signs: *Salt and pepper-like grains about the size of sand in the coat usually around the dog's back, tail, groin and hindquarters.*

Every dog owner at one point or another will have to do battle with the dreaded flea. Adult fleas comprise only five percent of the total flea population, their eggs comprise fifty percent, larvae thirty-five percent and pupae ten percent. Fleas are most prevalent in warm weather. Fleas spend most of their life off the pet so treatment of the dog is only partly effective. To be successful you must attack not only the flea, but the flea *eggs* and the *larvae* that are in your environment. Otherwise the dog will reinfect itself when new fleas emerge.

Simultaneously mount a three-pronged attack. The main weapons are: insecticides such as *Dips*, which last about one week in Southern California, *Shampoos* especially formulated to kill adult fleas, *Powders*, which cling to a dogs coat, *Sprays*, to instantly kill adult fleas, *Bombs*, to cover large indoor areas and dog houses, *Granules*, used for the outdoor areas or on carpets to penetrate deep into the base.

Treat the dog with safe dips, shampoos. Treat inside the house with bombs, sprays, granules. Treat the yard with sprays, granules.

The Plan: Spray or use granules in the yard then treat the dogs by taking them to the groomers or give them a bath inside the home using a safe shampoo and dip (make sure the dog's eyes and ears are protected). Once the yard is safe, release the dogs in the yard and then vacuum (dispose of the bag when done), spray and bomb inside the home, or for long-term results have your house treated by an exterminator company or ask your pet supply store if they recommend a safe inorganic salt product. Don't forget to treat crates, kennel runs, bedding, garages and the car. Most insecticides will only kill adult fleas, a slow vacuum will take up eggs and larvae. To make sure, vacuum often!

TIP Buy a fine-toothed flea comb. Collect the fleas in the comb and then drown them in water laced with dish soap or flea shampoo (this can be very effective for short haired dogs).

Choose a product based on the recommendation of your veterinarian or pet store professional. Insecticides are poisons!

Pyrethrums, which are made from chrysanthemums, are claimed to be safe and effective but, like any pesticide, can be toxic if not properly used.

Use chemical flea products with caution and only as directed. Don't mix products!

Many dogs suffer allergies to flea bites called flea bite dermatitis. Some owners rub on aloe vera for relief. Consult with your veterinarian for an effective course of treatment.

Check with your veterinarian before applying an insecticide to a dog that has been wormed within a week.

Natural Flea Fighters

The following methods are natural flea treatments not scientifically proven but some owners say they work:

Avon's Skin-So-Soft diluted w/ water as a spray.
Cedar chips.
Garlic, vinegar or brewers yeast added to food.
Fine-toothed flea comb. Collect the fleas in the comb and then drown them in water laced with dish soap or flea shampoo. (This can be very effective for short haired dogs.)
Herbal flea collars.
Aloe vera drink for pets
Citrus shampoos.

Lyme Disease

Lyme disease is transmitted by the deer tick. Symptoms of the disease include fatigue, fever and swollen glands in the neck. Avoid walks in areas where deer ticks are common. Consult your veterinarian about the number of incidences in your area and check to see if he or she recommends a vaccination.

Dental Care   It is just as important for dogs to take good care of their teeth as it is for humans. Your veterinarian is also your dog's dentist. Dogs get a build up of tartar that must be removed periodically to help prevent major organ damage, tooth loss and unnecessary pain.

TIP   Brush your dog's teeth regularly. Get your puppy accustomed to someone opening and examining its mouth.

10

Responsible Dog Ownership

Your Dog and Your Neighbors

All dog owners are responsible for making their dogs good neighbors. Excessive barking, unleashed roaming and unattended excretion are the major problems in urban and suburban areas. Civic leaders are banning more and more places of use for dogs because of a few irresponsible owners. Be considerate of your neighbor. If your dog barks, consider taking it inside or, for more severe problems, consult with a dog behaviorist. Always carry plastic bags on a walk. Leash your dog in public places and always practice responsible dog ownership.

Canine Good Citizenship

The AKC promotes Canine Good Citizenship with their program that encourages responsible dog ownership through training.

Your dog should be conditioned always to behave in the home, in public places, and in the presence of other dogs. The program is an evaluation that consists of ten different activities that a good canine citizen would be expected to be capable of performing. Included are such requirements as allowing a stranger to approach, walking naturally on a loose lead, walking through a crowd, sitting for examination, reacting to a strange dog and reacting to a distraction such as a door suddenly closing or a jogger running by the dog. The evaluator will inspect your dog's grooming, appearance and will evaluate your dog's performance of the sit, down and stay in position commands. The last requirement is that the dog demonstrate good manners when left alone.

General Dog Laws

Dog owners should be aware of local and state laws concerning dog ownership, some of which are described here.

Lemon Law for New Dog Owners

Retail sellers of dogs cannot sell very sick or defective dogs. Certain non-disabling problems can be disclosed and the dog can be certified as acceptable for sale by a veterinarian. If you are sold a sick or defective dog, first contact the place where you obtained the dog and seek an amicable solution to the situation. If the seller is unwilling to rectify the problem, you may be able to exercise rights under the Dog Lemon Law.

License Required

All dog owners shall apply for and obtain a separate dog license for each dog they own after it is four months old. All dog owners must possess a license at the time the dog is four months of age or thirty days after obtaining or bringing any dog four months of age into the area in which the Department of Animal Control provides licensing or animal control services. Dog owners need to renew the dog license *before* it becomes delinquent.

Restraint of Dogs by Owner

Dog owners shall at all times prevent their dogs from being at large and from being in violation of any other animal-related municipal code.

Conditions of Animal Ownership

Animal premises shall be kept sanitary and shall not constitute a fly breeding reservoir, a source of offensive odors or human or animal disease.

Public Protection from Dogs

Dog owners shall at all times prevent their dogs from biting or harassing any person engaged in a lawful act and from interfering with the lawful use of public or private property. Any person who violates any provision of this section is guilty of a misdemeanor.

Committing Nuisance

No person shall allow a dog in his/her custody to defecate or to urinate on property other than that of the owner or person having control of the dog. The failure to curb such dog and to immediately remove any feces to a proper receptacle constitutes a violation of this section. Unsighted persons relying on a guide dog shall be exempt from this section.

Female Dogs in Season

Dog owners shall securely confine their female dogs while in season within an enclosure in a manner that will prevent the attraction of male dogs in the immediate vicinity.

Disturbing the Peace Prohibited

No person shall own or harbor an animal in such a manner that the peace or quiet of the public is unreasonably disturbed. Any person who violates any provision of this section is guilty of a misdemeanor.

Inhumane Treatment and Abandonment

No person shall treat an animal in a cruel or inhumane manner or willingly or negligently cause or permit any animal to suffer unnecessary torture or pain. No person shall abandon any domestic animal without care on any public or private property. Any person who violates any provision of this section is guilty of a misdemeanor.

Transportation of Animals

No person shall transport or carry, on any public highway or public roadway, any animal in a motor vehicle not protected by a device that will prevent the animal from falling to the highway.

Animals in Unattended Vehicles

No person shall leave an animal in any unattended vehicle without adequate ventilation or in such a manner as to subject the animal to extreme temperatures which adversely affect the animal's health or welfare.

Dog Bites

Most laws state that dog owners are responsible for any dog bite injuries caused by the dog whether or not the dog was at fault. Consult your attorney for exact local and state statutes. Authorities may impound your dog for quarantine, or, if your rabies vaccine and license is up-to-date, the quarantine may be at your home. "If you are sued, the damages to the injured party may be increased if you are found to have harbored a vicious dog," according to Michael Rotsten, an Encino attorney who specializes in animal rights law.

Liability Insurance

In most states, dog owners are financially liable for any personal injury or property damage their pet causes. Someone else may be responsible if: the dog owner is less than 18 or someone other than the owner was taking care of the dog. Dog owners may be responsible for medical bills, time off work, pain and suffering, property damage, and, if the owner is found to be careless, double or triple damages or punitive damages could be declared. Consult your insurance agent to see if you are adequately covered against any risks and your local government for the laws in your area.

11

Lost & Found

The speed and thoroughness with which you react can make the difference in whether you recover your pet.

1. Organize a search party — call your friends and relatives and direct a search by foot or by car as soon as possible.

2. Ask mail carriers, paperboys, utility workers, delivery people, etc., if they have seen a stray dog. Tell a patrolling policeman.

3. Make up a card or flyer with a picture of your dog, description of your dog, your name and telephone number where you can be reached in case they spot your pet.

4. Distribute flyers to homes or mail boxes in the area you lost your dog.

5. Check all local shelters. Go in person. Don't rely on office staff to properly identify your dog over the phone. Enter your pet's information in the "lost" log and review the "found" log. Dogs without ID are held a minimum of 3 days.

6 Offer a reward, especially to neighborhood kids on bikes or skateboards.

7. Check with local veterinarians, pet shops and groomers — give them a flyer.

8. Advertise in all local newspapers. Watch the "found" ads — respond to any that might possibly be your dog.

9. Put up signs at intersections, in shopping centers, laundromats, in vet offices, pet stores and grooming parlors. Make up flyers that include a picture of your pet and both your home and work telephone numbers.

10. Don't Give Up. Often well meaning people keep a stray in their home for weeks in hopes of finding the owner.

TIP It is important that you physically go to the shelter to see if your dog is there.

Unclaimed Pets State law mandates a 72 hour hold on strays. Policy varies from shelter to shelter but usually dogs that have identification are usually kept five days while officers try to make contact with owners. After that, unclaimed pets are evaluated to determine physical condition and overall adoptability. Based on the evaluation animals are either placed up for adoption or killed by injection method. The length of time most shelters hold strays depends on their capacity at the time. Because there is a lack of space, many healthy, good tempered, highly adoptable animals are killed.

Found Pets Ask around the neighborhood. The pet may live close to you. Ask children.

Call animal control, or take the pet to the shelter yourself. That's where the owner will be looking. Use the "Found" log. Notify all shelters within a ten mile radius. Don't wait too long—some owners lose heart after a week of looking.

You could also place an advertisement in the "found" section of the newspaper (some papers do not charge), put up signs in your neighborhood and at intersections.

Call local veterinarians and groomers.

12

Travel

Airline Travel   Some airlines allow pets to be transported in the passenger cabin if the pet is in an approved carrier and can fit under the seat. Other, larger pets are placed in a pressurized compartment in the underbelly of the plane. Contact the cargo department of your airlines to receive specific information, especially if you are planning a foreign trip where quarantine time and medical certification is necessary.

TIPS You must make reservations *well in advance* preferably on a non-stop early morning flight.

Obtain an airline-approved crate in advance of your flight date. (Don't rely on the airlines.) Some airlines require a health certificate that is signed by your vet no later than 10 days prior to flight. Check with your airline. Prepare the crate. On the outside tape a piece of paper covered in plastic with your name, address, telephone numbers for both arriving and departing points, your dog's call name, the flight number, destination, and state on the paper if you are on board. Do not feed your adult pet for twelve hours before the flight, puppies sooner; allow water up until the time you leave for the airport. Check liability limitations from the airlines. Seek veterinary advice if you are considering tranquilization.

Note: In summer if the temperature is 85 degrees or higher at departure or arrival times airlines by law cannot transport your pet.

TIP Line the bottom of the carrier with a thick layer of newspaper. This will absorb any moisture and insulate against cold temperatures.

Help your dog become accustomed to the crate well in advance of the flight.

Car Travel & Vacations

Give your pet about one hour to digest a meal, Make a stop about every two to three hours for exercise, have a drink, and for relief.

Put a leash on your dog before you open the door to exit. Consider a collapsible wire crate. They are safe for motor travel and a nice place for your pet to relax.

TIP Dogs could get eye infections or injury from hanging their head out the car window.

Give your dog a chance to urinate or defecate before the trip.

Use a crate or seat harness for safety.

Choosing A Boarding Kennel

If you decide you absolutely cannot take your dog with you, then you must choose between a kennel and a dog sitter. You must use care in choosing.

To get into a good kennel, it will be necessary to make advanced reservations, especially during the summer months and around the holidays.

Visit the kennel. Ask the following questions: How big are the cages? How many dogs occupy each cage? Will they allow a special reminder of home like a favorite blanket or toy in the cage? Do they have runs so your dog does not have to be in the kennel all day? Is there shading? What about safety procedures like fire alarms, smoke detectors, and overhead sprinklers? Ask how long they have been in business and how many dogs they board. Make sure the place is well staffed during off hours. Ask if they groom at the facility or do they transport to another location. (There could be a risk of the dogs getting loose if transported.) Ask about veterinary facilities and payment in the event of medical emergency or make arrangements with your vet. Ask for a written confirmation of prices quoted and any "extras." Is the kennel clean? Is it air conditioned in the summer months? Ask about the food they provide or if you have to bring your own.

A good kennel will request proof of current vaccinations. They are required by law. You may be required to sign a release of liability. The kennel operator should be interested in your dog. Inquiries about the dog's medical history, needs, routines, food and nicknames are positive signs that your dog should receive good care. You may feel better if the kennel belongs to the American Boarding Kennel Association. This association inspects kennels, has education programs and requires members to pledge a code of ethics.

Note: Vaccines are required for boarding dogs in California. Bordetella (every 6 mo.), DHLP-CV (every year) and Rabies (every 3 years in adult dogs) are the current requirements. Check with your kennel and your veterinarian.

Ten Items for the Canine Travel Kit

1 Collar and leash.
2 ID tags with home and vacation addresses to be attached to collar.
3 Dog food and water bowls.
4 Its blanket and a couple of towels.
5 A bottle of water and a supply of food.
6 Health records & license (if required).
7 A first-aid kit with medication for motion sickness and diarrhea, etc.
8 Bedding and grooming aids.
9 Scooper, plastic bags and paper towels.
10 Favorite toy.

13

Activities & Sporting Groups

Running

Dogs need regular exercise. A big benefit of owning a dog is that a dog encourages walks and or runs that are good for both owner and dog. Before you begin running with your dog consider his breed, age and health condition. Make sure your dog is safe and on leash. Start slowly and protect your dog's feet. Be aware of extreme weather conditions. Make sure you provide plenty of water after the run, watch for injury and make sure you take plastic bags to clean up any droppings.

Dogs on the Beach

In Southern California dogs are allowed on the following beaches only:

San Diego County
City of Del Mar
June 1 to Sept 30 permitted leashed south of 17th and North of 29th Streets. Off leash allowed Oct 1 to June 1 at same location.
City of San Diego
North end of Ocean Beach and Fiesta Island dogs are permitted off leash.
All other areas dogs are only allowed leashed after 6 pm and before 9 am.
City of Coronado
Permitted north of lifeguard tower and south of naval base only.

City of Imperial Beach
> Allowed on leash south of Imperial Beach
> Blvd. & north of Palm Ave.

San Elijo State Beach
> Permitted on leash south of life guard tower
> 7 only.

Orange County

Huntington City Beach
> Leashed at end of Goldenwest St., not
> allowed elsewhere

City of Newport Beach
> Allowed leashed before 9 am & after 5 pm,
> Sept 15 to June 15 only

City of Laguna Beach
> Allowed leashed on beaches, Sept to June,
> summer before 8 a.m. after 6 p.m.

Los Angeles County
> Dogs are not allowed on the beaches

Dogs in the Park

Most parks require a dog to be on a leash. A few progressive communities have created special parks just for dogs. They are:

Long Beach Recreation Park 7th & Park
Laguna Beach Laguna Canyon by Humane Society
Costa Mesa Tewinkle Park (opens soon)

Hiking with Your Dog

When you want to enjoy the great outdoors with your dog follow these tips:

Make sure your dog is up to date on its vaccinations (Lymes, Heartworm, etc.) and is in good health. Consult with your vet.

Train your dog with walks that increase in distance and ultimately equal the length of the planned hike.

Check in advance to see if dogs are allowed on the trail. Some parks ban dogs, others require leashed dogs, and others will allow dogs to be off leash.

Bring doggie snacks

Consider a dog pack but remember your dog is not a pack mule.

Use a leash, preferably a retractable one. Dogs that are off leash can spot a wild animal and be gone in a split second, especially the hunting breeds. Unleashed dogs can also damage sensitive plant life.

Make sure your dog has ID tags and they are securely fastened before you leave for your hike.

Bring plenty of water and a plastic bowl and don't let your pet drink stagnant water. They are susceptible to the same diseases, like giardia, that we are.

Watch out for rushing water — make sure your dog is leashed when crossing streams.

Don't let your dog approach other hikers unless the other hikers initiate the approach.

Don't forget a first aid kit that includes gauze pads, gauze, adhesive tape, disinfectant (a snake-bite kit if your area is known for snakes is a good idea) and tweezers.

Check your dog for ticks and remove immediately (make sure you get the head).

Make sure your dog does not overheat. Try to stop and rest in a shady area, if you see your dog excessively panting. Cool by giving water both internally and externally.

Consider apparel that glows in the dark or can be easily identified by hunters like a bright orange vest.

For organized on-leash hikes see service directory under Hiking.

American Kennel Club (AKC)

The AKC is a club of clubs, founded by 462 show-giving clubs to help organize the sport. The AKC is "dedicated to advancing the study, breeding, exhibiting, running and maintenance of thoroughbred dogs." There are 145 breeds and over 1.2 million purebred dogs registered every year.

The AKC licenses dog shows, field trials, obedience trials, tracking tests, hunting and lure coursing tests, herding tests and trials, and coonhound hunts. It maintains the official record of these events and also maintains various systems of administrative review.

To enter a show or obtain show date information see Superindendents in Service Directory.

Dog Shows

Dog shows are evaluations of a dog's conformation. Most dogs seen at shows are competing for points toward their championship.

After examination of the entry, each judge decides how close the dog measures up, in his or her opinion, to the official *breed standard.* The dogs are compared against each other and placed from first to fourth. It takes fifteen points to become a champion of record and use the "CH" Title. The number of points awarded are based on the number of dogs at the show, the more dogs, the more points. Also, the points are adjusted depending on breed, the sex and the geographical location of the show. A dog can earn from one to five points at a show. Wins of three, four or five points are considered "majors." The fifteen points required for championship must be won under at least three different judges, and must include two majors won under different judges.

Obedience Trials

Obedience Trials test a dog's ability to perform a prescribed set of exercises.

A judge scores three different levels, with each level being more difficult. AKC awards titles for successful completion of Novice (CD), Open (CDX) and the third, and most difficult, Utility (UD). A competitor who gets more than 50% of the points on each exercise and a total score of 170 or more out of a possible 200 earns a "leg" towards an obedience degree or title. Three legs are required for a degree. The ultimate distinction, for those dogs that have earned their utility titles, is an Obedience Trial Champion (OTCH) title.

Junior Showmanship

This is an entire class of AKC competition for youngsters between the ages of 10 and 18 that helps them develop handling skills. This class of competition is judged solely on the ability and skills of the handler.

Title Terminology

CD	Companion Dog
CDX	Companion Dog Excellent
CG	Certificate of Gameness
UD	Utility Dog
OTCh	Obedience Trial Champion
Ch	Champion
FCh	Field Champion
HCH	Herding Championship
HI	Herding Intermediate
HIC	Herding Instinct Certificate
HS	Herding Started
HX	Herding Excellent
JH	Junior Hunter
LCM	Lure Courser of Merit
ROM	Register of Merit
SH	Senior Hunter
TD	Tracking Dog
TDX	Tracking Dog Excellent
TT	Temperament Tested
WC	Working Certificate
WCX	Working Certificate Excellent
WDX	Working Dog Excellent

Triple Champion, title awarded to a dog that has won show, obedience and trial championships.

Professional Handlers

Anyone aspiring to have a career as a professional dog handler or anyone requiring the services of a professional dog handler may write or call:

Professional Handlers Association
Kathleen Bowser, Secretary (No Joke)
15810 Mount Everest Lane
Silver Springs, MD 20906
301 924-0089

Herding Dogs

For information on herding instinct testing, trials and training contact:

Jerome M Stewart
Herding Classes
714 968-7051

Candy Kennedy
714 685-8696

Blazin' Border Collies
Terry Parrish
619 739-8673

Whiskers 'N Wool
Linda Lee Merritt
619 442-7640

In the testing section, dogs can earn titles of Herding Test Dog (HT) and Pre-Trial Tested Dog (PT).

AKC trials offer four titles, beginning with the Herding Started (HS), Herding Intermediate (HI), and Herding Excellent (HX). After earning an HX, dogs can then accumulate the necessary fifteen championship points for the Herding Championship (HCH).

Contact your local breed club or the following speciality clubs:

American Herding
Breed Association
Peggy Richter
619 377-5926

San Fernando Herding Assoc.
Janna & Ted Ondrak
818 343-1989

The Herdsman (AKC)
Rte 1, Box 52-A
Putman, Oklahoma 73659
405 661-2262

San Diego Co. Stock
Dog
Janet Seweryn
6130 W Manor Dr.
La Mesa, CA 91942

Mutton Punchers
Ken & Gayle Dugan
805 366-2437

Herding Breed Club of
San Diego
619 484-4377

Den Trials

Group of hunt instinct tests for breeds bred to hunt underground. Open to all terrier breeds and Dachshunds that can fit into a 9" square tunnel. Dogs stalk rats through tunnels ranging 10 to 30 feet. (This is a bloodless sport.)

Contact Jim Tibbits
805 945-5874

Dog Sledding Clubs

International Federation of
Sled Dog Sports
Glenda Walling
7118 N Beehive Rd.
Pocatello, Id 83201
208 234-1608

International Sled Dog
Racing Assoc
Donna Hawley
P O Box 446
Norman, ID 83848-0446
208 443-3153

Agility Training

Agility is a lot of fun. This sport is like a visit to a doggy amusement park that provides an outlet for energy and a great way to spend some free time with your companion.

In this sport dogs traverse a maze of obstacles and compete for speed and accuracy. Dogs jump through tires, zip through tunnels, scale a 6-foot-tall A-frame, walk a narrow "dog walk," negotiate a see-saw, zig-zag through poles and soar over a variety of hurdles. Dogs can participate early. They learn to improve their skill with practice.

U S Dog Agility Assoc.
P O Box 850955
Richardson, TX 75085
214 231-9700

National Agility Club
401 Bluemont Circle
Manhattan, KS 66502
913 537-7022

San Diego Agility Club
Gail Huston
619 569-4875

Agility Club of
Santa Ana
Cheryl Malooly
310 692-0183

West Valley Dog Sports
Jack Mathieson
5802 Jumilla Ave.
Woodland Hills, 91367
818 347-3247

Stuart Mah (Judge)
Chino
909 590-1170

Nat Committee for Agility
916 966-5287

Carting

Carting Classes
Paula Ciagoda
619 445-8309

Dog Owners Guide

Carting Equipment

Summerfield Specialties
PO Box 2346
Spring Valley, CA 91979
619 461-7324
Cart & Harness

Field Trial and Hunting Clubs

Field trials are held separately for Pointing breeds, Retrievers and Spaniels, as well as Beagles, Basset Hounds and Dachshunds. Field trials are practical demonstrations of the dog's ability to perform in the field, the function for which they were bred. AKC titles that are awarded are Field Champion and Amateur Field Champion.

Hunting tests are for retrievers, pointing breeds and spaniels. AKC evaluates the dog's performance on three levels, with each level increasing in difficulty. The levels are Junior (JH), Senior (SH) and Master Hunter (MH). Dogs are judged on their hunting, bird finding, marking, retrieving and trained ability.

American Kennel Club
5580 Centerview Dr
Raleigh,NC 27690-0636
919 233-9767

San Diego Hunting
& Retrieving Club
619 689-2573 or 579-2376

Antelope Vly Dachshund
805 943-3221

Inland Valley Retriever Club
Fran Young

United Kennel Club
100 E Kilgore Rd.
Kalamazoo, MI 49001
616 343-9020

San Diego Sporting
Dog Club
619 583-8392

Cal So Coast Retriever Cl
909 689-8668

Tracking Tests

Tracking tests the dog's ability to follow a scent. A dog that passes this test earns a AKC Tracking Dog title (TD). Advanced work can earn a Tracking Dog Excellent (TDX) title.

American Kennel Club
51 Madison Ave.
New York, NY 10010
212 696-8286

Gus Paul in San Diego
619 453-0690
Nick Hammond
714 629-6374

United Kennel Club
100 E Kilgore Rd.
Kalamazoo, MI 49001-5592
616 343-9020

Betty Regan
714 982-1238

Flyball

This is a great team sport that requires your dog to jump over four small obstacles and retrieve a tennis ball by thumping a container that is set to spring-out the ball and return with the ball to the start area. The next team member then starts, and so on, until all team members have finished. You are racing against another team and the team that finishes first wins.

North American Flyball Association
5325 W Hope Rd
Lansing, MI 48917
517 322-2221
or inquire at your local breed or obedience club.

Scent Hurdle Racing

Dogs run over the same hurdles as flyball, but they must pick out their owners' dumbell by scent from a set of four and return. Also run as a relay. Check with your local obedience club.

Frisbee Competition

To be put on a mailing list to receive event info :

FriskiesCanine Frisbee
Disc Championship
4060-D Peachtree Rd. #326
Atlanta, GA 30319
800 786-9240
(Free training Manual)

in California write/call:
Box 725
Encino, CA 91426
1 800 423-3268
818 780-4913

Lure Coursing

Dogs chase a simulated game over an open course of some 550 to 1800 yards that tests speed and agility. Breeds allowed to run by the American Sighthound Field Association are: Afghans, Basenjis, Borzois, Greyhounds, Ibizans, Irish Wolfhounds, Pharaoh Hounds, Salukis, Scottish Deerhounds and Whippets, all of which follow their quarry by sight. The purpose is "to preserve and further develop the natural beauty, grace, speed, and coursing skill of the sighthound." The association accepts only registered dogs from AKC, UKC, National Greyhound Assoc., or must possess a critic number from the Saluki Club of America. For information call:

American Sighthound
Field Assoc.
2108 Tranon Ct.
Tallahassee, FL 32308
904 877-6795

AKC Lure Coursing
Director
1235 Pine Grove Rd.
Hanover, PA 17331
717 637-3011 (Day)
717 632-6806 (Night)

Inland Widerness Hunt Club
Chino, CA
Dixie Hirsch
714 649-2770

So Cal Whippet Assoc.
Riverside, CA
Cheryl Smith
909 699-0856

Cal Coursing Assoc
Pam Roberts
18481 Roberts Rd.
Woodcrest, CA 92508

Mo Aiken, Open Field
714 961-0413

Local Judges

Lyndell Ackerman
Riverside, CA
909 780-5872

George Martin
Garden Grove, CA
714 636-1798

Howard Lowell
Hesperia, CA
619 334-9354

Michael Hussey
Perris, CA
909 943-6908

Ann Billups
818 963-1038

Coleen Sayre
805 497-7305

Schutzhund

This rigorous German sport combines tracking, obedience and protection exercises. While dogs of other breeds are admitted, this sport is primarily for the German Shepherd Dog. Schutzhund, meaning "protection dog," measures endurance, ability to scent, courage, mental stability and trainability. The sport recognizes both the handler's ability to train and the dog's ability to perform. Choose your trainer with great care.

United Schutzhund
Club of America
3704 Lemoy Ferry Rd.
St. Louis, MO 63125
314 638-9686

Landersverband DVG
America Inc.
Sandi Nethercutt
113 Vickie Dr
Del City, OK 73115
405 672-3947

Golden State Schutzhund
Chuck Buehler
714 633-8517

San Diego Diensthund
Maurice Bullock
619 264-1796

San Diego Schutzhund
John McKinney
619 789-4494

Big West
619 956-3647

West Hills WDA
June Lamb
818 246-6287

Mildred & Leo Muller
Coast SC 909 350-8730

Weight Pulling

International Weight Pulling Assoc.
P O Box 994
Greeley, CO 80632

Appendix A

Local Breeders and Breed Club Directory

Southern California Breeders Directory

The following list of breeders is offered as an aid to the public in obtaining purebred dogs. Breeders listed were obtained from AKC show guides, national and local breed clubs and word of mouth. *Southern California Dog Owners Guide* does not recommend, guarantee, endorse, nor rate breeders and kennels. Although we strive hard to include reputable breeders, we do not assume any liability. You must exercise good judgement. Read Chapter 3, what to look for from a quality breeder. Buyer beware.

Breeders — If you are a local breeder and you would like to be included in this directory, please submit a letter of application with qualifications to the publisher at the address in the front of the book. Please include references from other breeders or clubs. If you need to change a listing, please fill out a change form located in the back of this book.

Puppy Owners — If you have a complaint against any breeder listed, please write a detailed letter to the publisher at the address in the front of the book.

Affenpinscher
Affenpinscher Club of America
2006 Scenic Rd Tallahassee, FL 32303 Ms. Terry Graham, Sec

Mary Ostrand		805 682-8388
Judi Benjamin		818 830-0377
Norma Cacka	Siblu	909 887-3703

Afghan Hounds
Afghan Hound Club of America, Inc
2408A Rt 31, Oswego, IL 60543 Ms. Norma Cozzoni, Sec

Afghan Hound Club of California	Breed Club	310 863-3097

Dog Owners Guide

Western Hound Assoc of So California	Puppy Referrals	818 364-1203
Carol Chapek	Magistelle	619 443-7605
Richard & Janis Reital	Tifarah	619 756-2273
Bruce Sutton	Summerwinds	619 756-2273
Suzanne Neill	Sura	714 921-8473
Denise & Jerry Willieford	Shenandoah	805 492-6204
Mary Cutherell	Donmar	909 795-4867
Giselle Ringwald	Rialto	909 873-9989
Gaston & Claudette Piette	Kamour	909 882-3220

Airedale Terrier

Airedale Terrier Club of America
47 Tulip Ave., Ringwood, NJ 07456 Dr Suzanne Hampton, Sec

Southern California Airedale Association	Puppy Referral	818 360-9701
Kenneth & Kaye Jolgren	Kayekids	619 294-3483
Rose Richards	BlazonCrest	714 220-2473
Dee Chase		714 544-0975
June & Robin Dutcher	Coppercrest	714 827-8013
Karah Curtis		714 831-1272
Theresa Beyerle	Blackheath	805 237-0558
Tom & Sandy Pesota	Blackjack	805 245-1257
Teresa Beyerle		805 434-2887
Judie Jensen	Santana	805 646-5304
Frances & Joseph Sikorski		818 360-9701
Ron & Martha Gouw		818 546-1604
Elinor Mero		818 769-3629
Jeannine Berry		818 846-9674
Linda & Richard Benson		818 848-4549
Robert Bannon		909 735-4498

Akita

Akita Club of America
761 Lonesome Dove Lane Copper Canyon, TX 75067 Nancy Henry, Sec

Channel Islands Akita Club	Breed Club	805 386-3400
Inland Empire Akita Club	Breed Club	619 949-8199
Akita Club of America	Breed Club	818 446-2486
Akita Club By The Sea	Breed Club	619 283-8093
David & Gail Lowrie	Red Dawn	619 328-0350
Susan Cargill	Kobu	619 941-3406
Bill Bobrow	Rippa-Na	619 949-8199
Bonnie Lutz	Kaigan	714 499-3729
Tony & Dawn Marcova	Okii Nami	714 858-1364
Manny & Sharon Lundberg	White Cap	805 386-3400
Steve & Tammy Crome	Ninjutsu	805 583-3576
Roger & Lesley McCleery	Top Gun	805 529-7546
Bruce & Kathy Mandell	Nishi Taiyo	805 646-5374
Carol Parker	Sashimo	818 446-2486
Camille Kam Wong	Triple K	818 446-2486
Gilbert & Elaine McMoran	Sunrise	909 354-7529
Robert & Anna Sanchez	Sun-Rae	909 355-0547

Appendix A: Local Breeders and Breed Club Directory

Cindy Carlson		909 621-9435
Sylvia & Frank Thomas	Chiheisen	909 684-8230
Gail Nishijima	Nishijima's	909 734-4338
Jan & Randy Ballou	R-J's	909 829-2808
Mardell Denny	Jer-Mar's	909 829-1139
Dave & Catherine Shifflet	Kantara	619 724-8455
Jim & Debbie Stewart	Daitan	909 943-1811

Alaskan Malamute

Alaskan Malamute Club of America
187 Grouse Creek Rd, Grants Pass, OR 97526 Ms Sharon Weston, Sec

Southern California Alaskan Malamute Club	Breed Club	714 998-9579
Carl & Genia Dolbee	Moondance	310 947-6660
Susan Sholar	Sholyn	619 753-2466
Steve & Bonnie Cox	Thunder Storm	714 449-8442
Carol Mannella	Sno-Mann	714 998-9579
Betty Macy	Funquest	805 269-5021
Tina Dunn	Double T	805 583-8280
Pat & Steve Starks	Kodiak	818 352-5828
Cynthia & Keith Chauvie	Joshua	818 894-7458
Paul & Michelle Talalay	Tundra	909 340-3292
Beverly Turner	Tikiluk	909 685-5099
Terry & Gloria Toussaint	Terra Glow	909 798-0819

American Eskimo (Standard)

American Eskimo Dogs Club of America
Rt 3 Box 211-B Stroud, OK 74079 Carolyn Jester, Sec

American Eskimo Dog Club of San Diego	Breed Club	619 286-0837
California American Eskimo Assoc., Inc	Breed Club	805 833-6377
San Fernando Valley Am Eskimo Assoc	Breed Club	818 993-7825
Nancy Hofman	Country	310 864-7626
Gail Shealy (Miniatures)	Sunshine	619 246-8856
Sandy Tocco	Lucky's	619 561-0570
Pam & Mike Neil (Miniaures)	Snobitz	619 672-3250
Dan & Mimi Nila	Celestials	619 949-8167
Lynn Martin (Miniatures)	Starlight	714 840-8874
Kathleen Cella	Cellas	818 348-2725
Mary Stevens	Stevens	818 993-7825

American Foxhound

American Foxhound Club
1221 Oakwood Ave Dayton, OH 45419 Mrs Jack Heck, Sec

American Staffordshire Terrier

Staffordshire Terrier Club of America
785 Valley View Rd Forney, TX 75126 H Richard Pascoe, Sec

Am Staffordshire Terrier Club of Greater LA	Breed Club	818 716-8224
Candice Eggart	Candy's	310 423-1352
Leri Hanson	Knockout	310 988-8644
Lydia Castagna	Raging Moon Amstaff	818 716 8224
Debra Jackson	Talk O' Town	909 279-8205

American Water Spaniel
American Water Spaniel Club
2600 Grand St NE Minneapolis, MN 55418 Carolyn Kraskey, Sec
Linda Ford   619 723-1706

American Wirehaired Pointing Griffon
36340 Hillside Lane Lebanon, OR 97355 Kathryn Haberkorn, Sec

Anatolian Shepherd
Anatolian Shepherd Dog Club of America
PO Box 880-D Alpine, CA 91903 Quinn Harned, Sec

Quinn & Marilyn Harned	Sakarya	619 445-3334
Robert Ballard	Chomarji	619 445-8475
Candice Wolf	Kandira	619 561-9595
Roberta Rogers	Kayan	619 473-8706

Australian Cattle Dog
Australian Cattle Dog Club of America
24605 Lewiston Blvd Hampton, MN 55031, Bellie Johnson, Sec

Australian Cattle Dog Club of Greater LA	Breed Club	909 943-5553
Rhonda Rhodes	Blue	619 561-0880
John & Danielle Lowrie	Stonecrest	619 669-0081
Kimberly Allgeier	Blu-Buk	619 758-1904
Linda Alain	Wagtail	805 944-2478
Jana Gianelli	Keoni	805 933-3775
Marty Griffith	Dawn Heir	818 357-8720
Joyce Rowland	Renegade	818 794-7788
Rosalie Baker	Rosestone	909 686-5363
Lorna Perez	Aqui	909 688-1978
Evelyn Stone	Redstone	909 825-4471
Denise Frick	Hit-N-Heel	909 943-5553

Australian Shepherd
United States Australian Shepherd Assoc.
PO Box 4317, Irving, TX 75015, Sherry Ball, Sec

West Coast Australian Shepherd Assoc	Breed Club	619 868-5711
Sandy Sakal	Summertime	310 924-8732
Tom, Donna & Andrea Armstrong	Upncomin	310 925-1508
Kathy A Steele	Spectrum	310 929-2787
Lynn Sugiura-Hamon	Taisho	619 285-9767
Wendy & Maury Finsterwald	Los Chicos	619 423-1884
Herm Fohlin	Riverview Farms	619 443-6866
Rick Pittman	Sundown	619 443-7822
John & Danielle Lowrie	Stonecrest	909 654-8091
Ron & Dayle Moden	Foxpointe	619 670-7249
Jon & Laurie Friberg	Woodlake	619 749-3928
Debra, Renee & Angela Roberts	Ro-Bar	714 538-1129
Pamala Levin	Aguadulce	805 684-2459
Becky De Leon	Summercrest	805 438-3077
Barbara & Erika Peters	Jubilee	805 944-3117
Florence Toombs	Running T	818 362-7850

Appendix A: Local Breeders and Breed Club Directory

Danielle Henderson	Fire Point	818 577-1928
Alice Wise	Down Under	818 784-8148
Charmaine Melton	Moonlight	909 672-0225
Tony Keyfel	Naskarade	909 681-5855
Jerry & Pat Burner	Ramblewood	909 794-8105
Catherine & John Seveland	Summerland	909 797-1165
Judy Humeston	Heart Fire	909 798-1100
Karyl,Mark & Nikole Heathman	Dreamtime	909 943-8830

Australian Terrier
Australian Terrier Club of America
1515 Davon Lane, Nassau Bay, TX 77058 Ms Marilyn Harban, Sec

Donna Minor	Cross Winds	714 970-5437
Nedra Adams	Jana	805 266-1557

Basenji
Basenji Club of America, Inc
PO Box 1076, South Bend, IN 46624 Ms Susan Patterson-Wilson, Sec

Basenji Club of Southern California	Breed Club	818 917-0367
Western Hound Assoc of So California	Puppy Referrals	818 364-1203
Nancy Brown	Tamba	619 366-3305
Barbara Naddy	Gala	619 583-3644
Douglas Joy	Dune	619 660-2401
Edwin & Joni Boese	Shika	619 788-1350
Carol Webb	Kazor	714 777-2256
Anne Ductor	Dharian	619 437-0686
JoAnn Fimlaid	Jamila	714 898-3826
June Young	Changa	714 996-2432
Stella Sapios	Astarte	805 684-5513
Julie Jones	Jasiri	818 705-5631
Richard & Amber McGee	Red Jhinn	909 943-0310

Basset Hound
Basset Hound Club of America, Inc
2343 Peters Rd Ann Arbor, MI 48103 Andrea Field, Sec

Greater San Diego Basset Hound Club	Breed Club	619 426-8174
Basset Hound Club of SC, Inc	Breed Club	310 390-7171
Western Hound Assoc of So California	Breed Club	818 364-1203
Pam Heine		310 697-0729
Andy & Sue Shoemaker	Shoe Fly	310 697-5522
Sandra Hopper	Windblown	619 375-7780
Chuck & Sheila Cunningham	Helix	619 426-8174
Mary & Acy Lund	I Bee	619 429-4338
Gail Allen	Tailgate	619 443-3151
Kathie & Jerry Spencer	Jercat	619 480-1261
Elain & Melissa Cortner	Bolain	619 722-1016
Douglas & Judith Mack	A Mack	714 498-0888
Barbara Humphrey	Sunshine	714 528-9756
Kevin & Debbie Whelan	Symphony	714 836-6918
Jeff Schulze		714 870-7731
Ralph Scarrow	Fascination	818 286-6069

Stephanie Hobbs	Encore	909 244-1211
Jan Kano	Arrowhead	909 624-5953
Barbara Dunning	Bar-B	909 781-8373
Fran Wooster	Woodhaven	909 829-0750
Sandy Huddleston	Shylo	909 864-5955

Beagle

National Beagle Club
River Rd Bedminster, NJ 07921 Mr Joseph Wiley Jr., Sec

Southern California Beagle Club	Puppy Referral	714 826-0928
Western Hound Assoc of So California	Puppy Referrals	818 364-1203
Penny Petrille	Ha'Penny	209 275-5493
Ray & Sue Jacksen	Rowdy's	213 893-3542
Julie Wright	Just-Wright	619 249-6898
Ada Lueke	Saga	619 460-1805
Claude & Nancy Brown	Ms Behavins	714 527-6448
Lois Lambert	Brightons	714 539-6702
Bill & Janet Nieland	Nieland	714 826-0928
Andres & Esther Tomatis	Lothan	909 822-5050

Bearded Collie

Bearded Collie Club of America
1116 Carpenter's Trace, Villa Hills, KY 41017, Ms Diana Siebert, Sec

Sandy Elington	Shiloh Beardies	909 353-0249
Alice Goodman	Castle Combe	213 656-0822
Lisa Kampff	Silvercrest	818 891-0395
Lori Fournier	Surfsong	619 757-1993
Kathy Smith	Kaelyn	818 848-4208

Beauceron

North American Beauceron Club
106 Halteman Rd Pottstown, PA 19461 S Bulanda, Sec

Ron & Debbie Skinner	Les Ombres Valeureux	909 767-9163
Karla Davis	DuChateau Rocher	209 564-3993

Bedlington Terrier

Bedlington Terrier Club of America
PO Box 11, Morrison, IL 61270, Mr Robert Bull, Sec

Bedlington Terrier Club of the West	Breed Club	619 576-9714
Marjorie Hanson	Valgos	619 435-7393
Robin Boyett	Mutt Hutt	619 576-9714
Chris Williams		619 747-4492

Belgian Malinois

American Belgian Malinois Club
1717 Deer Creek Rd Central Valley, CA 96019 Ms Barbara Peach, Sec

Jean-Claude Balu	Balu	909 823-4386
Janet Wheeler		310-641-4560
Gary O'Hare	Chenil Victoire	619 697-4062
Ron & Debbie Skinner		909 767-9163

Appendix A: Local Breeders and Breed Club Directory

Belgian Tervuren
American Belgian Tervuren Club, Inc
4970 Chinook Trail Casper, WY 82604 Ms Nancy Carman, Sec

Belgian Tervuren Club of SC	Breed Club	818 899-3407
Cathy Modica	Labarse	619 480-8826
Lynn Morgan	duParc Roux-Sel	714 549-3176
Pat Weymouth	TLC	714 544-2459
Mike & Eileen Hudak	Coastwynds	714 751-6137
Mary Cutherall	Donmar	909 795-4867
Greg Garrity		909 886-2674

Belgian Sheepdog
Belgian Sheepdog Club of America, Inc
2530 Harbison Rd Cedarville, OH 45314 Mrs. Phyllis Davis, Sec

Kim Potvin		619 443-4352
Randy & Sharon Thomsen		619 698-0420
Kurt Marti	Siegestor	909 593-6980
Norm & Holly Benfer		909 371-3536

Bernese Mountain Dog
Bernese Mountain Dog Club of America, Inc
812 Warren Landing Fort Collins, CO 80525 Ms Roxanne Bortnick, Sec

Jolaine Scheurenbr		619 267-6397
Linda Graham	Puppy Referral	619 296-1027

Bichon Frises
Bichon Frises Club of America, Inc
Route 2, Gulch Lane, Twin Falls, ID 83301 Mrs Bernice Richardson, Sec

Bichon Frises Club of Greater LA	Breed Club	213 461-7190
Bichon Frises Club of San Diego	Breed Club	619 454-6984
Kay Hughes	Diamant	213 461-7190
Stanley & Jill Cohen	Sea Star	310 457-9684
Bill Dreker	Nuage	310 479-8654
Gene & Mary Ellen Mills	Drewlaine	619 479-4188
Allison Hardy		619 753-7657
Barbara Chappell	Taywyn	909 276-4822
Linda Douglas	Honey Hill	714 898-4923
Lianne Bordurant	Scarlett	805 581-1418
Phoebe Caldwell	Enfim	805 963-2986
Gloria Crowell	Bonheur	909 785-8921

Black & Tan Coonhound
American Black & Tan Coonhound Club, Inc
700 Grand Ave Elgin, IL 60120 Victoria Blackburn, Sec

Western Hound Assoc of So California	Puppy Referrals	818 364-1203
Debbie Sitzinger	Hook Creek	909 336-1733

Bloodhound
American Bloodhound Club
1914 Berry Lane, Daytona Beach, FL 32124 Mr Ed Kilby, Sec

Western Hound Assoc of So California	Puppy Referral	818 364-1203
John & Diane Bowen		619 427-2982

Susan Hamil	Quiet Creek	714 494-9506
Stacy Matson	Rancho Sabuesos	714 858-0442
Lynne Aguirre	Ritz	909 737-4439
Andre & Esther Tomatis	Lothan	909 822-5050

Bolognese

Bolognese Club of America
PO Box 1461 Montrose, CO 81402 Dorothy Goodale, Sec 303 249-6492

Border Collies

Border Collie Club of America
6 Pinecrest Lane Durham, NH 03824 Janet Larson, Sec

Richard O'Brien	Cloverfield	619 242-9637
Pamela Giffin	Border Gang	619 388-4310
Bob & Patsy Musson	Highpine	619 277-8162
Linda Lee Merritt	Whiskers 'N Wool	619 442-7640
John & Robin Elliott	On the Lamb	619 445-9465
Kay Leary		619 669-0638
Terri Parrish	Blazin	619 739-8673
JC McDowell		714 521-7170
Doug Mead	Meade	714 684-1858
Laura Bridges	Bridges	818 352-0405
Bob Meadows		805 529-6134
Russell & Darlene Drake	River Ridge	805 688-8250
Doug Mead	Meade Arabian Farms	909 684-1858
Candy Kennedy	Candy-Bar	909 685-8696

Border Terrier

Border Terrier Club of America,Inc
832 Lincoln Blvd Manitowoc, WI 54220 Mrs Laurale Stern, Sec

Brenda Werbelow	Tweed Hill	310 690-0798
Rob & Carol Planavilla	Skibo	619 669-1133

Borzoi

Borzoi Club of America, Inc
29 Crown Dr Warren, NJ 07059 Mrs Karen Mays, Sec

Western Hound Assoc of So California	Puppy Referrals	818 364-1203
Borzoi Club of California	Breed Club	818 915-4456
Linda Richardson	Yalyn	619 479-4128
Torrea Leborn	Swanmanor	619 582-0023
Barbara Sloan	Arcobellini	619 632-7154
Patricia & Ken Burton	Kifka	805 297-3090
Linda Greco		818 768-5329
Ellen Hall	Ellens	818 768-6076
Bozena Thompson	Bozena	818 793-8319

Appendix A: Local Breeders and Breed Club Directory

Boston Terrier

Boston Terrier Club of America, Inc
8537 East San Burno Dr Scottsdale, AZ 85258 Ms Marian Sheehan, Sec

Pacific Coast Boston Terrier Club	Breed Club	818 344-3487
Boston Terrier Club of San Diego	Breed Club	619 561-0652
Pasadena Boston Terrier Club	Breed Club	714 774-5362
Ethel & Lisa Braunstein-LaMere		619 243-3830
Marie C Nery	Jay Bee's	619 463-0207
Terry & Chris Pratt	Bar None	619 561-0652
Maxine Pittser		714 541-3092
Rita Otteson & Mae Wiger	Bonnie	714 774-5362
Gisele Schiffer	Gi-Gi	818 342-0385
Anne & Bob Catterson	Bobcat	909 736-1763

Bouvier des Flandres

American Bouvier des Flanders Club, Inc
Rt 1 Box 201, Delaplane, VA 22025 Ms Diane Ring, Sec

SC Bouvier des Flandres Club	Puppy Referral	818 355-2650
Marcia Bittner	Tradewynd	619 788-0686
Bruce Edens		619 581-8005
Dave & Joan Galbraith	Galbraith	909 928-9225

Boxer

American Boxer Club, Inc
6310 Edward Dr Clinton, MD 20735 Mrs Barbara Wagner, Sec

Boxer Club Of San Diego County	Puppy Referral	619 561-5122
Boxer Club of San Fernando Valley	Puppy Referral	818 894-3596
Boxer Club Of Southern California	Puppy Referral	909 780-3948
Orange Coast Boxer Club	Puppy Referral	909 927-0802
Bill & Sandy Brown	York Hill	310 696-7165
J J Delmar	Main Event	619 222-1719
Bridget Reinhold	Bridgewood	619 561-5122
Susan Peterson	Sur's	619 672-1909
Jennifer Tellier	Telstar	619 672-2428
Judy Gordon	PAWZ IV	619 747-2098
Robert & Peg Butler	U-Turn	714 495-0915
Grace Lamoreaux	Celestial	714 557-6020
John & Betty Aikenhead		818 363-4410
Hugh Lynas	Hugh-Roy	909 350-2876
Margi Roberson	Heleva	909 360-1242
Sherri Gilmour	Sher'ed	909 371-3374
Jerry & Elaine Hunt	Vision	909 626-1635
Sharon Reek	Shar-In	909 653-4685
Hanna Renno	Renno	909 681-3224
Gail Metzger	Gamet	909 780-3948

Briard

Briard Club of America, Inc
547 Sussex Ct Elk Grove Village, IL 60007 Ms Janet Wall, Sec

Pacific States Briards	Puppy Referral	213 877-6282

Dog Owners Guide

Mike & Michelle Clevenger	Blackwater	909 789-1230
Bob & Pat Davidson	Mt Shadows	909 883-2805
Nancy Mandeville	Nanjere	909 928-3244

Brittany

American Brittany Club, Inc
800 Hillmont Ranch Rd Aledo, TX 76008 Ms Joy Searcy, Sec

California Brittany Club	Breed Club	714 240-3444
Dr. Cheri Bednarck		619 561-8905
Eva & Gerald Klein	Twnactn	714 240-3444
Barbara & Arthur Weddell	Sandbar	714 761-3094

Brussels Griffon

American Brussels Griffon Association
Box 56 221 E Scott Grand Ledge, MI 48837 Mr Terry Smith, Sec

Darryl Vice	Rrydal	619 322-3275
Robin Boyett	Mutt Hutt	619 576-9714
Anne & Bob Catterson	Bobcat	909 736-1763
Susan Duke	Xotic	909 887-8426

Bull Terrier

Bull Terrier Club of America
10477 Ethel Cr Cypress, CA 90630 Susan Murphy, Sec

Golden State Bull Terrier Club	Breed Club	714 821-4605
Cheryl Clemmensen	Action	619 445-1201
Linda Lethin	Kingsmere	714 774-4266
Susan Murphy	Jarrogue	714 821-4605
PJ & Michelle Gilbert		805 269-4910
Bill & Pat Edwards	Shavin	818 956-1170
Anne & John Dreher	Etenna	909 685-7660

Bulldog

Bulldog Club of America
8810 M Street Omaha, NE 68127 Ms Linda Sims, Sec

Pacific Coast Bulldog Club	Breed Club	310 548-6382
Bulldog Club of Greater San Diego	Breed Club	619 748-8848
Roberta & Richard Anderson	Richie-Rob's	310 421-4958
John & Darlene Carlin	Tugboat	310 548-6382
Sharon Yeager	Ziggy	310 596-8424
Linda Exarhos	Saxon	619 596-2222
Betty Fisher	White Fang	619 588-6491
Marcie Dobkin	DeSoto	619 748-8848
Lillian Tiffany	Tiffany	619 868-6765
Lenora & Bob Kerr	Kenn'L Kerr	714 733-0944
	Von Haddon	805 466-9312
Jack Kittrell	Viggys	805 943-3330
Kim Lindemoen	Bufrod	818 353-2717
Carmella Zuniga	Crystalf	909 622-0949
Ben & Barbara Hill	Pedley	909 685-8523
Margaret Coon	Ken'L Coon	909 789-0374
Ruby Grogg	Dy-Gros	909 926-1312

Kathy Hairston	Kajim	909 980-4504

Bullmastiff

American Bullmastiff Association, Inc
Box 137D Burger Rd Melbourne, KY 41059 Ms Mary Anne Duchin, Sec

Patricia O'Brien	Bullmast	310 421-9354
Stanley & Jill Cohen	Sea Star	310 457-9684
Taun Brooks	Wild Heart	619 369-2400
Stan & Claudia Stankiewicz		619 575-0541
Terry Gaskins	Upper Crust	619 697-7075
Darrell & Evie Johnson		619 789-7425
Carol Beans	Tauralan	714 544-1824
Pat O'Brien	Bullmast	714 870-5235
Carol Haddon	Von Haddon	805 466-9312

Cairn Terrier

Cairn Terrier Club of America
8096 Chilson Rd Pinckney, MI 48169 Christine Bowlus, Sec

Cairn Terrier Club of Southern California	Puppy Referral	619 728-7133
Helen Hislop	Rutherglen	310 861-0064
Eileen Currier	Glynncuri	619 444-9974
Neoma & James Eberhardt	Dees	619 724-0932
Jack & Karen Smith	Redcoat	619 728-7133
Sheila Buckley	Castlecairn	619 749-0901
Nikki Clark		714 535-3647
George & Danielle Rackstraw	Greyfriar	714 832-1844
Kathleen Spelman	Ragtime	818 303-3041
Susan Kaczor	Bonawe	818 782-8612
Roy & Laura Srong	Glencairn	909 797-2707
Bob & Virginia DeGroff		909 884-3169

Canaan

Canaan Dog Club of America
PO Box 555 Newcastle, OK 73065 Lorraine Stephens, Sec 405 387-5576

Cane Corso

International Cane Corso Federation
PO Box 212 Hainesport, NJ 08036 609 265-0029

Catahoulas, Louisiana

National Association of Louisiana Catahoulas
PO Box 1040 Denham Springs, LA 70727 504 665-6082

Mary McInnes	Golden State	909 823-8279

Cavalier King Charles Spaniel

Cavalier King Charles Spaniel Club
434 Country Lane Louisville, KY 91401 Suzanne Brown 502 897-9148

Joanne & James Nash	Rambler	415 964-0181
Susan Rundles	Bentley Priory	619 267-0080
Wesely & David Schiffman	Crossbow	818 706-8789
Steve Shapiro		818 988-9926
Joan Letterly	Wyndcrest	909 887-3486

Lena Winter	Lakeside	909 928-9577
Hap & Bea Jones	Jo-Bea's	909 947-7554

Chesapeake Bay Retriever

American Chesapeake Club, Inc
1705 Rd 76 Pasco, WA 99301 Ms Janel Hopp

Annette Monugian	Marnetts	310 943-5090
Mary Ellen Mazzola	Z's	619 445-2711
Maurine Coleman	Coleman	714 894-4160
Debra Strayer	Quail Ridge	805 239-0677
Dana Bleifer DVM	Quail Run	818 780-2278
Lee Smith		909 689-8668
Mary Hautz	Gra-Ma's	909 883-1298

Chihuahua

Chihuahua Club of America, Inc
5019 Village Trail San Antonio, TX 78218 Ms Lynnie Bunten, Sec

Southern California Chihuahua Club	Breed Club	714 877-4707
Alberta Booth		310 323-5851
Bill & Trudy Kimball	Kimball	310 324-9356
Shirley Larson	Mi-Bar's	310 532-3727
Melodie DeFrates	Speedy	619 561-9634
Penny McAvoy (Smooths)	McAvoy's	619 466-8312
Rose King	Los Reyes	619 475-8046
Jeanne Ochoa	La Duende's	619 726-8246
Treva Johnson	J.R.J. TJ'S	619 475-7745
Carole Mills-Heiligers	Si Si	619 244-6919
Farrie Paul	Paul's	619 443-6490
Tim & Marie Eller		619 723-1955
William & Donna Greenamyer	Greenhaven	619 868-1755
Junko Guichon		619 945-5942
Loretta Bakken		619 582-4298
Francis & Shirley Hericks	Hericks	619 741-3655
Nancy Wright		714 770-4720
Robert Clegg	Prizm	818 448-1601
Frank & Muriel Kauffman		818 812-0429
Paul & Carol Starjack		818 884-5291
Carole Heiligers	Si Si	909 278-2063
Don & Peggy Scharf	Scharf	909 622-5070
Joy Ater		909 688-3036
Ursula Legere		909 734-6209
Dale Van Camp	Hot Shot	909 877-4707
Della Mae Wasson	Wasson	909 880-1185

Chinese Crested Dog

American Chinese Crested Club
3101 E Blount St Pensacola, FL 32503 Ms Lynda Nagel, Sec

Joy Yonkman	Amy's	310 424-2803
Mary Bockstadter	Babylon	619 868-5357
Gayle M Good	Goodacres	909 887-2324
Chuck & Patty Stokke	Chatty	909 395-9357

Appendix A: Local Breeders and Breed Club Directory

Jan & Tim Noland	Orient Expression	909 624-7960
Carol Montgomery	China Road	909 980-1357

Chow Chow

Chow Chow Club, Inc
3580 Plover Place Seaford, NY 11783 Ms Irene Cartabio, Sec

Chow Fanciers Assoc Of Southern Cal	Puppy Referral	619 366-2860
Golden State Chow Chow Club	Breed Club	714 241-9805
Dr. Clif & Marlene Shryock		213 865-7369
Lloyd & Charlotte Palmer		619 267-2444
Dex Hansard		619 371-4809
Peter Gores	Windsong	619 440-6464
Lisa DelGuzzi		619 459-4544
Myra Price		619 479-3597
Clyde H. Means		619 575-2616
Donald Carl Harrington		619 951-7918
Marlo Romero		619 951-7918
Bob & Linda Banghart	Rebelrun	714 241-9805
Harry & Isabelle Pearson		714 624-7740
Pat Pearson		714 676-8770
Rick & Reba Donnelly		714 897-6126
Carin Prelesnik		714 962-8424
Dr. W. Van & Jan Willis		714 992-2601
Tara Quinn		805 251-2847
Cindy Hooks		805 257-6955
Harvey & Penny Kent		805 273-2469
Harold & Cecil Lee		805 481-2131
Gloria & Barrie Mogg		805 583-8867
Lois Burk		805 646-8249
Tyrobe & Mechelle Moore		805 664-8627
Harvey & Penny Kent	Sunburst	805 943-6035
Frances Schilling		818 360-1790
Barbara Johnson		818 997-6091
Roy & Judy Bailey	Chowlam	909 681-4711
Lorraine Kazlauskas		909 780-2718
Shelly Dillingham		909 698-6835
George & Kathy Beliew	Imagine	909 792-2122
Lanny & Susan Carr		909 946-6708

Clumber Spaniel

Clumber Spaniel Club of America
9 Cedar Street Selden, NY 11784 Ms Barbara Stebbins, Sec

Bobby Rench		909 874-1242

Cocker Spaniel

American Spaniel Club, Inc
845 Old Stevens Creek Rd Martinez, GA 30907 Margaret Ciezkowski, Sec

Cocker Spaniel Club of San Diego	Breed Club	619 945-1186
Cocker Spaniel Club of So California	Breed Club	818 768-2146
West Coast Cocker Spaniel Club	Breed Club	909 599-8851
Cocker Spaniel Club of Orange County	Breed Club	619 724-0527

Judy Bjelland	Loma Point	619 226-1433
Pete & Patti Hine	Ris'n Star	619 323-2970
John Zolezzi	Searidge	619 436-4960
Pam Kelly	Misty Isle	619 444-1877
Dawne Christy	Hi-Acres	619 448-4252
Ruth Bartholomew	Ha-Bar's	619 463-8364
Lola Roto	Eboncars	619 464-1377
John Agrella	Cosmic	619 561-5474
Maggi Escudero	Kamay	619 561-8544
Pat Fleming	Live Oak	619 728-8537
Jean Miles		619 421-0124
Linda Scott		619 945-1186
Helen Rice	Corwin	714 828-0962
Bonnie Compas	Excetera	714 961-1641
Mara Biggs		805 499-9409
Kim Stanley		805 647-7623
Brandon & Jeannie Nelson		805 949-3749
Ken & Kathy Mitoma	Damon	909 245-4201
Linda Wheeler-Goldbaum	Ralyn's	909 272-0717
Dorothy McCoy	Glen Arden	909 599-8851
Diane Morgan	Redhill	909 678-2033
Ken & Charlotte Lambert	Lambert	909 887-1813
Shirley Sanders	Kasino	909 943-3047
Lois Wilson	Glenmurry	909 947-2257
Hap & Bea Jones	Jo-Bea's	909 947-7554
Geri Roy	Carousel	909 980-3325
Max & Gloria Spaulding	Glory-B	909 985-3353

Collie

Collie Club of America, Inc
1119 South Fleming Rd Woodstock, IL 60098 Mrs Carmen Leonard, Sec

Area Puppy Coordinator	Puppy Referral	818 888-1172
Area Puppy Coordinator	Puppy Referral	818 287-6372
Area Puppy Coordinator	Puppy Referral	818 912-0977
South Bay Collie Fanciers	Breed Club	310 598-7742
Collie Club of America	Breed Club	818 912-0977
Los Padres Collie Club	Breed Club	805 642-1492
California Collie Clan	Breed Club	213 728-9343
San Diego Collie Club	Breed Club	619 565-4600
San Gabriel Valley Collie Club	Breed Club	714 594-9356
Southern California Collie Club	Breed Club	818 360-9903
Elaine & Tomie Goto	Triumph	213 294-9603
Susan Royds	Skyview	310 370-9769
Allen & Karen Sanderfer	Karal	310 499-6836
Helga & Peter Kane	Kanebriar	310 547-1053
Joe & Cecilia Fouty	Jola's	310 834-7535
Robert & Alex York	Yorkridge	619 272-7277
Theresa Walsh	Silverlake	619 278-2877
Mary Sadler	Edenrock	619 469-8116
Janine Walker-Keith	Incandescent	619 565-4600
Michele & Steve Gilmore	Kountrytime	619 789-0156
Sayuri Harami	Spring	619 868-6150

Appendix A: Local Breeders and Breed Club Directory

Judy Sherwin	Almasi	714 242-0242
Dennis Fyda	Windrift	714 376-1776
Maureen Grosky	McMaur	714 527-4535
Vicky & Heather Newcomb	Keepsake	714 531-5449
Jim & Pat Martin	Wonderland	714 537-2351
Jody Ostrowski	Bellvue	714 540-3021
Brinda & Edward Chavez	Cameo	714 594-9356
Judith Byrant	Dea Haven	714 668-9514
Vicki Sizemore	Horizon	714 737-2053
Bob & Connie Del Rio	White River	714 785-1317
Paula Rice	Willamere	714 892-4870
William & Gail Whitson	Sun Country	805 523-7061
Mordecai & Grace Eskenazi	Graymor	805 526-7895
Leslie & Anita Hernandez	Classique	805 583-5073
Karen Anderson	Nordic	805 589-1650
Janice Grillo	Sunkist	805 589-9087
William Brokken	Foremost	805 682-8317
Bob & Ros Tolliver	Stirling	805 833-1476
Joan Grantham	Cranbrook	805 934-1102
Laura Mitobe	Care	805 946-3977
Terrie Parker & Ellie McCullough	Cinderella	818 285-8977
Martha Ramer	Society	818 287-6375
Meredith Ponedel	Meridel	818 345-3012
Lisa Friedman	Shondell	818 352-1569
Linda Garcia & Virginia Kruthoff	Elite	818 355-5038
Denise Greskoviak	Shannon	818 506-0830
Teri Konoske	London	818 579-6469
Arleen Lemus	Penrose	818 798-3027
Ed & Shelly Degner	Canyon	818 812-0508
Joan & Bob Berfield	Stoneypoint	818 888-1172
Carol Schopf	Missionbrae	818 894-4491
Norman Nicholson	Royal Crest	818 912-0977
Linda Robbins & Barbara O'Keefe	Gambit	909 465-1161
Al & Helene Forthal	Shoreham	909 677-6651

Corgi, Cardigan Welsh

Cardigan Welsh Corgi Club of America,Inc
PO Box 141 Moody, AL 35004 Dr Kathleen Harper, Sec

Cardigan Welsh Corgi of SC	Breed Club	714 897-2685
Kathy Steele	Spectrum	310 929-2787
Kim Shira-Rauber	Coedwig	619 287-5104
Virginia Taurasi		619 436-4721
Sueannette Wood	Su-Ets	619 448-8760
Helen Cramer	Dorre Don	619 478-5655
Karen Harbert	Aelwyd	619 670-1147
Susanne Roberson	Oak Creek	619 788-3246
Chuck & Barbara Nauman	Vintage	714 492-0823
John & Maureen Tomlinson	Medley	714 897-2685
Lorraine Struck		714 997-0784
Gerry Greenfield	Toromar	909 736-7734

Corgi, Pembroke Welsh

Pembroke Welsh Corgi Club of America, Inc
2601 Bancroft Lane Louisville, KY 40241 Mr John Vahaly, Sec

Pembroke Welsh Corgi Club of SC	Puppy Referrals	619 480-8348

111

Pembroke Welsh Corgi Club	Breed Club	818 842-1431
Mildred Paul		213 650-2050
Jan Scott		213 851-5063
Lamer Morrell	Bantry Bay	310 394-1897
Susan Yamaguchi	Shenanigan's	310 421-0181
Arleen Rooney		310 830-8126
Margaret Anne Shallanberg	Shallanmar	310 832-6654
Marlin & Nancy Smith		619 442-2756
Gwen Platt	Rojanway	619 480-8348
Rick Bellhof		619 669-7246
Lisa & Mike Coit	Rosewood	619 670-3444
Lynne Cable	Crown Jewels	619 748-0390
Deborah & Maurice Blais	Crysmont	619 941-6599
Conni Hughes	Royalfox	714 852-1003
James & Edie Richards	Roderic	805 522-2778
Jan Lewis		805 640-8356
Margaret Stewart	Jandon	818 842-1431
Lowell & Arlene Davis		818 339-9649
Barbara Ryan	Ryan's Corgies	909 676-1868
Debra De Los Rios		909 689-9045
Cynthia Campbell	Stablemate	909 780-5986
Thomas Conway	Locksley Hall	909 781-9790
Lowell Jameson	Tydden	909 795-9495
Barbara Morris	San B	909 886-4355
Selwyn & Harriett Smith	Harlwyn	909 899-9845

Curly-Coated Retriever

Curly-Coated Retriever Club of America
24 Holmes Blvd Ft Walton Beach, FL 32548 Gina Columbo, Sec

Stephanie Doerr	Solimar	619 424-9217
Diann Tongco	Tika	619 464-2461
Kathleen Kardash	Eclypse	619 569-1311
Carol Kail	Aarowag	714 557-1668
Weddell & Jaqua Sandbar	Sandbar Sporting Dogs	714 761-3094
Rick & Kathy Kail	Sharwin	714 557-1668

Dachshund

Dachshund Club of America, Inc
390 Eminence Pike Shelbyville, KY 40065 Mr Walter Jones, Sec

San Diego Dachshund Club	Breed Club	619 274-3655
Dachshund Club of Santa Ana Valley	Breed Club	714 724-0300
Antelope Valley Dachshund Club	Breed Club	805 943-3221
Dachshund Club of California	Breed Club	310 323-2961
Sierra Dachshund Breeders Club of LA	Breed Club	714 771-1010
Western Hound Assoc of So California	Puppy Referrals	818 364-1203
Barbara Powers	Distlefink	213 257-8962
Polly Fleming		213 472-4912
John Mohme		310 276-2149
Gail Laidoner-Hernandez	Galadachs	310 323-2961
Steve & Denise		310 433-1815
Mary Lou / Mercedes		619 329-7951
Pat & Sanford Roberts	Robdach	619 443-7711
Wes & Betty Martin		619 274-3655

Appendix A: Local Breeders and Breed Club Directory

Jeanine/ Michelle Sudinski	Lucene	619 463-0610
William & Kathleen Adams	Rancho Wilheen	619 724-6791
Jan Metzger	Fallbrook Cty	619 728-6317
Marj Lewis		619 753-7032
Mary & Craig Lee	Dachslee's	714 630-4998
Gene & Jan French	Gejan	714 679-4871
Marlene Perez		714 761-4945
Polly Fleming	Fleming	714 796-4453
Kathy Hume		714 821-8837
Jerri Smith/ Jan Oswald		714 849-3460
Arvilla Mayhall	Wavecrest	714 998-3460
Irva McDougald	Raisin'L	805 256-6834
Mary Pyle	Raisin'L	805 943-3221
Cynthia Kennard		818 303-0057
Judy Anderson	Schoolhouse	818 353-3017
Sandy McFadden		818 365-0476
Franz & Gretchen Neuwirth		818 780-5553
Marge Dwyer		818 843-2232
Janet Georgeanne		818 890-2265
Beth Ann Mills		818 996-8172
Marcie Sartor	Woodwind	909 391-4784
Harry & Joyce Tufts		909 629-7614
Amanda Hodges	Teckelwood	909 682-5590

Dalmatian

Dalmatian Club of America, Inc
4390 Chickasaw Rd Memphis, TN 38117 Mrs Anne Fleming, Sec

Dalmatian Club of San Diego	Breed Club	619 756-3836
Dalmatian Club of Southern California	Puppy Referral	310 403-2930
Diane Bartholomew	Dalwood	310 530-8484
Thomas & Carole Harris	Daisydot	310 594-9993
Linda Peters	Clearly	310 867-5917
Connie Light	Lighthouse	310 944-8571
Dennis & Carol Herbold		310 944-8497
Cinda Lyford	Echo	619 390-2770
Jan Hill	Hill-N-Dal	619 561-7382
Randy Thomsen	Ra-Shar	619 698-0420
Deborah Goddard	Rdalmar	619 756-3836
Brooke Barnett	Brookshire	714 460-0137
Jim & Barbara Lyons	Quiksilver	714 494-5150
Patricia Wallace-Jones	Chalkhills	714 996-6099
Julie Stubbings	Easytospot	805 252-6303
Toni Shackleford	Talamora	805 520-0637
Mary Widder	Sunnyglen	805 583-5914
Lou & Evelyn Cabral	Briarfield	818 333-7473
Maria Johnson	Altamar	818 340-1992
Barbara Ann Harrison	Majestic	818 353-7235
Lyra Partch	DotzInk	818 447-6017
Lauren Schmitz	Frontier	818 560-4722
Elaine & Steve Gewirtz	Firebuster	818 889-6848
Brooke Temple Barnett	Brookeshire	909 460-0137
Tim & Rochelle Romano	Wayfarer	909 353-8871
Sandy Turney	Whinemaker	310 539-4455

Dog Owners Guide

Dandie Dinmont
Dandie Dinmont Terrier Club of America, Inc
25 Ridgeview Rd Staunton, VA 24401 Mrs Mixon Darracott, Sec

Dora & John Watson	Carngorm	619 249-3187
Karen Dorn	Biskra	619 568-3164
George & Carol Hamilton		818 330-4708
Joanne Moxham	Truehart	818 887-9742

Doberman Pinscher
Doberman Pinscher Club of America
10316 NE 136th Pl Kirkland, WA 98034 Ms Judy Reams

San Fernando Valley Doberman Pisncher Club	Breed Club	310 457-4460
Santa Ana Valley Doberman Pinscher Club	Breed Club	714 956-2685
Aztec Doberman Pinscher Club of San Diego	Breed Club	619 443-8944
LA Doberman Pinscher Club	Breed Club	818 289-9421
Cal Sierra Doberman Pinscher Club	Breed Club	714 884-9604
Vic & Angie Monteleon	Montwood	619 443-8944
Robi Marx	Tahoe	619 445-5494
Cinthia Miyagawa	Cinderwood	619 475-3850
Mary Mulligan	Delcrest	619 579-9366
Lynn Webber	Coral Tree	619 660-1175
Mort and Lois Rohter	Morlo	619 788-0172
Judy Munyon & Terry Buice	Yellow Rose	714 776-1508
Bob & Cherie Floyd	Aryan	714 858-3983
Doris Bandoian	Vahdor	714 996-2787
Darla Dorr	House of Dorr	818 342-3334
Toby Bloom	Del Mar	909 350-1926
Teri Dugan	Terra Dell	909 590-0181
Alyce Dixon	Dixfire	909 687-9843
Roz Wheelock	Revimar	909 734-7565
Jean-Claude Balu	Balu	909 823-4386
Judy Bingham	Electra	909 845-8272
Rita Lowman	Retz	909 926-2640

Dogo Argentino
4575 Lebanon Rd Danville, KY 40422 606 236-3702

Dogue de Bordeaux
John & Ricki Toole	Martel	909 763-4715
Dottie Warino		714 771-4121

English Cocker Spaniel
English Cocker Spaniel Club of America, Inc
PO Box 252 Hales Corners, WI 53130 Mrs Kate Romanski, Sec

English Cocker Spaniel Club of San Diego	Breed Club	619 466-9792
English Cocker Spaniel Club of So California	Breed Club	818 332-6775
Perry & Barbara Scott	Coprfyld	619 262-2885
Susan Carson	Heritage	619 423-1152
Dave Schneider	Canon	619 443-8250
Alexis Mathy	Wyndsonnet	619 445-0686
Lea Schneider	Alibi	619 445-3618
Carolyn Sisson	Prima	619 466 9792

114

Appendix A: Local Breeders and Breed Club Directory

Doug McFarlane	Marimac	619 724-0527
Cathie Yager	Hyland	619 789-7233
David Flanagan	Decorum	714 536-5120
Rebec & Harvey Riggs	Cabin Hill	714 662-1244
Louise Southard	Winchimes	714 827-5006
Linda Gall	Lynann	805 498-5347
Eileen Weston	Bobwhite	818 332-6775

English Setter

English Setter Assoc of America, Inc
114 S Burlington Oval Dr Chardon, OH 44024 Mrs Dawn S Ronyak, Sec

California English Setter Club	Breed Club	909 941-0313
Chuck Oldham	Thenderin	310 821-8742
Karen Kennedy	Kelyric	619 443-8687
Georjean Jensen	Jensen's	619 479-5437
Rebec & Harvey Riggs	Cabin Hill	714 662-1244
Diane Beal	Gold Rush	909 593-2595
Laura Reynolds	Santan	909 685-5803
Harry & Marlene Uva	Allspice	909 941-0313
Dean & Jane Matteson	McErin	909 986-8055

English Springer Spaniels

English Springer Spaniel Field Trial Assoc, Inc
29512 47th Ave S Auburn, WA 98001 Ms Marie Andersen, Sec

Eng Springer Spaniel Assoc San Fernando Vly	Breed Club	805 522-0687
Gateway Cities English Springer Spaniel	Breed Club	909 946-3362
Carolyn Sisson	Prima Spaniels	619 466-9792
Carol Murphy	Birdwood	619 447-8020
Becky Gifford	Diego	619 697-8144
Charles & Jean Feth	Charjean	619 298-6429
Dawn Barker	Windcrest	619 443-4985
Carol & William Murphy	Birdwood	619 447-8020
Carolyn & Judy Sisson	Prima Avocado	619 466-9792
Peggy & Vern Johnson	Marjon	714 731-6428
Bob & Patricia Ramsey	Bel Canto	714 761-7144
Don & Bonnie Dobbins	Mindon	714 530-3812
Carrie Racey	Caran	805 522-0687
Bonnie Buchanan	Riley	818 331-6746
Gary & Linda Wheeler-Goldbaum	Ralyn's	909 272-0717
Kathy Grayson	Dignity	909 672-3965
Diane Morgan	Redhill	909 678-2033
Pat Stechenfinger	Royals	909 884-0601
Geri Roy	Carousel	909 980-3325

English Toy Spaniel

English Toy Spaniel Club of America
18451 Sheffield Lane Bristol, IN 46507 Ms Susan Jackson, Sec

Barbara Latimer	Fairoaks	503 632-6698
Pauline Paterson		805 947-7320

Dog Owners Guide

Field Spaniel
Field Spaniel Society of America
11197 Keystone Lowell, MI 49331 Mrs Sally Herweyer, Sec
CC Blatter   909 792-4184
Bob & Patricia Ramsey   Bel Canto   714 761-7144

Fila Brasileiro
Fila Brasileiro Club of America
244 Flat Rock Church Zebulon, GA 30295 706 567-8085

Finnish Spitz
Finnish Spitz Club of America
110 Knots Landing Macon, GA 31210 Mr Richard Yates, Sec
William & Donna Greenamyer   Greenhaven   619 868-1755
Richard & Dawn Woods   Lobitos   310 532-7121
Mary Ellis   Velvet Hills   805 528-3429
Peggy Olsen   Japego   909 947-5986

Flat-Coated Retriever
Flat-Coated Retriever Society of America, Inc
6608 Lynwood Blvd Richfield, MN 55423 Ann Mortenson, Sec
Great Western Flat-Coated Retriever Club   Breed Club   805 943-5037
Flat-Coated Retriever Club of San Diego   Breed Club   619 279-7690
Jay & Beth Desjardins   Raisin   310 338-1096
Richard & Cynthia Trotter   Belstar   310 439-0828
Nanci Hanover   Holly Creek   310 459-8761
Sarah Messick   Folly   619 662-1811
Judith Dexter   Dexmoor   619 868-6005
Bill & Barbara Fisher   Desertwynd   805 943-5037
John & Karen Sack   Alpha   818 507-7606
Ruth Deming   Blucrest   909 685-6484
Roger & Peachie Orton   Omega   909 797-9512
Neal Goodwin   Altair   909 947-5539
Adrienne Ayles   Sterling   909 983-5493

Fox Terrier (Smooth)
American Fox Terrier Club
PO Box 604 South Plainfield, NJ 07080 Mr Martin Goldstein, Sec
Western Fox Terrier Breeders Assoc   Breed Club   909 672-4987
Elaine Grittman   310 925-6558
Marjorie Hanson   619 435-6131
Dr. L.J. Lockwood   Alcala   619 436-6619
Richard & Janet McCann   Ram   619 726-6477
Mary Lou Hammond   Lizabethan   714 527-5985
Cheri & Heather Alderson   714 968-5058
Linda Fodor   805 254-4560
Barbara Cross   805 489-2680
AJ Baron   805 929-4565
Karen Grande   805 983-4385
Katie Cross   Rudolph   805 984-2091
Robert Johnson   818 795-6608

Pam Bishop		909 679-0187
Eileen Olmstead, DVM		909 946-6421
Charlotte LeVecque	Charbone	909 862-3416
Alyce Dixon	Dixfire	909 884-9604
Sue Pucci	Windfall	909 944-0097
Richard & Virginia Ashlock		909 983-0369
Edna McGinnis	Leedmar	909 985-7118

Fox Terrier (Wire)

Kathleen Reges		213 225-8878
Mari Morrisey	Brookhaven	310 375-8656
Deborah Lambert		310 439-0501
Jene` Thomas		310 439-0501
Stanley & Jill Cohen	Sea Star	310 457-9684
Bruce Schwartz		310 559-6016
Moonlighter		619 949-9387
Marjory Sonoga		714 768-6751
Denise Roberts		805 482-8674
Lee McTaggart	Dalayre	818 767-7212
Ursula Diel	Dekoupage	818 918-0396
Geri Grogg	Gam-B	909 794-9265

Fox Terrier (Wire, Smooth)

Richard & Laura Forkel	Wendywyre	714 974-7374
J Wood Wornall Jr.		818 768-1885

French Bulldog

French Bulldog Club of America
1141 Constantinople St New Orleans, LA 70115David Kruger   209 299-3693

Luca Carbone	Jaguar	209 291-0175
George Niles		209 299-3693
Betty Littschwager	Blue Max	909 798-4058

German Pinscher

German Pinscher Club of America
Rt 1 Box 290 Champion, MI 49814 906 339-2953

Dianna Jones	Blazers	909 795-1162

German Shepherd

German Shepherd Dog Club of America, Inc
17 West Ivy Lane Englewood, NJ 07631 Blanche Beisswenger, Sec

German Shepherd DC of LA Co	Breed Club	818 841-2823
German Shepherd DC of San Diego	Breed Club	619 748-3970
Orange Coast German Shepherd DC*	Breed Club	714 542-3518
San Bernardino/Riverside GSDC	Breed Club	619 252-4446
German Shepherd DC of Long Beach	Breed Club	310 697-6216
German Shepherd DC of San Gabriel Valley	Breed Club	818 285-5223
German Shepherd DC of Ventura	Breed Club	805 647-3027
Kathy Aubrey	Utopia	310 429-1181
Jerome Amerman	Jagan	310 541-7833
Terry Ryan		310 694-2563
Tedi Ginsburg	Asgard	310 697-6216

Lillian Fuller	Del Prado	310 697-0535
Bob & Darlene Ghigleri	Schatzmar	310 944-0424
Bob & Star Ott	Double Ott	619 252-4446
Angie Stegner		619 561-6813
Alice Marie Cox	Rasenhof	619 461-6180
Vickie Loeschnig	Masestatisch Schaferhunde	619 669-1859
Dave & Janet Coleman	Rocknoll	619 745-4694
Robert Burkhardt		619 748-7943
Don Haseman		619 748-3970
Dyan Merkel	Merkel's	619 759-9966
Howard & Loree Poole	Von Unserhund	619 789-7624
Bob & Marla Taylor	Haus Lobenswert	619 956-3647
Jacque Viszolay		714 496-9616
Mario & Carrie Carrasco	Carico	714 680-0438
Joyce Shelp	Mariner	714 893-5549
Cindy Tellefsen		805 481-6126
Al & Joanna Rand	Randheim	818 285-5223
Robert Penny		818 355-6191
Andy Strasser	Silstra	818 713-0729
Adele Hysen		818 767-2991
Jack & Blythe Brosal	Blyjac	818 992-5465
Clint & Beth Pederson	Nordmark	818 448-6715
Dick & Jean Whalen	Jericho	909 242-4188
Leo & Mildred Muller	Vom Westerland	909 350-8730
Mary Cutherall	Donmar	909 795-4867
Jean-Claude Balu	Balu	909 823-4386
Joe & Marie Bevacqua	Sunny Bee	909 947-1202
Maurice & Shirley McWilliams	Sin's	909 672-2955
Twyla Miner	Lorien	909 780-5084
Doris & John Rossini	West Wind	909 947-3726
Bill & Eileen Danlap	Danleen	909 984-2091
Katie Rudolph	Rudolph	909 984-2091

Giant Schnauzer

Giant Schnauzer Club of America, Inc
4220 S Wallace Chicago, IL 60609 Ms Dorothy Wright, Sec

Lois Barleman		619 967-7976
Kevin Schrum	Stylus	714 588-7959
Lee & Carol Herd	Palm Run	714 893-5821

Golden Retriever

Golden Retriever Club of America
2005 NE 78th St Kansas City, MO 64118 Ms Catherine Bird, Sec

Golden Retriever Club of San Diego	Breed Club	619 449-1991
Golden Retriever Club of Greater LA	Breed Club	310 437-3796
Golden Retriever Club Riverside/San Brdo	Breed Club	909 688-7602
Donna Jacobs	Fable	310 376-1306
Tryna Kemmer	Sea Breeze	310 424-1801
Ann Leatherbury	Leatherbury	310 541-7833
Norma Shipman	Donnor	310 696-1666

Appendix A: Local Breeders and Breed Club Directory

Gloria Henderson	Miraleste	310 831-8793
Barbara Smith	Laurelridge	619 286-0901
Barbara Hoxel		619 486-4144
Sheila Clark	Desert Sun	619 569-6818
Lynn Cooper	Lynn's	619 591-7608
Jan Sageser	Placer	619 940-6331
Myra Moldawsky	Ashwel	714 360-1438
Nancy Young	Ambervale	714 637-8994
Michelle Anderson		714 780-0849
Mary Bowman	Calico	714 994-6353
Clairyce Dolson	RDO	805 256-8056
Marjorie Blake	Quailwood	805 397-4715
Sylvia Corbett	Golden Light	805 522-8114
Joyce Davis	Sunset	818 716-9128
Sharon Shilkoff	Woodland	818 225-0807
Bea Goldblatt	Goldleaves	909 788-4408
Jean Marie Messinger	My-Magical	909 788-4408
Cathie Kunkel	Bulgold	909 988-3997

Gordon Setter

Gordon Setter Club of America
945 Front Rd Glenmoore, PA 19343 Ms Alison Rosskamp, Sec

Cindy Huber	Cinkell	619 222-3735
Jane Matteson		909 986-8055
Linda Sanders		702 649-6383

Great Dane

Great Dane Club of America,Inc
442 Country View Lane Garland, TX 75043 Mrs. Marie Fint, Sec

Great Dane Club of California	Breed Club	714 639-4805
Great Dane Club of San Diego	Breed Club	619 445-6558
Karen Lindsay	Brierdane	619 440-5556
Kareen Mcllwaine	Temple Dell	619 445-2845
Jack & Cheryl Goodwin	Patchwork	619 588-5293
Susan Wells	Canyon	619 745-3324
Bruce & Gene Mitchell	Von Raseac	619 758-7745
Carol Ann Chaney	Chaney Dane	619 765-0626
Horkey Pierce	Ana Dane'Reg	714 639-4805
Alice Bonne		714 972-9441
Glen & Gloria Bearss	Glen-Glo	714 995-3121
Doug & Ann Toomey	Warwick	818 708-3374
Eileen Rosenblum	Horizon	909 590-9798
Malcolm & Virginia Helman	Rancho Del Sol	909 622-7819
Tanya & Bruce Blauw	Witches Rune	909 685-6066
Judith Murdock	Sir Blu Danes	909 780-2293
Jill Swedlow	Sunnyside Farm	909 797-1855
Pat Lewis	L-Rancho	909 829-8218
Gloria Desart	DeSart	909 845-1856
Carmella & Manuel Zuniga	Colours Danes	909 984-9825

Great Pyrenees

Great Pyrenees Club of America, Inc
Rt 1 Box 119 Midland, VA 22728 Mrs Charlotte Perry, Sec

Great Pyrenees Assoc of So California	Breed Club	310 946-6985
Robin Comer	Sheep Hills	619 759-0166
James & Kim Lasley	Mistry	619 788-6799
Terri Demey-Combs	Euzkle	619 949-0318
Doug Stitt	Mantu	909 355-6943
Sue King	Partager	909 789-9125
Dorothy Sisco	Shadowrun	909 887-8201

Greater Swiss Mt Dog

Greater Swiss Mt Dog Club of America
Rd 8 Box 203 Sinking Spring, PA 19608 215 678-3631

K Shell & J Cortez	Zetroc	909 945-1798

Greyhound

Greyhound Club of America
227 Hattertown Rd Newton, CT 06470 Ms Patricia Clark, Sec

Western Hound Assoc of So California	Puppy Referrals	818 364-1203
Don & Pat Ide	Huzzah	714 838-4381

Harrier

George Toliver	De Amo	619 375-2319
Betty Burnell	Seaview	805 642-8758

Havanese

Sue & David Nelson	Shaggyluv	714 523-1311

Ibizan Hound

Ibizan Hound Club of the US
4312 E Nisbet Rd Phoenix, AZ 85032 Lisa Puskas, Sec

Margaret Piazza		619 427-6249
Judy Umeck	Bel Canto	714 761-7144
Cherie Ringwald	Rialto	909 873-9989

Irish Setter

Irish Setter Club of America, Inc
16717 Ledge Falls San Antonio, TX 78232 Mrs Marion Pahy

Irish Setter Club of Southern California	Breed Club	310 372-7613
Irish Setter Club of San Diego	Breed Club	619 789-3956
Burt & Cynthia Reinherz	Reddwing	310 372-7613
Joyce Nilsen	Thenderin	310 392-0619
Jo Ann Medica	Shenandoah	310 641-6371
Charles Oldham	Candy	310 821-8742
Alexis Mathy	Wyndsonnet	619 445-0686
Jim & Claudia Prescott		619 453-2597
Aileen Frazier	Witchwynd	619 670-1146
Ronald & Vicki Larmour	Sierra-Lyn	619 789-3060
Tina Bienefeld	Sunrise	714 774-5181
Pat Haigler	Rendition	714 871-0665
Marilyn Title	Marilyn	818 708-3785

Appendix A: Local Breeders and Breed Club Directory

Kathy Whiteis	Sunshine	909 676-4436
Kristy Hanes	Brookfield	909 735-9069
Dick & Shirley Farrington	Shawnee	909 780-7333
Linda Thomas	Swashbuckler	909 780-2403
Eleanor Heist	Red Arrow	909 822-4727

Irish Terrier
Irish Terrier Club of America
RR 3, Box 449 Bloomington, IL 61704 Mr Bruce Petersen, Sec

Irish Terrier Club of SC	Breed Club	818 963-9871
Linda Honey		310 519-8642
Mary Roberts		310 864-5080
Nancy Anne Bruner		714 633-5156
Ruth Cudigan		805 484-2364
Martha Salem		805 485-2364
James Cassity		818 366-6233
Juliana Swanson		818 790-7687
Betty & Don Jameson		818 887-7800
Jeanene MacDonald		818 963-9871
Marion & Cruse Honey		909 780-7419
Barbara Hoffman		909 780-8245
Roberta Massey		909 825-4497
Cory Rivera	Trackways	909 943-4396
Steve Senger		909 947-3892
Shari Halldane	Snowmist	909 874-4270

Irish Water Spaniel
Irish Water Spaniel Club of America
24712 SE 380 Enumclaw, WA 98022 Ms Renae Peterson, Sec

James Brennan	Jaybren	206 235-1140
Florence Blecher		213 874-0944
Ruth Roes	Co-R's	805 682-2668

Irish Wolfhound
Irish Wolfhound Club of America
8855 US Route 40 New Carlisle, OH 45344 Mrs William Pfarrer, Sec

Irish Wolfhound Assoc of the West Coast	Breed Club	310 434-0576
Western Hound Assoc of So California	Puppy Referrals	818 364-1203
Cheryl Rice	Ap Rhys	310 434-0576
Gerald & Sonja Colcun	Blythehounds	619 922-9500
Dixie Hirsch	Sunstag	714 649-2770
Kathy Smith	Kaelyn	818 848-4202
Pat Huntley	Referral	818 894-8988

Italian Greyhound
Italian Greyhound Club of America, Inc
35648 Menifee Rd Murrieta, CA 92563 Lillian Barber, Sec

Kathy Holmes		310 477-8023
Debora Avila	Imaje	310 699-2474
Claire Gaynor	Bilair	619 463-0700
Suzanne Butler	Banneco	619 481-4442

Dog Owners Guide

Alene Eden	Paradiso	619 789-1476
Dana & Jim Bosch	Lani	714 538-4333
Linda Williams	Lacey	805 946-3647
Marie Stern	Banzai	909 594-0461
Lilian Barber		909 679-5084
Lynn Poston	Kalon	909 829-4744

Jack Russell Terrier
The Jack Russell Terrier Club of America
PO Box 365 Far Hills, NJ 07931 908 234-1860

South Coast JRT Club	Breed Club	619 748-0523
Kathy & Steve Padilla	Ruff'N Tumble	310 547-5478
Peter & Liz Littmann	Hopdiggity	619 742-1977
Mary Abbott	Shenanigans	619 748-0523
Ron & Donna Sinderud	Incahoots	619 765-2304
Jo Paddison	Foxton Locks	714 633-0294
Suzanne Rodriguez	Kango	714 676-1352
Michelle Farrace	Runamuk	714 680-0247
Cindy Van Coops	Golden Hills	805 238-5829
Jill & Robert Paul	Fisticuffs	805 239-7679
Jackie Kaptan	Desert Sage	805 269-1467
John & Lissa Cortenbach	Cortenbach	805 687-8209
Darlene Boyland	Lickity Split	805 688-2770
Gail Bloom		805 497-2506

Japanese Chin
Japanese Chin Club of America
2113 Tract Rd Fairfield, PA 17320 Ms Faith Milton, Sec

Michele Blake	Blake	619 436-1579

Keeshond
Keeshond Club of America, Inc
8535 N 10th Ave Phoenix, AZ 85021 Ms Shannon Kelly, Sec

Keeshond Club of Southern California	Breed Club	714 586-5989
Dennis & Colleen LeHouillier	Cari-On	310 323-1292
Barbara Brown	Kan Du	310 439-4519
Linda Weiss	Panda	310 455-1572
Tawn & John Sinclair	Shoreline	310 457-3569
Barbara Ann Brown	Kan Du	310 599-3175
Mel & DeeWildenstein	Wildstone	310 697-1345
Bonnie Norman	Valley Kees	619 562-5796
Sandra Lambright	DOGS USA	714 581-7933
Kristine Arnds	Winsome	714 586-5989
Connie Jankowski		714 780-2514
John & Rita Jacobs	Designer	714 830-4748
Jim & Eileen Parr	Parrkees	714 892-0672
Tom & Marlene Pierce	Keewicke	714 894-7470
Joanie Fraser	Frazaira	805 245-2217
Jack & Sharon Pierce	Van d Pier	805 527-7363
Jan & John Corrington	Kemont	909 626-6962
Carol & Dennis Mollberg	Kadenja	909 780-1522

Appendix A: Local Breeders and Breed Club Directory

Arthur & Sandra Knudsen	Shadowood	909 924-9106

Kerry Blue Terrier

United States Kerry Blue Terrier Club
2458 Eastridge Dr Hamilton, OH 45011 Ms Barbara Beuter, Sec

Kerry Blue Terrier Club of SC	Breed Club	805 269-0709
Helen Eiden	Eidenbock	310 398-1750
Stephen Clark	Tontine	619 562-2376
Richard & Carol Basler		714 551-2040
Joan Berry	Valentia	714 846-4692
Ellen Smith Wexler	Kehalen	805 269-0709
Mary Lou Perry		909 780-3861

Komondor

Komondor Club of America, Inc
W358 S10708 Nature Rd Eagle, WI 53119 Ms Sandra Hanson

Kuvasz

Kuvasz Club of America
RR1 Box 121, Hannibal, NY 13074 Ms Nancy Schefcick, Sec   818 999-1543

Kuvasz Club of Southern California	Breed Club	714 946-6265
Sally Furgeson	Santa's	206 793-0098
Connie Roe		818 443-2944

Labrador Retriever

Labrador Retriever Club, Inc
9690 Wilson Mills Rd Chardon, OH 44024 Mr Chris Wincek, Sec

Labrador Retriever Club of So California	Breed Club	714 581-2057
Jane Thompson Babbitt	Norfield	310 391-3396
Alexandra Flanigan	Kintra	310 944-1194
Jane & James O'Grady	Hathersage	619 435-7393
Barbara Nowak	Broyhill	619 444-5829
Liz Jarrett	Goosechase	619 445-5829
Robert & Kathy Besser	Beshire	619 437-1318
Roberta Halley		619 445-6177
Robin McBain	Sweetwater	619 480-9008
Eric & Trudy Soneson	Prospect	714 581-2057
Nancy & Bill VanSickle	Heatherbourne	714 636-3475
Susan & Bill Eberhardt	Saddlehill	714 639-0882
Karen Jobke		619 746-0711
Margaret Stanard	Markflite	714 832-8549
Weddell & Jaqua	Sandbar Sporting Dogs	714 761-3094
Diane Welle	Blue Knight	805 269-0603
Candice Stormes	Classic's	805 269-1533
Winnie Limbourne	Wingmaster	805 269-5252
Sharon Liccardi		805 273-1240
Jeff Gleason		805 274-8660
Doris Engbertson		818 785-3609
Doug Henderson		818 919 3421
Lorraine McKerracher	Paisley	818 969-9654
Kimberly Flowers		818 339-8301

Dave & Claudia Schmidt	Oakridge	909 628-0652
Nancy Hope Love	Brookland Labs	909 672-2667
Dennis & Carol Mollberg	Kadenja	909 780-2514
Cherie & Robert Hudson	Joseph's Labs	909 923-4757

Lakeland Terrier

United States Lakeland Terrier Club
PO Box 214 Bayport, NY 11705 Ms Carol Griffin, Sec

Christopher Kit Marks		619 353-2442
Bill Burns	St. Roques	714 771-7091

Leonberger

Leonberger Club of America
PO Box 97 Georgetown, CT 06829

Kerilyn & Brown Campbell	Hause Der Lowen	818 896-0654

Lhasa Apsos

American Lhasa Apsos Club, Inc
18105 Kirkshire Birmingham, MI 48025 Ms Amy Andrews, Sec

San Diego Co Lhasa Apsos Club	Breed Club	619 278-2484
Lhasa Apso Club of Southern California	Breed Club	310 859-3930
Lynn Lowrey	Marlo	310 859-3930
Shirley Benedict	San Jo	619 278-2484
Lois J. Nelson	Kilo's	619 741-8272
Judy O'Dell	Ladell	714 494-8322
Kitty Littlejohn	B-My Lori Shan	714 839-2813
Michelle O'Sullivan	O Lori Shan	714 891-5516
Ken Sharpton & Bill Dawson	Cameo	714 986-2968
Gayle Chase	Bobbet	805 526-8453
Sylvia Nestle	Tingdene	818 889-7958
Lorraine Shannon	Lori Shan	909 371-5061
Dianna Jones	Blazers	909 795-1162
Judith Camacho	Harrow	909 984-7177
Bill Dawson	Cameo	909 986-2968

Maltese

American Maltese Assoc
6145 Coley Ave Las Vegas, NV 89102 Ms Pamela Rightmyer, Sec

Pauline & Tom Bowen		213 745-4649
Jeanne Uzelac	Vik tors	310 274-3588
Janet Lance	Hunter	310 863-7957
Martha Thomas	Marlee	619 365-1679
Anne Hill Kohl	Deborah Hill	619 426-9460
Steve Cloud		619 464-7218
Nicki Shemanshi	Silky Doll	619 480-7374
Victoria Daily	Victoria	714 525-9931
Ramonita Whitney	Mona	805 251-4199
Sheila Gordon	Shadow Hills	818 503-0587
Mary Day	C & M	818 914-0380
Frances Glionna		909 686-3073
Bill Dawson	Cameo	909 986-2968

Appendix A: Local Breeders and Breed Club Directory

Manchester Terrier (Toy) ;
American Manchester Terrier Club
52 Hampton Rd Pitttown, NJ 08867 Diane Haywood, Sec

Phillip Shane	Rosewood	310 374-4931
Betty Hodges	Rosewood	909 926-1673

Mastiff
Mastiff Club of America, Inc
45935 Via Esparanza Temecula, CA 92590 Ms Carla Sanchez, Sec

Pacific Southwest Mastiff Club	Breed Club	909 272-9244
Robert & Catherine Huling	Mystic	310 925-3098
William & Virginia Gebhardt	Sunny	619 422-8238
Phyllis Miller	Seacoast	619 454-8984
Mike & Dee Gensburger	Gulph Mills	714 763-8443
Ron & Caroline Tobin	Comstock	805 498-6135
James & Edie Richards	Roderic	805 522-2778
Andy & Betsy Harvey	Thunderpaws	805 525-4980
Richard & Mary Greaver	Thunder Sky	805 943-5698
Marge Levine	Hale	818 597-1653
Carla & Joe Sanchez	Southport	909 676-1161
Cynthia Campbell	Stablemate	909 780-5986
Jon & Pam Mettrick	MQH	909 780-9677
Beverly Fritz	Suniglen	909 988 0059

Mastiff, Neopolitan
United States Neapolitan Mastiff Association
920 Bonnie Lane Auburn, CA 91343 818 892-4944

	Dog Star	818 767-8442

Mastiff, Tibetan
American Tibetan Mastiff Association
920 Bonnie Lane Auburn, CA 95603 916 888-6888

Miniature Bull Terrier
Miniature Bull Terrier Club of America
17 Fremont Rd Sandown, NH 03873 Marilyn Drewes, Sec

Southern California Miniature Bull Terrier	Breed Club	714 245-7786
Trudy Pizer	Hobbit Hill/LuvaBull	619 249-4848
Priscilla David		818 366-3890
Genelle Olrey		909 272-9244
Doug & Bonnie Price	Windeville	909 681-8744
Debra Mannon		909 242-9047
Patti Holt		909 653-9466
Dot Smith	Akemo	909 947-1571

Miniature Pinscher
Miniature Pinscher Club of America
Rt 1 Box 173 Temple, TX 76501 Ms Kay Phillips, Sec

Miniature Pinscher Club of Greater LA	Breed Club	909 887-3703
Shirley & Ray Larson	Mi-Bar	310 532-3727
Jeff & Jan Cox	Oakhills	619 244-6228

Barbara Mahan	Memories	619 364-4472
Jan Miller	Mill Anns	619 449-7871
Delores Zobel	Mel-Dee's	619 489-6261
Nelda Haun	Siblu	805 581-4903
Larry & Connie Wick	Larcon	818 781-5367
Patricia Campbell	TJ's	909 734-8958
Norma D Cacka	Bluehen	909 887-3703
Dorothy Lamb	Fireside	909 887-3703
Rita Lowman	Retz	909 926-2640

Miniature Schnauzer

American Miniature Schnauzer Club
RR2 Box 3570 Bartlesville, OK 74003 Mrs Susan Atherton, Sec

Miniature Schnauzer Club of So Cal	Breed Club	714 692-2877
Miniature Schnauzer Club of So Cal	Breed Club	310 838-3252
Gene Matic	Matic	213 460-4412
Ruth Ziegler	Allaruth	213 472-7993
Janet Brown-Corpin	Sandcastle	310 533-1344
Carol Hansen	Hansen House	310 493-5005
Ivan Mayberry	Dorovan	619 463-9897
Jan Mosely	Mag's Minis	619 661-6444
Bonnie Warrell	Belgar	619 728-7246
Leanne Tousey	Elete	714 529-8636
Margaret & Jerry Blakley	B-Major	714 531-7473
Stephe Marquart	St. Roque	714 639-0219
Vi & Robert Baws	Bows	818 443-6156
John & Muriel Brown	Jonmuir	818 914-9343
Yvonne Phelps	Solebate	818 448-3424
Vera Poliker	Kelvercrest	909 780-6284
Linda Ramsay	Yasmar	909 922-9562

Newfoundland

Newfoundland Club of America
RR3 Box 155 Carlinville, IL 62626 Clyde Dunphy, Sec

Stephen & Linda Barkas	Seaworthy	619 222-0677
Blair Schultze	Affenbar	619 445-1222
Claire Carr	Wynship	619 578-7561
Carol Elaine Thompson	Susana	805 583-8423
Joann Givens	Springhaven	805 724-1630
Janis Kiseskey	Ebb-N-Tide	805 845-9598
Virginia Hoag		818 349-6770
Christine Grey	Kipjack	818 367-1404
Shirley Brown	Barasway	909 788-0968

Norwegian Elkhound

Norwegian Elkhound Association of America
4772 Mentzer Church Rd Convoy, OH 45832 Mrs Diane Coleman, Sec

Norwegian Elkhound Assoc of SC	Breed Club	805 685-1219
Western Hound Assoc of So California	Puppy Referrals	818 364-1203
Jeanne Smolley	Bomark	310 541-3413
Margaret Williamson	Seacrest	619 423-8654

Appendix A: Local Breeders and Breed Club Directory

Freeman & Betty Claus	Redhill	714 544-9372
Mike & Sue Tweddell	Eventyr	805 257-1717
Rudy & Maureen Lux	Tarroma	805 498-0588
Maureen Kenton	Republik	805 522-7396
Mary Kater	Camelot	805 685-1219
Harry & Kay Hawn	Harka	909 242-2184
Lori Webster	Tioka	909 685-2166

Norwegian Lunderhund
Norwegian Lunderhund Club of America   619 246-8856
Jo Ellen Schmudlack   Nereng   818 951-2083

Norwich Terrier
Norwich & Norfolk Terrier Club
407 Grenoble Dr Sellersville, PA 18960 Mrs Maurice Matteson, Sec

Susan Lawrence	Castle Bar	310 313-2104
Donn La Vigne		619 444-2799
Peggy Blakeley	B Major	714 774-8863
David Powers		818 367-5785

Nova Scotia Duck Tolling Retriever
Diana Humanik   National Club   402 493-4411

Old English Sheepdog
Old English Sheepdog Club of America
14219 E 79th St South Derby, KS 67037 Ms Kathryn Bunnell, Sec

Old English Sheepdog Club of SC	Breed Club	818 570-0185
Dee Dee Caswell	Cottonwood	619 445-3517
Sue & David Nelson	Shaggyluv	714 523-1311
Tina Dugan	For-Pause	714 644-7907
Kristi & Marilyn Marshall	Love'N-Stuff	805 269-1661
Jo O'Dell	Allydon	818 286-9443
Penny Morgan	Birchfield	818 570-0185
Dody Glassco	Fuzzy Acres	818 339-0376
Darlene Glazebrook	Huggybears	818 894-6775

Otter Hound
Otter Hound Club of America
Rt1 Box 247 Palmyra, NE 68418 Dian Quist-Sulek, Sec

Jenell		908 591-0706
Kristi & Marilyn Marshall	Love'N-Stuff	805 269-1661

Papillon
Papillon Club of America
551 Birch Hill Rd Shoemakersville, PA 19555 Mrs Janice Dougherty, Sec

Papillon Club of Southern California	Breed Club	909 861-6595
Mary Lou Sandvik	Marsan	213 965-2325
Muriel Bohlman	Starview	619 244-0317
Susan Nikkel	Clear Sky	619 728-2139
James Pattison	Boni-Cal	619 751-1277
Don & Mary Bockstadter	Mardon	619 868-5357
Rosemary Warthen	Charada	619 944-4550

Gloria Coleman	Glorycole	714 531-7650
Sharon & Jim Kinney	Issibaa	714 532-4582
Betty Omohundro	Omi's	909 861-5248
Edythe Wise	Wise	909 861-6595
B. Eleanor MacDonald	Elmac	909 984-9849

Pekingese

Pekingese Club of America
Rt 1 Box 321 Bergton, VA 22811 Mrs Leonie Marie Schultz, Sec

Pacific Coast Pekingese Club	Breed Club	619 367-4090
Bonnie Eriksson	Kismet	310 455-1681
Adell Lantz	Lantzlot	619 327-1747
Harold Fraser	Dragonhai	619 365-8292
Misty Snow	MYFU	619 367-4090
Jacqueline Ragland	Ja-Ling	619 434-8654
Bill & Shirley Dumas	Du-Ma	805 483-0969
Patricia Andrusenki	Citilites	818 286-3552
June Strange	Mor-Lane	818 994-3594
Elizabeth Wilkie	Wilkie Way	909 627-9966
Jeanette Franklin	Corralitos	909 984-5154

Petit Basset Griffon Vendeen

Petit Basset Griffon Vendeen Club of America
426 Laguna Way Simi Valley, CA 93065 Ms Shirley Knipe, Sec

Western Hound Assoc of So California	Puppy Referrals	818 364-1203
Ruth & Paulsson Balladone	Balmar	717 823-4543
Jim & Stephanie Gibbons	Golden Rule	800 366-7006
Debbie Parrott	Hootwire	805 527-6327
Carol Parker	Le Cirque	818 446-2486
Ray & Sue Jacksen	Le Cirque	818 893-3542

Pharoah Hound

Pharaoh Hound Club of America
Rt 209 Box 285 Stone Ridge, NY 12484 Rita Sacks, Sec

Western Hound Assoc of So California	Puppy Referrals	818 364-1203
Joyce Martin	Shema Pharoah, Reg	714 636-1798
Linda Heim	Spirit	714 892-8266
Vickie Belitto	Wadjet	909 682-0796
Libby Leone	Lileo	408 663-2550
Don Delmore		510 865-9418
Mariah Cook		915 855-4636

Pointer

American Pointer Club
Rt 1 Box 10 Branch, LA 70516 Ms Lee Ann Stagg, Sec

Pointer Club of Southern California	Breed Club	909 685-5744
Lucy Goodman	Beagood	619 435-8069
David & Lisa Severy		818 897-4149
Donna Glenn	Shufield	909 780-4276
Henri Tuthill	Cumbrian	909 928-5801
Karen Detterich	Paladen	909 359-6960

Appendix A: Local Breeders and Breed Club Directory

Pointer, German Shorthaired
German Shorthaired Pointer Club of America
1101 West Quincy Englewood, CO 80110 Ms Geraldine Irwin, Sec

German Shorthair Pointer Club of So Cal	Breed Club	805 948-6271
German Shorthair Pointer Club of San Diego	Breed Club	619 748-5771
German Shorthair Pointer Club of Orange Co.	Breed Club	714 359-6960
German Shorthair Pointer Club of Riverside	Breed Club	909 798-3491
Duane Sisson	Pine Hills	619 445-4451
Glen & Piedad Harris	P'arris	619 469-3538
Inge Clody	Minado	619 748-5771
Milton & Mae Taylor	Liebe	619 748-6178
Mike & Judy Sanders	Gunnars	714 495-8575
Marilyn & Lee Stockland	Marilee	714 544-7483
Carole & Hal Griffen	Oak Leaf	805 269-1594
Daisy Schapheer	Von Hainholz	805 948-6271
Karen Detterich	Paladen	909 359-9660
Rhonda Storm	Zeigenfeld	909 681-1470
Andrea Ammel-Owens	Un-willyn	909 780-5537
Philip & Stephanie Casdorph	Von Kasdorf	909 798-3491

Pointer, German Wirehaired
German Wirehaired Pointer Club of America
3838 Davison Lake Rd Ortonville, MI 48462 Ms Barbara Hein, Sec

German Wirehair Pointer Club of SC*	Breed Club	310 530-3264
Harry Rawn	Vomweisen	310 454-0405

Pomeranian
American Pomeranian Club
RR3 Box 429 Washington, IN 47501 Ms Frances Stoll, Sec

San Diego Pomeranian Club	Breed Club	619 475-2531
City of Angeles Pomeranian Club	Breed Club	310 618-9905
Cande Freeman	Pominique	310 549-2707
Annaray Rhien	Sungold	619 270-8470
Antonia Diamond	Diadem	619 371-1550
Fern Rodrigues	Sun Ray	619 443-9946
Margaret Ontiveros		619 475-2531
Pauline Hughes	Point Loma	619 753-5807
Kimberly Read	Luv-N	714 992-4195
Fran Smith	VIP	805 272-9527
Patricia Andrusenki	Citilites	818 286-3552
Theresa Cortez	Cortez's	909 597-3354
Gaila Brickus	Brickus	909 763-0433
Sherri Mason	Mason's Pom Heaven	909 657-8166
Nancy Chadwick	Chadwick's	909 735-4877
Penny Dees	Pen's	909 849-3904
Tula Demas	Tula's	909 883-1944
Sherri Wedell	Wedell's	909 944-4860

Dog Owners Guide

Poodle
Poodle Club of America
2514 Custer Pky Richardson, TX 75080 Mrs Harold Kinne, Sec

Poodle Club of SC	Breed Club	818 701-5306
San Diego Poodle Club	Breed Club	619 724-9134
Hub Poodle Club of Orange	Breed Club	714 530-1826
San Bernardino/Riverside Poodle Club	Breed Club	909 682-3164
Barbara & Dennis Adler	Celebrity	714 530-9231
Sherry Ann Hilf	Sherry's	714 546-2848

Poodle, Toy
Shirley Larson	Mi-Bar	310 532-3727
Mary Jane Norman	Tiny Tim	619 444-5527
Tracy Chiapetta	Tra-Ris	619 464-4373
Joyce Hitz	Grooming by Joyce	619 464-4373
Allan Chambers	Varsity	619 561-3037
John Pilkington	Calafia	619 670-4779
Norma Strait	Norjean	619 724-9134
Joseph & Lisa Cannarozzo	Calisa	619 749-4480
Dorothy Carlson	Chez Doral	619 758-2776
Sharon Campbell-Black	SharBelle	619 758-7322
Janet Lockyear	Jan'l	714 528-4353
Alison Dodge	Ali's Toys & Minis	714 646-9795
Doris Scott	Tudor	909 943-6630
Beverly Fritz	Suniglen	909 988-0059

Poodle, Miniature
Pam & Tony Woods		310 323-0811
Dorothy Norvell		619 223-1021
Janice Teller-West	Tellers	619 432-8408
Dr. L.J. Lockwood	Alc, Mala	619 436-6619
Sonna Bartling	Rogonna Miniature	619 440-7566
John Campbell	Dhubhne	619 479-8670
Michelle Mixon	Michou	619 281-1932
Dorothy Cangson	Candoran	714 530-1826
Alison Dodge	Ali's Toys & Minis	714 646-9795
Victor Hansom	Farcay	818 788-1482
Dianna Jones	Blazers	909 795-1162

Poodle, Standard
Janice Teller-West (Browns)	Tellers	619 432-8408
Julie Borst-Willard (Blacks)	Tiera	619 488-9500
Wendy Conkrite	Baroque	619 669-6457
John & Sheila Fowler (Black & White)	Summermist	619 744-7886
Sharon Campbell-Black (White & Blacks)	SharBelle	619 758-7322
Robert & Peggy McDill	Espree	714 380-0885
Cindy Parish (White)	Kolgemme	714 496-1042
Gloria Coleman	Glorycole	714 531-7650
Mary Sperling (Black & White)		714 751-1539
Lois Deangelis		818 351-5382

Francine Shipman	Starlight	818 710-1328
Victor Hansom (Black)	Farcay	818 788-1482
Charlie Holloway (White)	Wessex	909 682-3164
Katherine & Marc Higgins (Blacks)	Carme Lamarka	909 734-0277
Gwenneth Mosdale (White & Black)	Kingdown	909 888-7042
Penny Harney (Silver & Blue)	Pinafore	909 944-8884

Portuguese Water Dog

Portuguese Water Dog Club of America
176 Beech St Islip, NY 11751 Ms Virginia Santoli, Sec

SC Portuguse Water Dog Club	Breed Club	619 967-0967
Bobbe Kurtz	Starview	619 251-3210
Marilyn Ott	Questar	619 454-5882
Roberta & Floyd Corkill	C-Water	619 967-0967
Nedra Adams	Jana	805 266-1557
Norman Bogdadow	Deadwood	818 285-2888

Pug

Pug Dog Club of America
1820 Shadowlawn St Jacksonville, Fl 32205 Mr James Cavallaro, Sec

City of Angels Pug Club	Breed Club	818 703-5026
Paul Winfield	Avoncliff	213 463-4833
Susan Nelson	Hollyvel	310 921-5146
Paul V. Lipka	Paulaines	619 447-9128
Hazel Martens	Larimar	619 479-9588
Bud Shaver	B.E.'s	619 726-4907
Tony Nunes	Garnet	714 971-2685
Dolly & Kathy Lupo	Kadlu	805 584-1007
Blanche Roberts	City of Angels	818 703-5026
Celia Cradit	C's	909 359-6155
Ann Carpentier	Shadow Valley	909 865-7874
Diana Geerling	Lazy G	909 928-3129

Puli (Hungarian)

Puli Club of America
5109 Kathy Way Livermore, CA 94550 Ms Barbara Stelz, Sec   510 449-4190

Rat Terrier

Rat Terrier Club of Southern California
Loyal Penicks   714 737-6446

Rhodesian Ridgeback

Rhodesian Ridgeback Club of the United States
PO Box 121817 Ft Worth, TX 76121 Ms Betty Epperson, Sec

Orange Coast Rhodesian Ridgeback Club	Breed Club	714 532-5559
Western Hound Assoc of So California	Puppy Referrals	818 364-1203
Kate Graham	Filmmakers	213 874-7204
Anne Miller	Rajataru	619 320-8288
Peggy Davis	Neema	619 669-1787
Dana Steadley		619 749-6358
Jill & Steve Davis	Rainbow Hill	619 765-2010
Helen Brunner	Tropaco	619 789-3112
Dick & Barbara Rupert	Oakhurst	714 532-5559

Dog Owners Guide

A Kathleen Main	Raintree	714 870-9986
Myrna & Joe Berger	Rob-Norm's	818 985-8617
Jacque Rex	Starland	909 381-3064
Troy Abney	Rivercity	909 780-7080

Rottweiler

American Rottweiler Club
960 South Main St Pascoag, RI 02859 Ms Doreen LePage, Sec

Golden State Rottweiler Club	Breed Club	909 592-7718
Southwestern Rottweiler Club of SD	Breed Club	619 263-8268
San Bernardino Rottweiler Fanciers	Breed Club	909 883-1944
Inland Empire Rottweiler Club	Breed Club	909 485-0055
Hi-Desert Rottweiler Club	Breed Club	619 244-4655
Daviann Brooks	Nighthawk	310 278-6645
Lynn Brown	Ebonystar	310 599-6422
Irene Diano	Auserlesen	310 828-8918
Raul & Lisa Maurin		310 929-3797
Glenn Nutgrass	Blau Gras Haus	619 266-8155
Ron Seidler		619 263-8268
Marlin Smith		619 442-2756
Amy & Bryon Stermon	Zeus	619 443-8863
Crystal Pearson	Triple Oak	619 445-7011
Cindy D'Ambrosia	Eisenherzen	619 470-8636
Denise Sisneroz	Gipfel	619 670-1810
Dr. Wm. C Adams	Rancho Wilheen	619 724-6791
Ed & Sylvia Boyle	Gemstone	619 789-5802
Gladys Trout		619 947-7960
Carolyn Schumacher	Von Sshu	619 967-6263
Mickey Curtis	Pinecreek	714 645-7246
Marianne Zavala	Magic Z	714 771-5791
Carolyn Kaufman		805 473-0135
Jim & Edie Richards	Roderic	805 522-2778
Bob & Jeannie Tappan		818 357-0222
Michael Grossman	Windcreas	818 889-9514
Laura Jane Worsham	Von Der Lors	909 592-7718
Patricia Burton	Hi Sierra	909 628-2880
Rene & Tina Valencia	Tin-Ritz	909 734-8324
Jean-Claude Balu	Balu	909 823-4386
Tula Demas		909 883-1944
Virgil Herring	Country Resort	909 943-6542
Dot Smith	Akemo	909 947-1571
Hap & Bea Jones	Jo-Bea's	909 947-7554

Saluki

Saluki Club of America
Po Box 753 Mercer Island, WA 98040 Marilyn LaBrache Brown, Sec

San Angeles Saluki Club	Breed Club	818 364-1203
Western Hound Assoc of So California	Puppy Referrals	818 364-1203

Appendix A: Local Breeders and Breed Club Directory

Cori Solomon	Teri Kor	310 471-6672
Sharon Kinney	Issibaa	714 532-4582
Valerie Preston	Khiva	818 364-1203
Jackie & Ron Wassenaar	Ranesaw	909 681-4984
Lyndell Ackerman	Carmas	909 780-5872

Samoyed

Samoyed Club of America
W6434 Francis Rd Cascade, WI 53011 Kathie Lensen, Sec

Samoyed Club of San Diego	Breed Club	619 789-4797
Samoyed Club of Los Angeles	Breed Club	213 261-0912
Samoyed Club of Orange Co	Breed Club	714 637-7236
Samoyed Club of Southern Cal	Breed Club	310 861-7016
Barbara Arno	Arno	213 933-4314
Eric Endahl	Snowdahl	310 493-0235
Jerry & Barbara Mathe	Whie Artic	310 516 8424
Lia & Larry Benson	Starlite	310 861-7016
Rudy Munoz	White Bear	619 463-0527
Linda Jennings		619 322-9489
Marcia Sandusky	Delmar	619 753-3664
Mark & Terri Ward	Syn-y-Mar	619 757-4476
Gary & Gail Oesterreich	Artic Brite	619 789-4797
Chris & Dick Higley	Sitkins	619 789-9324
Carole Cheesman	Sassile	619 945-3198
Mike & Diane Hoffeker	Serako	714 637-7236
Donna Hollingsworth	Holly	805 482-6025
Virgil & Sandy Pellegrino		805 498-4467
Clu Carradine	Alta	805 568-6756
Barbara Allen		805 821-2817
Terry Bednarczyk	Samusz	818 249-7539
Sue & Tom Bailey	Fireside	909 874-3221

Schipperke

Schipperke Club of America
5205 Chaparral Laramie, WY 82070 Ms Diana Dick, Sec

Schipperke Club of Southern California	Breed Club	310 599-6422
Lynn Brown	Ebonystar	310 599-6422
Gretchen Sears	Glaeser Haus	619 468-3433
Virginia Larioza	Raffinee	619 630-7297
Diana Alderete	Sunhillo	619 868-3350
Eileen Lane	Spindrift	805 947-7812
Lisa Navarrete		805 943-6362
Sam & June Walden	Chinome	909 653-0572
Tanya Blauw	Witches Rune	909 685-6066
Cynthia Campbell	Stablemate	909 780-5986
Lester & Helen Karlton	Jetaway	909 789-1574
Betty Littschwager	Blue Max	909 798-4058
Betty Witt	Jeyall	909 928-9469

Scottish Deerhounds

Scottish Deerhound Club of America
545 Cummings Lane Cottontown, TN 37048 Mrs Joan Shagan, Sec

Western Hound Assoc of So California	Puppy Referrals	818 364-1203
Joan Giles		

Scottish Terrier

Scottish Terrier Club of America
PO Box 1893 Woodinville, WA 98072 Ms Diane Zollinger, Sec

Scottish Terrier Club of California	Breed Club	818 353-0657
Sueannette Wood	Su-ets	619 448-3098
Robin Starr	R-Starr	619 489-0334
Patt Bennett		619 741-0388
Karen Gallow		818 353-0657
Elaine Carrington	Finnvarra Rex	909 359-0989
Gussie Burros	The Last Resort	909 657-9203
Jacki & Glen Herron	Jacglen	909 797-6982

Sealyham Terrier

American Sealyham Terrier Club
Box 76 Sharon Center, OH 44274 Mrs Barbara Carmany, Sec

Sealyham Terrier Club of So California	Breed Club	818 353-5565
Howard Stone	Stonebroke	209 522-8957
Margaret Schools	Hapi-Dal	714 537-1474
Daniel Sackos	Helen	818 286-4942

Shar-Pei

Chinese Shar-Pei Club of America
PO Box 113809 Anchorage, AK 99511 Ms Jocelyn Barker, Sec

Golden State Shar-Pei Club	Breed Club	818 335-1665
San Diego Co Shar-Pei Club	Breed Club	909 780-4503
Shar-Pei Club of Riverside	Breed Club	714 838-1091
Desert to Sea Shar-Pei Club	Breed Club	909 884-0747
Jan Schwartz		213 254-1268
Sandra Szladek		310 437-4523
Verla & Bruce Randell		310 519-7788
Elizabeth & William Straube		310 539-5356
Christine Palmer		310 633-3354
Roz Williams		310 867-6808
Sandy Rude		310 928-1491
Thomas & Alta Germany		619 228-0117
Charles & Irma James	House of Cuddles	619 342-3206
Billie Jo Swanson	Ver Million	619 561-6643
Charlene Tompkins		619 669-5375
Beth Boyer		619 727-7522
Mara & Bob Snyder	Prunehill	619 789-5175
Henri & Marianne Casteel	Casteels	619 868-6908
Mike & Anita Dice	House of Hu'll	714 838-1091
Roberta Libman	Mikobi	714 661-1175
Lynn Olds		805 727-1718
Linda & Jay Trustman		805 946-2557

Mozelle Chandler		818 343-2201
Richard Morgan		818 443-5064
John Tuck		818 965-2246
Greta Link		818 752-8539
Melinda Murphy		909 592-1345
Harriet Land		909 595-2380
Bobbie Coughlin	KDK	909 676-2086
Christine Palmer		909 681-4639
Judy Welch	El Jay	909 685-2518
Doreen & Jeff Hunter	Hun Do Je	909 780-4503
Judy Clark	Swe-Pea's	909 943-2580
Darlene Wilson		909 884-0747
Judy & Buddy Dorough	Tuj	909 989-9501

Shetland Sheepdog

American Shetland Sheepdog Association
2125 E 16th Ave Post Falls, ID 83854 Ms Susan Beacham, Sec

Shetland Sheepdog Club of SC	Breed Club	714 537-8460
Shetland Sheepdog Club of San Diego	Breed Club	619 579-9265
Santiago Shetland Sheepdog Club	Breed Club	714 531-1853
Del Dios Shetland Sheepdog Club, Inc.	Breed Club	619 276-9295
Michael Macnamara	Esquire	619 276-9295
Bob Green	Highgate	619 461-4995
Bernice Lockmann	Capri	619 462-5698
Sharon Morgan	Showmor	619 479-3417
Willa Gregory	O'Scotia	619 484-4377
Steve Brooks	Summer Brook	619 579-9265
Linda Jackson	Sallette	619 670-1312
Linda McCoard	Ohana	619 748-2111
Marie Arbeiter		619 748-6030
Carol Foster-Nobel MD	Orange Hill	619 756-3438
Marcia Bittner	Tradewynd	619 788-0686
Beth Sullivan	Crown	619 789-3995
Patricia Houston	Midday	714 494-2787
Andrea Linden	Surfside	714 499-2470
Judy Todd		714 537-8460
Peggy & Jan Haderlie	Summersong	714 649-2511
Patricia Thomas	Paradale	714 821-5456
Shirlee Brundage DVM	Kylin	714 870-9662
Dottie Atkins	Show Biz	818 367-6795
Bonnie Smith	Tara Hill	909 780-6784
Brandol & Gayle Eads	Bangay	909 883-4623

Shiba-Inu

National Shiba Club of America
101 Peaceful Dr Converse, TX 78109 Frances Thorton, Sec

Bob Bobrow	Rippa-Na	619 949-8199
Frank & Alice Sakayeda	Satori	714 633-7498
Mitze Reid	Paladin	714 738-4640
Manny & Sharon Lundberg	White Cap	805 386-3400

Camille Kam Wong	Triple K	818 446-2486
Carol Parker	Sashimo	818 446-2486
Jim & Karen Church	Toki-O	909 689-8376
Stephanie Young	Desert Shiba's	909 766-2002

Shih Tzu
American Shih Tzu Club
837 Auburn Ave Ridgewood, NJ 07450 JoAnn Regelman, Sec

Shih Tzu Fanciers of Southern California	Breed Club	909 597-1248
Lois Magette	Majestic	310 430-4429
Sharon Bilicich	Shar-Ming	310 831-6992
Linda Myzer	Puppy Love	619 443-1335
Penny McAvoy	McAvoys	619 466-8312
Susan Sholar	Sho-Lin	619 942-8668
Jan Russell	Misha	619 461-3836
Victoria Dailey	Victoria Dailey	714 525-9931
Joe & Bobbie Walton	Shen Wah	714 730-5189
Jody Neal	Wingate	714 960-5003
June Young	Changa	714 996-2432
Sheila Gordon	Windsor House	818 503-0587
Jill & Boyd Bailey	Joy Toi	909 653-3236
Virginia Mundy	Mundy	909 683-7730
Norma Hewiston	Shado	909 781-6631
Lorra & Mike Craig	Sabar	909 862-8623
Gege Cane	Cane	909 882-3061
Penny Harney	Pinafore	909 944-8884
Ena Lane	Show Off	909 597-1248

Shiloh Shepherd
Russ & Judy McElroy	McElroy	909 272-9850
Gwyn Poor	Lla-Ess's	818 352-3078

Siberian Husky
Siberian Husky Club of America
18 Greenwood St Elkton, MD 21921 Ms Barbara Palmer, Sec

Camino Real Siberian Husky Club	Breed Club	310 946-5950
Siberian Husky Club of SC	Breed Club	818 282-6805
Shirley McCarthy	Hi Tail It	310 322-5058
John & Kathy Regan	Lil Paws	310 322-9413
Clyde Porter	Clymara	310 693-5103
Toni Daniels	Datona	310 421-1878
Betsy Korbonski	Tovarin	310 459-2230
Sherri Del Pozo	Karamad	310 693-9953
Dow Bryant		310 861-0166
Gail Shealy	Miroskima	619 246-8856
Frederick & Joann Koperski	Tsarskaya	619 375-8695
Kim & Kirk Schwartzah	Sterling	619 424-6332
Connie & Willie Dansby	Conwil	619 443-5127
Frank & Mickey Polimeni	Poli	619 630-2005
Lisa & Barbara McMillan	Shadowfox	714 637-5006
Verla McFayden	Aneechee	714 892-5087

Appendix A: Local Breeders and Breed Club Directory

Nancy Sumida	Sumiro	714 992-0558
Michael & Karen Burnside	Sierra	805 495-5037
Suzanne Wilson	Newbury	805 498-3788
Bill & Ann Henry	Anbi	805 529-3796
Susan Adams	Midsummer	805 943-8808
Richard & Susan Jung	Cyberia	818 282-6805
Linda Longshore	Foxfire	818 330-6074
Peggy Arnett	Frostipaws	909 244-2482
Tony Keyfel	Maskarade	909 681-5855
Diana Butts	Helmcrest	909 681-8242
Deborah Blanchard		909 685-2320
Carmen Petersen	Crakara	909 685-4632
Carolyn Warren	Lakmat	909 780-3322
Beverly Kittle	Nailutchij	909 984-4130

Silky Terrier
Silky Terrier Club of America
2783 S Saulsbury St Denver, CO 80227 Ms Louise Rosewell, Sec

City of Angels Silky Terrier Club	Breed Club	714 527-3116
Mary Isabel	Mi-Ohn	310 436-9521
Burt D Fried	Jemsal	310 454-5456
Marge Gagliardi	Anahab	619 375-4735
Mimi Lorie	Alegre	619 423-9422
Zella Flood	Billabong	619 561-7691
Dorothy Hicks	Cypress Mi-Ohn	714 527-3116
Gloria Coleman	GloryCole	714 531-7650
Flo M Kotecki	Flo-Co	714 894-3922
Wilma L Awana	Franmas	805 248-6163
Robert A Farron	Royaline	818 351-0553
Ann E Tolley	Mar-An	818 574-5079
Betty King	Redtone	909 657-2490
Pat Gesler	Jampat	909 735-5295
Jean Eliker	Saturn	909 882-0816
Phyllis L Schneider	Blu-N-Tan Ranch	909 926-2191

Skye Terriers
Skye Terrier Club of America
11567 Sutters Mill Circle Gold River, CA 95670 Mrs Karen Sanders, Sec

Skye Terrier Club of Southern California	Breed Club	818 248-5569
Judy Davis	Talkan	916 674-2682
Carol Sumonds	Rover Run	415 897-1144
Judy Umeck	Bel Canto	714 761-7144

Soft Coated Wheaten Terrier
Soft Coated Wheaten Terrier Club of America
4607 Willow Lane Nazareth, PA 18064 Mrs Mary Anne Dallas, Sec

SCWT Club of SC	Breed Club	310 947-1770
Carlie Hofemann	Gaeshill	310 644-4812
Barnard & Ilze Barron	Westridge	310 457-7778
Doug & Naomi Stewart	Dounam	310 947-1770
Roxanna & Leo Springer	Springsong	619 297 7573
Judith L. Pitman	Aranbriar	619 569-1810

Dog Owners Guide

Henri & Laura Corbin		619 427-3448
Lee & Carol Herd	Palm Run	714 893-5821
Lucille Aiken	Ballyhagen	805 484-3071
Susan & Steve Sakauye	Harbour Hill	805 967-0953
Ann Leigh & Francine Shipman	Starlight	818 710-1328
Beverly Streicher	Hilltop	818 789-8328
John Caliri	Legacy	818 797-4556
Sally Tatum	Sundial	818 892-9469
Alan & Barbara Goldie	Carrigan	909 793-9291

Spinoni Italiano
Spinoni Club of America
PO Box 307 Warsaw, VA 22572 Jim Channon Sec 804 333-0309

Springer Spaniel, Welsh
Welsh Springer Spaniel Club of America
4225 N 147th St Brookfield, WI 53005 Ms Karen Lyle, Sec

Joan Hamaguchi	Bu-Gwyn	213 280-5338
Bob & Patricia Ramsey	Bel Canto	714 761-7144
Sandy Ilminen		909 686-8384
Linda West	Krystal	818 353-3853

St. Bernard
St Bernard Club of America
719 East Main St Belleville, IL 62220 Ms Carol Wilson, Sec

St Bernard Club of San Diego	Breed Club	619 758-8319
St Bernard Club of Southern California	Breed Club	909 685-0813
Orange Coast St Bernard Fanciers	Breed Club	714 642-7106
Dianne Bowen	Oxford	619 427-2982
Phoebe & Howard Brown	Buena Vista	619 758-8319
Jan Goodwin/Ron Allerdice	Silvercrown	714 241-0747
David Burchell	South Shores	714 586-2636
Dr. Ernest Parks	Hacienda Ursula	714 637-1986
Mylle Frederiksen	Rosenborg	714 642-7106
Ladd & June Morris	Morris'	714 777-2359
Liz & Don Miller	Capistrano Saints	714 996-0739
Marion Ruiz		909 685-2076
Jack Landgraf	Sky Meadows	909 763-5231
Anthony & Roberta Nanfito		909 823-3642

Staffordshire Bull Terrier
Staffordshire Bull Terrier Club
PO Box 70213 Knoxville, TN 37918 Linda Barker, Sec

Nancy Harris Jones	Tuftown	310 634-5032
James & Melinda Cargill	McCrae	818 892-7180
Gary Smith		818 988-0380

Standard Schnauzer
Standard Schnauzer Club of America
4 Deerfield, CT 06804 Ms Kathy Donovan, Sec

Standard Schnauzer Club of So California	Breed Club	310 949-4114
Paula King	Konig	310 548-6236

138

Appendix A: Local Breeders and Breed Club Directory

Gordon & Karen Benson	KB 'S	619 292-4924
Sue Culbertson	Von Erivic	714 637-5765
Burton & Ellen Yamada	Yamada	909 337-2347

Sussex Spaniel

Sussex Spaniel Club of America
908 Cowan Dr Columbia, MO 65203 Mrs Barbara Barnard, Sec

Linda Legare	Rustwell	507 263-3436

Tibetan Spaniel

Tibetan Spaniel Club of America
29W028 River Glen Rd West Chicago, IL 60185 Ms Shirley Howard, Sec

Jody Thomas	BB Jo	805 947-0823

Tibetan Terrier

Tibetan Terrier Club of America
127 Springlea Dr Winfield, WV 25213 Ms Brenda Brown, Sec

Donna Slikkerveer	Angels	714 992-1331
Kathy L Peterson	Karessa	909 591-7224

Tosa, Japanese

TOSA of America
9707 Noble Ave North Hills, CA 91343   818 892-4944

Toy Fox Terrier

Toy Fox Terrier Club of America
111 Moose Dr Crosby, TX 77532 Douglas Gordon, Sec 713 324-4269

Julie Wells	Jewels	619 739-1144
Jan & Glen Stewart	Windjangle Ranch	619 240-3464

Vizsla

Vizsla Club of America
PO Box 639 Stevensville, MO 21666 Ms Patricia Carnes, Sec

Vizsla Club of So California	Breed Club	818 366-1054
South Coast Vizsla Club	Breed Club	714 830-6509
Central California Vizsla Club	Breed Club	805 831-5049
Robert Dorman	Delcrown	619 435-3322
Andre & Esther Tomatis	Lothan	909 822-5050
Ed & Beverly Wanjon	Russet Leather	805 296-9682
Larry & Shelley Coburn	Golden Empire	805 831-5049
Mark & Bonnie Goodwein	Koppertone	818 366-1054

Weimaraner

Weimaraner Club of America
PO Box 110708 Nashville,TN 37222 Mrs Dorthy Derr, Sec   615 832-9115

Southland Weimaraner Club	Breed Club	310 373-3060
Joan Valdez	Valmar	310 373-3060
Steve & Jill Davis	Rainbow Hill Farms	619 765-2010
Ken & Connie Williams	Wil Wins	619 940-1085
Robert Remeika	VS-Von Schatten	714 827-3019
Fa Farr	Fanthom	818 609-9085
Debbi Nusbaum	Altamar	818 773-9246
Mary McElwee	Marmac	909 923-3981

Dog Owners Guide

Welsh Terrier
Welsh Terrier Club of America
200 Hazelmere Dr Richmond, VA 23236 Mrs Marge McClung, Sec

Welsh Terrier Club Of SC	Breed Club	909 780-6284
Vera Potiker	Kelvercrest Terriers	909 780-6284
June Dutcher		714 827-8013

West Highland White Terrier
West Highland White Terrier Club of America
33101 44th Ave NW Stanwood, WA 98292 Mrs Anne Sanders, Sec

West Highland White Terrier Club of Cal	Breed Club	818 889-7904
Gina Standley	West Breeze	619 252-0232
Tom & Barbara Barrie	Peter Pan	619 749-4549
Shirley Goldman	Shirl's	714 780-3217
Mona Berkowitz	Momarv	805 498-2322
Shirley Jean Niehause	Whitehouse	805 987-3568
Thomas Powers		818 343-2239
Mary Kuhlman		818 353-1824
Joe Berger		818 985-8617
Linda Leavelle	Liberty	909 780-2358
Jeannine Price		909 944-7511

Whippet
American Whippet Club
14 Oak Circle Charlottesville, VA 22901 Mrs Harriett Nash Lee, Sec

Greater San Diego Whippet Assoc	Breed Club	619 477-4222
Southern California Whippet Assoc	Breed Club	714 649-2286
Western Hound Assoc of So California	Puppy Referrals	818 364-1203
Dianne Bowen	Oxford	619 427-2982
Elizabeth Wolkonsky	Folquin	619 443-1655
Bruce Sutton	Summerwind	619 445-1212
Rosanna Sutton	Winsmoor	619 463-6228
Dick & Livie Jensen	Limard	619 749-1356
Lori Lawrence	Star Line	619 755-5355
Susan Baker	Bonzoumet's	714 240-0538
Dana & Jim Bosch	Lanmarc	714 538-4333
BJ Rooney	Knightwood	714 775-5323
Tom & Ellen Hammett	Kezo	714 649-2286
Doris Bandoian	Vahdor	714 996-2782
Daniel Lockhart	Saxon Shore	805 646-6737
Lyra Partch	DitzInk	818 447-6017
Mike & Michelle Clevenger	Blackwater	909 789-1230
Mary Cutherell	Donmar	909 795-4867
Giselle Ringwald	Rialto	909 873-9989
Betsy Prior	Amir	909 928-4229
Katie Rudolph	Festiva	909 984-2091

Yorkshire Terrier
Yorkshire Terrier Club of America

PO Box 100 Porter, ME 04068 Mrs Betty Dullinger, Sec		818 571-0909
Yorkshire Terrier Club of Greater LA	Breed Club	310 410-4551

Appendix A: Local Breeders and Breed Club Directory

Pat Wakeman	Miss Pat	619 561-2657
Gloria Lipman	Nikko	619 741-9337
Yvonne Siler	Lynn-Mar	714 529-5908
Linda Bush	Bejaze	714 739-5662
Barbara Marches	Marchwyn	714 857-5154
Ken Sharpton & Bill Dawson	Cameo	714 986-2968
Yvonne Annan		818 330-6933
Mark Lytle	Artel	818 547-0345
Gale Kelley	Kel-Lee	818 571-0909
Jerry & Phyllis Ross	Bluebell	818 764-3614
Audrey Raymond	Raymondale	818 889-7877
Dorothy Gaunt	Dots	818 917-4034
Jane Ferguson	Dynasty	818 964-7912
Nancy Hadley	Scrumptious	909 780-6978
Deborah Meyer	Buttonbrite	909 883-3139
Maureen Vanderburg	Crystal	909 987-7985

Appendix B
Rescue Contacts

A number of individual dog lovers volunteer to rescue purebred dogs from shelters and put them up for adoption. Most dogs will have been spayed or neutered and will have received any necessary medical attention prior to placement. If you would like a purebred dog and are willing to forego the mixed blessing of puppy raising, consider adopting a dog from a breed rescue group. Local breed clubs are another source to contact. A donation is usually requested to help cover costs. You can also pick up a *Mutt-Matchers* paper. This publication is an excellent source and provides pictures of all dogs awaiting adoption and other animals.

Affenpinscher
Mary Ostrand	808 682-8388
Judi Benjamin	818 830-0377

Afghan Hound
Vicki Zayak	310 657-8237
Nancy Powell	818 347-1029
Andrea Augustine (Club)	818 545-7519
Pat Stephenson	310 455-1877

Airedale Terrier
Ruth Millington	805 386-3757
June Dutcher (Club)	714 827-8013
Elinor Hellmann	818 908-9828
Muriel & Ralph Prey	310 671-8695

Akita (Japanese)
Barbara Bouyet (Club)	805 492-2127
Leslie Thompson	619 283-8093
Sharon Lundberg (Club)	800 392-8414
Elizabeth Alsgaard	619 482-7220

Alaskan Malamute
Tina Dunn (Club)	805 583-8280

American Eskimo
Linda Voight (Club)	619 458-9029
Wendy Eastland (Club)	619 286-0837

American Staffordshire Terrier
Denise	805 668-2577
Lydia Castagna	818 716 8224

American Water Spaniel
Contact clubs	

Australian Cattle Dog
Colleen	805 687-8414

Anatolian Shepherd
Quinn Harned (Club)	619 445-3334

Australian Shepherd
Aussie Rescue	800 892-2722
Cherie Coakes	818 798-0336

Australian Terrier
Hal Wilcox	310 429-5035
Vela Woodward	714 530-6348

Basenji
Karen Jones (Club)	818 761-7668
Ken Linberg	805 685-1868
Dave Caslin	909 823-5821

Basset Hound
Adrianne Sherard	310 690-4579
Jerry (SD Area Only)	619 229-9016

Beagle
Dottie Ambrose	818 347-5529
Yvonne Jasinski	619 432-8247
Bill & Janet Nieland	714 826-0928
Ray & Sue Jacksen	818 893-3542

Bearded Collie
Ann Rambuad	909 822-6451

Dog Owners Guide

Sue Howey	805 968-8775
Sandy Ellington	909 353-0249

Bedlington Terrie

Marjorie Hanson	310 869-0164
Linda James	310 375-2317
Judy Smith	619 695-1122

Belgian Malinois

Mara Lee Giles	909 685-0828
Penny Gott	805 968-5230

Belgian Sheepdog

Mara Lee Giles	909 685-0828
Milard & Jeanne Brown	818 846-2221
Suzanne Castle	619 693-8254
Peri Norman	818 899-3407

Belgian Tervuren

Ann Howard	619 698-7401
Theresa Kaplan	310 472-0011
Pat Weymouth	714 544-2459
Larry Lovelace	619 686-3309
Gladys Clark	818 790-0196
Mary Lee Giles	909 685-0828

Bernese Mountain Dog

Roni Leighty	805 493-2738
Kathy Gray	714 738-8099
Irene Benson	619 296-1027
Dorothy Martin	909 585-3449

Bichon Frise

Margie Rickards	909 371-7464
Betty Ribble (Club)	619 751-1132
Barbara La Monte	714 828-5735
Phoebe Calwell (ref)	805 963-2986

Black and Tan Coonhound

Shawn Scott	909 943-9812
Debbie Seitzinger	714 336-1733

Bloodhound

Susan Hamil	714 494-9506
Frances Allen	714 794-3124
Stacy Mattson	714 858-0442
Lynne Aguippe	909 737-4439

Border Collies

Emily Miles	805 684-6177

Border Terrier

Randi Berger	818 986-0201
Elizabeth Grogan	909 887-2231

Borzoi (Russian Wolfhound)

Judy Lofgren	310 540-9695
Lenore Lee	714 786-7942
Torrea Le Born	619 756-4789
Peg Jemison	714 846-4192

Boston Terrier

Jody Davis	909 657-9112
Lil Huddleston	818 344-3487
Sherry Berry	909 798-0808
Allie Dell	310 436-8058
SD Rescue	619 561-0652

Cheryl Reynolds	805 684-4914

Bouvier des Flandres

Ted Ondrak	818 343-7565
Sally Imura	310 378-2691

Boxer

Ursula Sautier	818 343-6244
M Fairshter*	714 698-9496
June Collins (SD Only)	619 297-5749

Briard

Pat Cardone	714 529-8763
Virginia Engelhart	310 457-9697
Julie & Don Norman	213 851-3635

Brittany Spaniel

Theresa Kaplan	310 472-0011
Agnes Rodriquez	310 833-3458
William O'Brien	310 865-4323

Brussels Griffon

Eleanor McDonald	909 984-9849

Bulldog

Margaret Spinella	909 982-3864
Marcie Dobkin	619 748-8848
Betty Fisher	619 588-6491
Linda Exarhos	619 596-2222

Bulldog (French)

Denise Eltinge	805 682-0359
Friends Of The Frenchy	813 544-1824

Bullmastiff

Carol Beans	714 544-1824
Dina Case	818 889-0023
Alanna Grimm	310 457-1600

Bull Terrier

Jan & Randy Bisgaard	213 667-0582
Susan Murphy	714 821-4605
Christine Burton	310 457-2017
Bill Edwards	818 956-1170

Cairn Terrier

Jack & Karen Smith	619 728-7133
Laura Strong	909 797-2707
Kathhleen Spelman	818 303-3041
Susan Kaczor	818 782-8612
Candie Heffler	714 894-7707
Chris Frenk	805 733-3629

Cavalier King Charles Spaniel

Chuck Siemaker	310 375-4858
Leslie Mayer	310 459-9847
Theresa Kaplan	310 472-0011

Chesapeake Bay Retriever

Betsy Jones Moreland	818 443-7387

Chihuahua

Delynn Moutier (Club)	714 995-4641
Carol Starjack (Club)	818 884-5291
Ellen Wetenkamp	818 343-0360

Chinese Crested

Mary Buras	909 685-6026

144

Appendix B: Rescue Contacts

Clumber Spaniel

Bobby Rench	909 874-1242

Cocker Spaniel

Jacqi Killeen	909 986-6956
Ley O'Connor	909 923-2405
Jackie Rowe	619 466-6166
Linda Scott	619 645-1186

Collie (Rough)

Sue Baldwin	714 858 0298
Dini	909 797-8285
Stephen Colley (Club)	818 398-8987
Suzanne Castle	619 693-8254
Mo Roberts	909 780-8573
Chris Harmon	909 987-8617

Collie (Smooth)

Sue Baldwin	714 898-0298
Debby Robins	805 529-7139
Mo Roberts	909 780-8573
Diane Taylor	909 360-3815

Coonhound

Debbie Seitzinger	909 336-1733

Corgi, Cardigan Welsh

St Anthony (Jane Zweig)	213 654-5848
Arleen Rooney)	310 830-8126
Joyce Swain	714 871-1922
Sandie Coleville-Hyde	619 566-9644

Corgi, Pembroke Welsh

Meredith Brittain	909 887-5057
Gwen Platt (Club)	619 480-8348
Morrell Lamer	310 394-1897
Jan & Terry Lewis	805 640-8356
Margaret Stewart	818 842-1431

Curly-Coated Retriever

Lee Smith	909 689-8668
Kathleen Kardash	619 569-1311
Rick & Kathy Kail	714 557-1668

Dachshund

Wes Martin	619 274-3655
Marcie Sator	714 391-4784
Marge Dwyer	818 843-2232
Antelope Valley DC	805 256-6834
Marsha Eaton	909 789-9039

Dalmatian

Margaret Schools	714 537-1474
Marie Johnson	818 340-1992
Dal Club of SC	310 403-2930
Barbara Hoover	310 545-7915

Dandie Dinmont

Jim Hooper	310 945-7136
Gini Yamate	714 897-4737
June Reeley	213 256-8657
Carol Hamilton	818 330-4708
Mary Ostrand	805 687-8388

Doberman Pinscher

Nina Culver	818 767-1166

Aztec Club (Angie)	619 443-8944
San Diego Club	619 273-4265
Ardis Braun	805 524-5102

Dogue De Bordeaux

Kate Kimball	805 257-7879
Ricki Toole	909 763-4715

English Pointer

Pat Hargrove	310 530-2720
Karen Dietrich	909 359-6960

English Setter

Linda Gall	805 499-2913

English Toy Spaniel

Florence Treseder	818 767-0756

Field Spaniel

Contact clubs

Finnish Spitz

Mary Ellis	805 528-6768
Peggy Olsen	909 947-5986
Judi Buell	714 685-0813

Flat-Coated Retriever

Nanci Hanover	310 459-8761
John Sack	818 507-7606
Peachie Orton	909 824-3049

Fox Terrier

Pat Kelly	909 597-3082
SCFT Rescue (Pam)	909 672-2008
Ruth Millington	805 386-3757
Janet Hendrickson	714 642-4901
Kimberly Lehman	619 464-5454

Fox Terrier (Smooth)

Virginia Dickson	310 696-6985

Foxhound(American)

Sue Kane*	805 524-4542

Foxhound(English)

Sue Kane	805 524-4542

German Shepherd Dog

Monica Royalty	909 674-8363
Grace Konosky	818 558-7560
Melanie Buccola	818 848-3826
Deana Hungerford	619 931-5479
Willie Webster	619 566-1149

German Shorthaired Pointer

Stephanie Casdorph	909 798-3491

German Wirehaired Pointer

Terry Smith	909 682-5433
William O'Brien	310 865-4323
Carla Weber	805 265-8879

Golden Retriever

Susan Burrows (Club)	619 449-1991
Jeannette Poling (Club)	619 445-9216
Diane Monahan	818 701-0674
Jan Sager	619 940-6331

Dog Owners Guide

Gordon Setter
Jane Matteson*	909 986-8055
Perri Norman	818 899-3407

Great Dane
Diane Warren	909 792-6178

Great Pyrenees Mountain Dog
Christine Wagner	310 858-9208
Dottie Sisco	909 887-8201
Val Duke	909 780-2589
San Diego Rescue*	619 451-1815

Greater Swiss Mt. Dog
Betty Carroll	714 947-5363
Dave Caslin	714 823-5821
Kathy Ungar	805 255-1167

Greyhound
Greyhound Pets of Am	800 366-1472
Bruna	619 593-1238
Kay Rawson	714 467-1478
Operation Greyhound	619 593-1238
Cheryl Reynolds	805 684-4914

Harrier
Betty Burnell	805 642-8758

Ibizan Hound
Judy Umeck	714 761-7144

Irish Setter
Shirley Farrington	909 780-7333
Kathy Parsons	310 691-6038
Deanna Hugerford	619 942-6770
Ed & Glenna Durand	805 245-1241

Irish Terrier
Steve Senger	909 947-3892

Irish Water Spaniel
Florence Blecher	213 874-0944
Ruth Roes	805 682-2668
Dorothy Read	818 794-7585

Irish Wolfhound
Karen Chare	714 281-9167
Bill & Connie Davis	805 969-0160
Steve Hughes	619 746-8234
Greg & Brenda Ross	909 947-0415
Pat Huntley (Club)	818 894-8988

Italian Greyhound
Lynn Poston (Club)	909 829-4744
Claire Gaynor	619 463-0700

Jack Russell Terrier
JRTCA Rescue (Kathy)	310 547-5478
Cindy Drake	619 271-8933
Michelle Farrace	714 680-0247
Chris Levine	805 969-3885

Japanese Chin
Artis Downey	310 645-1598
Eleanor McDonald	909 984-9849
Margie Rickards	909 371-7464

Keeshond
Kris Amds	714 586-5989
Susan McCoy	805 527-4096
Kay Duffy	818 996-4049

Kerry Blue Terrier
Edith Izant	310 691-3450
Helen Bock	310 398-1750
Lonie & Doug Ward	619 457-4840
Catherine Wright	213 564-3536
Stephen Barry	818 914-1026
Ellen Smith-Wexler(Club)	805 269-0709
Janet Joers	805 688-2478

Komondor (Hungarian)
Trish Greer	909 780-9083

Kuvasz
Vicky Huguenen	714 737-1877
Gail Dash	818 366-5333

Labrador Retriever
Doyne Ladwig	714 646-5225
Nancy Nelson	909 679-1190
Kathy Besser	619 437-1318
Karen Jobke	619 746-0711
Barbara Peets	805 649-2095
Diane Matsuura	818 914-7881

Lakeland Terrier
Ruth Millington	805 386-3757
Peggy Privot	909 681-0527
Judy Jensen (SB Only)	805 646-5304

Lhasa Apso
Pat Majors*	619 475-0593
San Diego Rescue*	619 789-4864

Maltese
Nicki Shemanski	619 480-7374
Margie Rickards	909 371-7464
Caroline Rose	818 888-7613

Manchester Terrier (Standard & Toys)
Pete Ramsey	805 682-5939

Mastiff
Sue Giventer	909 829-3577
Alanna Grimm	310 457-1600
Marge Levine	818 597-9201
Bob Huling	310 925-3098

Mastiff, Neopolitan
NM Rescue	315 389-4028

Miniature Bull Terrier
Jan & Randy Bisgaard	213 667-0582

Miniature Pinscher
Norma Cacka	909 887-3703
Bobbi Schwinn	714 633-3266
Leanna Harwell	818 448-1213
Nelda Hawn	805 581-4903

Newfoundland
Denise Hatakeyama	818 912-4299

Appendix B: Rescue Contacts

San Diego Rescue 619 578-7561
Ginger Hohg 818 349-6770
Fran Dibble 805 498-6550

Norfolk Terrier
Margaret Stewart 818 842-1431

Norwegian Elkhound
Judy DeClercq 714 774-8863
Lori Webster 909 685-2166
Maureen Kenton 805 522-7396
Sue Tweddell 805 257-1717

Norwich Terrier
Peggy Blakeley 714 531-7473
Chris Fischer 818 899-4683

Old English Sheepdog
DeeDee Caswell 619 445-3517
Jane Dempsey 310 392-3366
Chris Bunsick 805 821-5004
Kathi Dudgeon 619 741-8432

Otterhound
Cheryl Reynolds 805 684-4914

Papillon
Margie Rickards 909 371-7464
Theresa Kaplan 310 472-0011
Kaye McDonald 714 433-6939
Eleanor McDonald 909 984-9849
Liz Palika 619 941-3221
Annabelle Hoffman 805 964-2446

Pekingese
Marie Martel 818 249-6354
Mary Ellen Kysor 818 342-8387

Petits Bassets Griffons Vendee
Wendy Jeffries 909 926-2277
Ray & Sue Jacksen 818 893-3542

Pharoah Hound
June Young 714 996-2432
Joyce Martin 714 636-1798
Randall Bullard 818 336-0780

Pointer, English
Karen Dietrich 714 688-4382

Pomeranian
Margie Richards 909 371-7464
Caroline Rose 818 888-7613
Connie Brown 805 270-1827

Poodle
Sallie Perkins 310 276-8982
Theresa Kaplan 310 472-0011
Jerry Klosson 619 945-2341
Yvonne Jasinski 619 432-8247
Carolyn Rose 818 888-7613
Linda Browring 805 527-8238
Beth Warther (Stds Only) 619 225-2158

Portuguese Water Dog
Marilyn Ott 619 454-5882
Susie Price 619 454-5807

Pug
Lisa Ultz 909 946-4958
John Eubanks 213 475-6992
Laurel Smith 805 682-0155
Little Angels PR (Sherri) 818 795-3944
Sherry Berry 909 798-0808
Ginger Julian 619 561-7742

Puli
Berni DeBus 310 828-2397

Rhodesian Ridgeback
Barbara Rupert 714 532-5559
Jackie Rex 909 381-3064
Mr & Mrs Berger 818 985-8617
Mary Trumbull 805 949-1383
Sandy Abney 909 780-7080
Bob & Shirley Howard 909 593-8461

Rottweiler
Roberta Banfield* 909 674-4849
Connie Rose* 619 726-8431
Cindy D'Ambrosia 619 470-8636
San Diego Club Rescue 619 470-8636
Beverly Berger 818 765-5997
Sandy Frantz 714 632-7966
Karen Ambrose 909 797-7840
Linda Benish (Inland Em) 909 350-0785

Saluki
Andrea Augustine 818 545-7519
Pam Philippi 909 985-8401
Sharon Kinney 714 532-4582
Cindy Shields 619 424-5684
Susan Price 619 486-4579
Joyce Tateo 805 947-1029

Samoyed
Mike Hoffecker 714 956-6180
Barbara Mathe 310 516-8424
Virginia Lariozo 619 630-7297

Schipperke
Lynn Brown 310 599-6422

Schnauzer, Miniature
Peggy Blakely 714 531-7473
Ruth Ziegler 310 472-7993

Schnauzer, Standard
Paula King 310 548-6236
Ray Schmalz 714 898-3557

Schnauzer, Giant
Carol Herd 714 893-5821
Ann Maldinado 916 966-3388

Scottish Deerhound
Joan Giles 909 591-4288
Mary Ann Reddin 310 697-8791
Frieda Pilat 805 269-4221
Carol Esterkin 818 996-0130

Scottish Terrier
Carol Herd 714 893-5821
Kathy Fish 619 484-2802

147

Jacki Herron | 909 797-6982
Elaine Carrington | 909 359-0989
Shiela Peavey | 805 735-0094
Phyllis Dabbs (Bkrsfld) | 805 871-2736
Sandra Priest | 619 441-0802

Sealyham Terrier
Howard Stone | 805 496-4566
Arnold Anderson | 818 353-5565

Shar-Pei (Chinese)
Charlene Tompkins | 619 669-5375
Erma James | 619 342-3206
Greta Link | 818 752-8539
Doreen Hunter (Club) | 909 780-4503
Darlene Wilson (Club) | 909 884-0747
E & W Straube (Club) | 310 539-5356

Shetland Sheepdog
Kathy Parsons | 310 691-6038
Kay Brunner | 310 943-5310
Del Dios Rescue | 619 276-9295
Connie Parrish (Club) | 619 789-9659
Willa Gregory (Club) | 619 484-4377
Janet Hendrickson | 714 642-4901
Judi Berry | 310 691-8118
Kathy Faulconer | 805 379-1208
Roz Cohen | 818 996-1269

Shiba Inu
Kay Brunner | 310 943-5310
Bruce & Jeri Braviroff | 909 596-1813

Shih Tzu
Phyllis Celmer | 619 942-0874
Sheila Gordon | 818 765-5592
Virginia Mundy | 909 683-7730
Ena Lane | 909 597-1248

Siberian Husky
Sandy Wirth | 818 597-8760
Deborah Blanchard | 909 685-2320
Peggy Arnett | 909 244-2482

Silky Terrier
Caroline Rose | 818 888-7613

Skye Terrier
Dodi Brand* | 818 248-5569
Patte Boyne* | 213 933-7467
Sue Emerson | 805 964-2446

Soft-Coated Wheaten Terrier
Carol Herd | 714 893-5821
Pat Slote | 213 661-5055
Ruth Millington | 805 987-2277
Susan Sakauye (SB Only) | 805 967-0953

Springer Spaniel, English
Jan Racey | 805 522-0687
Ellen Wetenkamp | 818 343-0360

Springer Spaniel, Welsh
Elizabeth Harward | 805 644-8190

St. Bernard
Dottie Lee | 714 496-5848
Susan Tran | 310 438-7169
Pam Katz | 805 524-3908

Staffordshire Bull Terrier
Cindy McNamara | 818 796-9547

Sussex Spaniel
Contact clubs

Tibetan Mastiff
Penny Melko | 212 257-5495

Tibetan Spaniel
Jody Thomas | 805 947-0823
Cheryl Reynolds (SB) | 805 684-4914

Tibetan Terrier
Margie Rickards | 714 371-7464
Randi Berger | 818 986-0201
Michelle Hiday | 818 335-4814

Tosa
International Tosa Rescue | 818 768-0691

Toy Fox Terrier
San Diego Rescue | 619 739-1144

Vizsla (Hungarian)
Kay Duffy | 818 996-4049
Beverly Wonjon | 805 296-9682
Lauren Horn | 714 495-0611

Weimaraner
Diane Monahan | 818 701-0674

Welsh Terrier
Ruth Millington | 805 386-3757
Jan Hexum (SB Area) | 805 964-7490

West Highland White Terrier
Jack Rennie | 310 377-1675
Lois Goldsworthy | 310 375-0344

Whippet
Dana Bosch | 714 538-4333
Norman Rufing | 619 477-4222
Ellen Hammett | 714 649-2286

Wirehaired Pointing Griffon
Contact clubs

Yorkshire Terrier
Theresa Kaplan | 310 472-0011
Andrea Blumenthal | 714 770-0916
Carolyn Rose | 818 888-7613
Bea Colten | 818 845-9237

Adoption/ Rescue Organizations

Adopt A Pet
805 527-8238 &
818 703-0903

Amanda Foundation
310 472-1742

Pet Orphans
818 901-0190

Pet Adoption Fund
818 340-1687 or
818 996-4049

Animal Assistance
League of Orange Co.
P O Box 38
Midway City, CA 92655
714 978-7387

Project Breed
202 244-0065

Actors and Others
for Animals
818 985-6263

Friends of Bajas Animal
Ellen Tousley
619 291-9223

St Anthony Canine Rescue
Arleen 310 830-8126 &
Jane 213 654-5848

Rancho Cucamonga
Friendship for Animals
Dianna Russell
909 944-9262

Shirley Cameron
Mixed Breed
619 439-7921

Foundation for the Care
of Indigent Animals
Penny Adams
619 466-0426

Focus/Snap
Candace Schumann
619 456-0452

Abandoned Animal
Relief Foundation
Joan Koch
619 753-3091

Greyhound Rescue

These groups work to save racing dogs that are scheduled to be killed.

Greyhound Pets of America
Darren Rigg
President & Founder
800 366-1472

Operation Greyhound
Bruna Palmatier
619 588-6611

Appendix C
Breed Cautions

This section is designed to offer the most serious and most common warnings prevalent in the breed. Buying from a quality breeder who offers certification will help reduce the likelihood of having to spend large sums of money on treatment, but remember, no breeder can be 100% sure.

Hip Dysplasia   An inherited problem where the hip does not fit properly into the socket. The best prevention is to X-ray the parents. X-rays are not 100% fool-proof, but they decrease the odds immensely.

Progressive Retinal Atrophy (PRA)   This inherited disease results in severe loss of vision and usually blindness. The best prevention is buying only puppies whose parents' eyes were examined by a canine ophthalmologist and found to be free of hereditary eye conditions before being bred. Usually the breeder sends the tests to the Canine Eye Registry Foundation (CERF) for evaluation and an official clearance certificate. If a breed is listed as having PRA or hereditary cataracts, ask to see the CERF certificates or a letter from a canine ophthalmologist.

von Willebrand's Disease   This is a blood-clotting disorder of genetic origin and produces external or internal hemorrhaging from a simple cut or illness. The best prevention is to buy only from parents whose blood was tested and found free of the condition before being bred.

Bloat This condition strikes large, deep chested breeds. The stomach swells with food, water or internal gases, seals itself off from relief, and may suddenly twist or flip over, resulting in death, unless there is surgical intervention. Feed small meals at least one to two hours after exercise.

Slipped Stifle This is a joint disorder.

List of Cautions by Breed. The name of the breed is printed in **bold type**, followed by the caution in plain type.

Note: All dogs listed below are good with children except as noted.

Affenpinscher: Susceptible to slipped stifle. Poor interaction with children.

Afghan Hound: Susceptible to hip dysplasia. Many breeders do not check hips because it requires anesthesia and the breed is sensitive to drugs. Needs extensive grooming, exercise. Poor interaction with children. Apartment not recommended.

Airedale Terrier: Susceptible to hip dysplasia. Buy only from OFA registered parents. Needs exercise. Tolerant with children.

Akita (Japanese): Susceptible to hip dysplasia and PRA. Buy only from OFA and CERF registered parents. Tolerant with children.

Alaskan Malamute: Susceptible to hip dysplasia, Does not like heat with his thick coat. Buy from OFA registered parents. Needs lots of exercise. Apartment not recommended.

American Eskimo: This breed has no real health problems and is considered a long-lived breed.

American Staffordshire Terrier: Susceptible to hip dysplasia. Buy only from OFA registered parents. Needs lots of exercise. Need caution around children.

American Water Spaniel: Susceptible to hip dysplasia. Buy only from OFA registered parents. Needs lots of exercise. Not good around children.

Australian Cattle Dog: Susceptible to hip dysplasia. Buy from OFA registered parents. Needs lots of exercise. Good with older children. Apartment not recommended.

Australian Shepherd: Hip dysplasia, buy only from OFA registered breeders, also Collie Eye Anomaly is present in some. Needs lots of exercise. Apartment not recommended.

Australian Terrier: Healthy breed, prone to no real problems. Tolerant of children.

Basenji: Comes in heat once a year. Tolerant with children. Fanconi Syndrome (kidney problem). Susceptible to PRA. Buy only from CERF registered parents.

Basset Hound: Susceptible to bloat. Buying from poor breeder can result in ill tempered, sickly dog.

Beagle: Susceptible to bloat. Poor breeding can result in ill-tempered, sickly dog. Needs lots of exercise.

Bearded Collie: Susceptible to hip dysplasia, epilepsy. Buy only from OFA registered parents. Apartment not recommended.

Bedlington Terrier: Susceptible to PRA. Tolerant with children.

Belgian Malinois: Susceptible to hip dysplasia. Buy only from OFA registered parents. Extensive grooming. Needs lots of exercise. Apartment not recommended.

Belgian Sheepdog: Susceptible to hip dysplasia. Buy only from OFA registered parents. Extensive grooming. Needs lots of exercise. OK with older children. Apartment not recommended.

Belgian Tervuren: Susceptible to hip dysplasia. Buy only from OFA registered parents. Extensive grooming. Needs lots of exercise. Apartment not recommended.

Bernese Mtn Dog: Short lived breed (10 Yrs.), Susceptible to hip and elbow dysplasia, bloat and some eye problems. With thick coat, does not like heat. Buy only from OFA registered parents (hips and elbows). Needs extensive grooming. Apartment not recommended.

Bichon Frise: Kartagener's disease, canine bladder stones, skin conditions. Needs regular grooming. may be hard to housebreak, not outside dogs.

Black and Tan Coonhound: Susceptible to hip dysplasia. Avoid field types if you want a household pet. Needs lots of exercise. Apartment not recommended.

Bloodhound: Short lived breed (10 yrs). Susceptible to hip dysplasia and bloat. Buy only from OFA registered parents. Needs lots of exercise. Apartment not recommended.

Border Collies: Susceptible to hip dysplasia and PRA. Buy only from OFA, CERF registered parents. Needs lots of exercise. Apartment not recommended.

Border Terrier: Susceptible to hip dysplasia. Buy only from OFA registered parents.

Borzoi: Susceptible to bloat. Sensitive to drugs. Needs extensive grooming. Poor interaction with children. Apartment not recommended.

Boston Terrier: Susceptible to infections and lacerations on protruding eyes, also respiratory difficulties and heatstroke because of his pushed-in-face. Avoid hot, stuffy conditions and closed cars. Protect from extremes of temperature.

Bouvier des Flandres: Susceptible to hip dysplasia and bloat. Buy only from OFA registered parents. Needs lots of exercise. Apartment not recommended.

Boxer: Short lived breed (10 Yrs.), susceptible to hip dysplasia and bloat. Sensitive to hot, stuffy weather, heatstroke. Careful of enclosed cars. Buy from OFA registered parents.

Briard: Susceptible to hip dysplasia, PRA, and bloat. Buy only from OFA and CERF registered parents. Apartment not recommended.

Brittany: Susceptible to hip dysplasia. Buy only from OFA registered owners. Needs lots of exercise.

Brussels Griffon: Susceptible to heatstroke and slipped stifle. Tolerant with children.

Bull Terrier: Susceptible to skin problems. Tolerant with children.

Bulldog: Shortlived breed (10 yrs). Hereditary throat problems, heat stroke, entropia, sensitive to anesthesia.

Bullmastiff: Short-lived breed, susceptible to hip dysplasia, bloat and eyelid problems. Buy only from OFA registered parents. Needs lots of exercise. Apartment not recommended.

Cairn Terrier: Susceptible to skin allergies. Tolerant with children.

Cavalier King Charles Spaniel: Susceptible to slipped stifle. Needs extensive grooming.

Chesapeake Bay Retriever: Susceptible to hip dysplasia and PRA. Buy only from OFA and CERF registered parents. Needs lots of exercise.

Chihuahua: Long lived breed (15 yrs), susceptible to slipped stifle. Poor interaction with children.

Chow Chow: Susceptible to hip dysplasia. Buy only from OFA registered parents. Does not like heat. Needs extensive grooming. Poor interaction with children.

Clumber Spaniel: Susceptible to hip dysplasia. Buy only from OFA registered parents. Needs lots of exercise.

Cocker Spaniel: Susceptible to hip dysplasia and PRA. Buy only from OFA, CERF registered parents. Needs extensive grooming. Needs lots of exercise.

Collie: Susceptible to PRA and CEA (Collie Eye Anomaly), Buy only from CERF registered parents. The Roughs need extensive grooming. Needs lots of exercise.

Curly-Coated Retriever: Susceptible to hip dysplasia and PRA. Buy only from OFA and CERF registered parents. Needs lots of exercise.

Dachshund: Long lived breed (15 yrs.) Susceptible to spinal disc problems. Miniatures have poor interaction with young children. Don't overfeed.

Dalmatian: Some puppies are born deaf or can only hear out of one ear. Buy only from OFA registered parents. Best breeders B.A.E.R. test puppies for hearing. Needs lots of exercise. Sheds a lot. Apartment not recommended.

Dandie Dinmont: Susceptible to spinal disc problems. Don't let him jump off high furniture. Poor interaction with children.

Doberman Pinscher: Susceptible to hip dysplasia, von Willebrand's disease, bloat. Buy only from OFA registered, VWD tested parents. Need lots of exercise. Tolerant with children. Happiest with family indoors. Protect from extremes in temperature.

English Cocker Spaniel: Susceptible to hip dysplasia and PRA. Buy only from OFA, CERF registered parents.

English Setter: Susceptible to hip dysplasia. Buy only from OFA registered parents. Needs lots of exercise. Apartment not recommended.

English Springer Spaniel: Susceptible to hip dysplasia and PRA. Buy only from OFA and CERF registered parents. Needs lots of exercise.

English Toy Spaniel : Susceptible to slipped stifle and heatstroke. Needs extensive grooming.

Field Spaniel: Susceptible to hip dysplasia. Buy only from OFA registered parents. Needs lots of exercise. Apartment not recommended.

Finnish Spitz: Susceptible to hip dysplasia and PRA. Buy only from OFA, CERF registered parents. Needs lots of exercise.

Flat-Coated Retriever: Susceptible to hip dysplasia and PRA. Buy only from OFA and CERF registered parents. Needs lots of exercise.

Fox Terrier, Smooth: Long lived breed (15 yrs.) Susceptible to deafness.

Fox Terrier, Wire: Long lived breed (15 yrs.) Susceptible to deafness.

Foxhound, American: Healthy breed, no real problems. Needs lots of exercise. Apartment not recommended.

Foxhound, English: Healthy breed, no real problems. Needs lots of exercise. Apartment not recommended.

French Bulldog: Susceptible to lacerations on eyes, respiratory difficulties and heatstroke. Protect from extreme heat, avoid enclosed cars. Large percentage of this breed die of carcinoma. Sensitive to anesthesia. Poor interaction with children.

German Shepherd: Susceptible to hip dysplasia and bloat. Buy only from OFA registered parents. Most frequent problem is personality and temperament. Buy only from reputable breeder. Needs lots of exercise.

German Shorthaired Pointer: Susceptible to hip dysplasia. Buy only from OFA registered parents. Needs lots of exercise. Poor interaction with children. Apartment not recommended.

German Wirehaired Pointer: Susceptible to hip dysplasia. Buy only from OFA registered parents. Needs lots of exercise. Poor interaction with children. Apartment not recommended.

Giant Schnauzer: Susceptible to hip dysplasi. Buy only from OFA registered parents. Needs lots of exercise. Poor interaction with children. Apartment not recommended.

Golden Retriever: Susceptible to hip dysplasia, PRA and von Willebrand's disease. Buy only from OFA and CERF registered parents. Needs extensive grooming. Needs lots of exercise.

Gordon Setter: Susceptible to hip dysplasia. Buy only from OFA registered parents. Needs lots of exercise. Apartment not recommended.

Great Dane: Short lived breed (10 yrs.), susceptible to hip dysplasia and bloat. Buy only from OFA registered parents. Low tolerance to tranquilizers. Apartment not recommended.

Great Pyrenees: Short lived breed (10 yrs.), susceptible to hip dysplasia and bloat. Buy only from OFA registered parents. Apartment not recommended.

Greyhound: Susceptible to bloat. Sensitive to drugs. Needs lots of exercise. OK in apartments.

Harrier: Healthy breed with no real problems. Needs lots of exercise. Apartment not recommended.

Ibizan Hound: Sensitive to drugs. Some hip dysplasia. Needs lots of exercise.

Irish Setter: Susceptible to hip dysplasia, PRA and bloat. Buy only from OFA and CERF registered parents. Needs extensive grooming. Needs lots of exercise. Apartment not recommended.

Irish Terrier: Healthy breed, prone to no real problems.

Irish Water Spaniel: Susceptible to hip dysplasia.. Buy only from OFA registered parents. Needs lots of exercise, extensive grooming. Poor interaction with children. Apartment not recommended.

Irish Wolfhound: Short lived breed (8-10 yrs)   Susceptible to hip dysplasia and bloat. Buy only from OFA registered parents. Extensive grooming. Apartment not recommended.

Italian Greyhound: Susceptible to slipped stifle. Poor interaction with children.

Jack Russell Terrier: Susceptible to a congenital dwarfism, where a puppy has a normal head and body but short legs. Apartment not recommended.

Japanese Chin: Susceptible to lacerations on eyes and heatstroke — avoid hot, stuffy conditions and cold and damp.

Keeshond: Susceptible to hip dysplasia. He does not like the heat. Needs extensive grooming.

Kerry Blue Terrier: Long-lived breed (15 yrs.) Susceptible to hip dysplasia. Buy only from OFA registered parents. Needs lots of exercise. Poor interaction with children.

Komondor: Susceptible to hip dysplasia and bloat. Buy only from OFA registered parents. Extensive grooming. Poor interaction with children. Apartment not recommended.

Kuvasz: Short lived breed (10yrs). Susceptible to hip dysplasia and bloat. Buy only from OFA registered parents. Needs lots of exercise. Poor interaction with children. Apartment not recommended.

Labrador Retriever: Susceptible to hip dysplasia, PRA, and bloat. Buy only from OFA and CERF registered parents.

Lakeland Terrier: Healthy breed, prone to no real problems.

Lhasa Apso: Susceptible to hip dysplasia. Buy only from OFA registered parents. Needs extensive grooming. Poor interaction with children.

Maltese: Susceptible to slipped stifle (a joint disorder). Needs extensive grooming. Poor interaction with children.

Manchester, Standard: Susceptible to bleeding disorders. Poor interaction with children.

Manchester, Toy: Susceptible to slipped stifle. Poor interaction with children.

Mastiff: Short-lived breed (10 yrs.), susceptible to hip dysplasia. Buy only from OFA registered parents. Apartment not recommended.

Miniature Pinscher: Prone to demodectic mange under stress. Poor interaction with children.

Miniature Schnauzer: Susceptible to cataracts and skin conditions. Extensive grooming.

Newfoundland: Short lived breed (10 years). Susceptible to hip dysplasia. Buy only from OFA registered parents. Needs extensive grooming. Apartment not recommended.

Norfolk Terrier: Healthy breed, prone to no real problems.

Norwegian Elkhound: Susceptible to hip dysplasia. Buy only from OFA registered parents. Poor interaction with children.

Norwich Terrier: Healthy breed, prone to no real problems.

Old English Sheepdog: Susceptible to hip dysplasia and PRA. Buy only from OFA, CERF registered parents. Needs extensive grooming. Apartment not recommended.

Otterhound: Susceptible to hip dysplasia and bloat. Buy only from OFA registered parents. Needs lots of exercise. Apartment not recommended.

Papillon: Susceptible to slipped stifle. Needs extensive grooming. Poor interaction with children.

Pekingese: Susceptible to eye problems, respiratory difficulties and heatstroke. Needs extensive grooming. Poor interaction with children.

Pharoah Hound: Sensitive to drugs. Needs lots of exercise. Apartment not recommended.

Pomeranian: Susceptible to slipped stifle. Needs extensive grooming. Poor interaction with children.

Poodle, Miniature: Susceptible to hip dysplasia, PRA. Buy from OFA, CERF registered parents. Needs extensive grooming.

Poodle,Standard: Susceptible to hip dysplasia, PRA, von Willebrand's Disease and bloat. Buy only from OFA and CERF registered and VWD tested parents. Needs extensive grooming. Needs exercise. Inside dogs.

Poodle, Toy: Susceptible to hip dysplasia and PRA. Buy only from OFA, CERF registered parents. Needs extensive grooming. Poor interaction with children.

Portuguese Water Dog: Susceptible to hip dysplasia and PRA. Buy only from OFA and CERF registered parents. Needs lots of exercise.

Pug: Susceptible to eye problems and heatstroke. Avoid hot stuffy conditions. Sensitive to anesthesia.

Puli: Susceptible to hip dysplasia. Buy only from OFA registered parents. Needs lots of exercise. Extensive grooming. Poor interaction with children.

Rhodesian Ridgeback: Susceptible to hip dysplasia. Buy only from OFA registered parents. Needs lots of exercise.

Rottweiler: Susceptible to hip dysplasia, elbow dysplasia and bloat. Buy only from OFA registered parents. Needs lots of exercise. Caution around children. Insurance in effect? Apartment not recommended.

Saluki: Susceptible to some hip dysplasia. Needs lots of exercise. Poor interaction with children. Apartment not recommended.

Samoyed: Susceptible to hip dysplasia and PRA. Buy only from OFA and CERF registered parents. Needs lots of attention. Requires regular brushings. Tendency to bark if left alone.

Schipperke: Long lived breed (15 years). Prone to no real problems

Scottish Deerhound: Short lived breed (10 yrs.) Susceptible to bloat. Needs lots of exercise.

Scottish Terrier: Susceptible to von Willebrand's disease, scotty cramp (minor discomfort walking). Needs extensive grooming. Apartment not recommended.

Sealyham Terrier: Long-lived breed (15 years). Susceptible to skin conditions.

Shar-Pei (Chinese): Short lived breed (10 yrs). Susceptible to hip dysplasia, skin problems and entropion. Buy only from OFA registered parents. Poor interaction with children.

Shetland Sheepdog: Susceptible to hip dysplasia, PRA, CEA (Collie Eye Anomaly). Buy only from OFA, CERF registered parents.

Shiba Inu: They are susceptible to hip dysplasia and PRA. Buy only from OFA and CERF registered parents.

Shih Tzu: Kidney problems. Needs extensive grooming.

Siberian Husky: Susceptible to some hip dysplasia, PRA, Buy only from OFA and CERF registered parents. Needs lots of exercise.

Silky Terrier: Healthy breed, no real problems. Extensive grooming.

Skye Terrier: Healthy breed, prone to no real problems. Needs extensive grooming.

Soft Coated Wheaten: Susceptible to PRA. Buy only from CERF registered parents. Needs lots of exercise. Extensive grooming.

St. Bernard: Short lived breed (10yrs.), Susceptible to hip dysplasia and bloat. Buy only from OFA registered parents. Needs extensive grooming. Apartment not recommended.

Staffordshire Bull Terrier: Susceptible to hip dysplasia. Buy only from OFA Registered breeder. Needs lots of exercise. Poor interaction with children.

Standard Pointer: Susceptible to hip dysplasia. Buy only from OFA registered parents. Needs lots of exercise.

Standard Schnauzer: A long-lived breed (15yrs.), susceptible to hip dysplasia. Buy only from OFA registered parents. Needs lots of exercise. Extensive grooming. Poor interaction with children.

Tibetan Spaniel: Healthy breed, prone to no real problems.

Tibetan Terrier: Susceptible to hip dysplasia and PRA. Buy only from OFA and CERF registered parents. Poor interaction with children.

Vizsla: Susceptible to hip dysplasia. Buy only from OFA registered parents. Needs lots of exercise. Apartment not recommended.

Weimaraner: Susceptible to hip dysplasia and bloat. Buy only from OFA registered parents. Needs lots of exercise. Apartment not recommended.

Welsh Corgi, Cardigan: Susceptible to hip dysplasia and PRA. Buy only from OFA and CERF registered parents.

Welsh Corgi, Pembroke : Susceptible to hip dysplasia and PRA. Buy only from OFA and CERF registered parents. ;

Welsh Springer Spaniel: Susceptible to hip dysplasia and PRA. Buy only from OFA and CERF registered parents. Needs lots of exercise.

Welsh Terrier: No apparent health problems

West Highland White Terrier: Long-lived breed (15 yrs.) Susceptible to skin conditions. Needs extensive grooming.

Whippet: Sensitive to drugs. Sensitive emotionally. Should be protected from cold. Needs lots of exercise. Poor interaction with children.

Wirehaired Pointing Griffon: Susceptible to hip dysplasia. Buy only from OFA registered parents. Needs lots of exercise. Poor interaction with children. Apartment not recommended.

Yorkshire Terrier: Susceptible to slipped stifle. Needs extensive grooming. Poor interaction with children.

Appendix D
Service Directory

The following list of service providers is offered as an aid to the public in finding dog-related services. *Southern California Dog Owners Guide* does not recommend, guarantee, endorse, nor rate service providers. We do not assume any liability.

Acupuncturist, Canine

There is growing interest in the use of acupuncture in the treatment of animals.

International Veterinary
Acupuncture Society
2140 Conestoga Rd.
Chester Springs, PA 19425
215 827-7245

John W Boyd DVM
31441 Avenida De La Vista
San Juan Capistrano 92675
714 661-8522

Henry Pasternak DVM
526 Palisades Drive
Pacific Palisades, 90272
310 454-2917

Don E Lundholm DVM
10130 Adams Ave.
Huntington Bch, CA 92646
714-964-1605

Robert Smatt DVM
5621 Balboa Ave.
San Diego, CA 92111
619 278-1575

Dr. Stephen Blake
DVM, CVA
9888 Carmel Mtn. Rd.
San Diego, CA
619 484-3490

Lauren A Bauer DVM
2801 Oceanside Blvd.
Oceanside, CA 92054
619 757-2442

Marshall E Scott DVM
2955 VanBuren Bl. H-8
Riverside, CA 92503
714 359-0363

Kevin James May DVM
560 North Johnson
El Cajon, CA 92020
619 444-9491

Priscilla Litehous DVM
10742 Riverside Dr.
North Hollywood CA
818 761-0787

Dog Owners Guide

Adoption Service for Seniors

Pets for People
1 800 345-5678

San Diego Humane Soc
Pets For People (Free
Adoptions for Seniors)
619 299-7012

Agility Clubs

U S Dog Agility Assoc.
P O Box 850955
Richardson, TX 75085
214 231-9700

San Diego Agility Club
Gail Huston
619 569-4875

National Agility Club
401 Bluemont Circle
Manhattan, KS 66502
913 537-7022

Agility Club of
Santa Ana
Cheryl Malooly
310 692-0183

AIDS/HIV Assistance

PAWS/LA
213 650-PAWS

PAWS/Orange Co
714 498-2898 or
714 558-1425

PAWS/San Diego
619 234-PAWS

All-Breed Clubs in Southern California

Long Beach Kennel Club
17919 Denker Ave.
Gardena, CA. 90248
Martha Olmos-Ollivier

South Bay Kennel Club
17817 La Salle Ave.
Gardena, CA 90248
Pamela Woods

Kennel Club of Pasadena
345 Highland Place
Monrovia,CA 91016
Eva Scanlan

Malibu Kennel Club
2222 Malcolm Ave
Los Angeles, CA 90064
Dana Pearl

San Fernando Kennel Club
5841 Fitzpatrick Road
Hidden Hills,CA 91302
Robert H Ward

Conejo Kennel Club
P O Box 1002
Thousand Oaks, CA 91358
Myron Stone

Kennel Club of Beverly Hills
17633 Community St.
Northridge, CA 91325
Mrs. Lani Powers

Los Encinos Kennel Club
13029 Gladstone Ave
Sylmar, CA 91342
Ms. Cathie Turner

Burbank Kennel Club
7 Skyline Dr.
Burbank,CA 91501
Marilyn Mayfield

San Gabriel Vly Kennel Club
7811 Shadyspring Drive
Burbank,CA 91504
Ralf L Reveley

Rio Hondo Kennel Club
2642 Buenos Aires Dr.
Covina,CA 91724
Arlene Davis

Del Sur Kennel Club
3036 Viejos View Place
Alpine, CA 91901
Ms. Diane Caswell

Silver Bay Kennel Club
13553 Avenida Del Charro
El Cajon, CA 92021
Catherine Shirley

Mt. Palomar Kennel Club
3719 Via Las Villas
Oceanside, CA 92056
Neoma Eberhardt

Cabrillo Kennel Club, Inc
9934 Pratt Court
Santee, CA 92071
Mark Joseph Walsh

Bahia Sur KC of Chula Vista
406 Julian St
Ramona, CA 92065
Connie Parrish

Imperial Valley Kennel Club
101 Vernardo Dr #72
Calexico, CA 92231
Adriana Rodriguez

Orange Empire Dog Club
7619 Alder
Fontana, CA 92336
Esther Tomatis

Apple Valley Kennel Club
PO Box 2755
Apple Valley, CA 92307
Ms Judy Long

Kennel Club of Riverside
39160 Liefer Rd
Temecula, CA 92591
Ms Margaret Sturgeon

Channel City Kennel Club
1140 Mission Ridge Rd
Santa Barbara, CA 93103
Naoma Ford

Lake Mathews Kennel Club
5740 Ave. Juan Bautista
Riverside, CA 92509
Elizabeth Matchett

Kennel Club of Palm Springs
26604 Green Ave.
Hemet,CA 92545
Phyllis Schneider

Shoreline Dog Fanciers Assoc.
1262 Debroah Dr.
Tustin,CA 92680
Betty Claus

Santa Ana Valley Kennel Club
4171 Prospect Ave.
Yorba Linda, CA 92686
Liz Miller

**Ventura Co. Dog Fanciers
Assoc.**
2315 Ramelli Ave.
Ventura, CA 93003
Richard Karle

Simi Valley Kennel Club
2711 Loganrita
Arcadia, CA 91006
Carol Parker

Antelope Valley Kennel Club
2545 E Garnet Ln
Lancaster, CA 93535
Janice Dearth

Santa Barbara Kennel Club
662 Prospect Blvd

Pasadena, CA 91103
Carmen M Visser

All-Breeds, Sanctioned

Great Western Terrier
Association of So Cal
7607 Whitegate Ave
Riverside, Ca 92506
Vera Potiker

Western Hound Assoc
of Southern California
722 S Loara St
Anaheim, CA 92802
Catherine Orgaro

Animal Abuse Hotline

San Diego Humane Society
1 800 98-ABUSE

Orange Co SPCA
714 536-0050

Golden State Humane Society
714 638-8111 (Orange Co)

Los Angeles SPCA
1 800 540 SPCA

Animal Agent for Film, TV & Ads

Brian McMillan's Animal Rentals
31305 Tick Canyon Rd
Canyon Country, CA 91351

Julie Sandoval Stubbings
805 252-4509

Animal Control Departments by County

San Diego County

Covers the unincorporated areas of San Diego Co. and the cities of
Carlsbad, Del Mar, Encinitas, Lemon Grove, Poway, San Diego, San
Marcos, Santee, and Solana Beach. They are responsible for
adoptions, as well as, enforcement of animal laws, investigation of
violations and initiation of prosecution as required, dog licensing,
Rabies prevention programs, control of vicious dogs, spay/neuter
referral programs, public education, owner notification of found, licensed dogs, kennel licensing and inspection and humane disposal of
old, injured or unwanted animals.

North County A S
2481 Palomar Airport Rd.
Carlsbad, CA 92008
619 438-3212
619 746-7307

Central County A S
5480 Gaines St.
San Diego, CA 92110
619 236-4250
619 291-3283

South County A S*
5821 Sweetwater Rd.
San Diego, CA 92002
619 263-7741
619 475-0372 Adoptions

San Diego County Animal Shelters are closed on Sunday and Monday

City Animal Shelters in San Diego Co.

Chula Vista Animal Shelter
690 Otay Valley Road
Chula Vista, CA
619 691-5123

El Cajon Animal Shelter
1275 N. Marshall Ave.
El Cajon, CA
619 448-7383

Coronado Animal Shelter
578 Orange Ave.
Coronado, CA
619 522-7371

Escondido Humane Soc
3000 Las Palmas Ave
Escondido, CA 92029
619 745-4362

Camp Pendleton
Bldg. 25132
Camp Pendleton, CA
619 725-4512

North County Humane Soc
2905 San Luis Rey Rd
Oceanside, CA 92054
619 757-4357

City Animal Control without shelters

Imperial Beach
Animal Control
619 423-8223
Animal Sheltered at
Chula Vista 619 691-5123

La Mesa
Animal Control
619 469-6111
Animals Sheltered at
El Cajon 619 448-7383

National City A C
619 336-4411
Animals Sheltered at
Chula Vista 619 691-5123

Vista Animal Control is
run and sheltered
at Oceanside
619 757-4357

Orange County

Orange County An Shelter
561 The City Drive South
Orange, CA 92668
714 935-7419

City Animal Shelters in Orange Co.

Costa Mesa
Bayshore Animal Hospital
2077 Harbor Blvd.
714 646-3800

Irvine
Irvine Animal Care Ctr
15129 Sand Canyon
714 559-7387

Laguna Beach
Laguna Beach AS
20612 Laguna Canyon Rd.
714 497-3552

Newport Beach
Dover Shores Pet Care
2075 Newport Blvd.
714 644-3656

Seal Beach
Seal Beach Animal Care
1700 Regency Drive
310 430-4993

Mission Viejo
714348-2045

San Clemente
San Clemente AS
320 Avenida Pico
714 492-1617

Westminster
Orange Co. H S
21632 Newland Street
714 536-8480

City Animal Control without Shelters

Costa Mesa
714 754-5311

Laguna Beach
714 497-0701

Newport Beach
714 644-3717

Santa Ana
714 647-5198

Westminster
714 898-3311

Irvine
714 559-7387

La Habra
310 905-9750

San Clemente
714 492-1617

Seal Beach
310 431-2541 x 225

Mission Veijo
714 348-2045

Los Angeles County

LA Co Animal Control
11258 S. Garfield
Downey, CA
310 940-8888
Services:Alhambra, Bell
Artesia, Cudahy, East LA
Florence, Hawaiian Gardens
La Habra, La Mirada
Long Beach Co., Maywood
South Gate, Whittier

LA Co Animal Control
216 W. Victoria
Carson, CA
213 321-5983
Services: Carson,
Compton, Inglewood
Rancho Dominguez,
Rolling Hills Est, Signal
Hill,

LA Co Animal Control
4275 Elton
Baldwin Park, CA
818 962-3579
Services: Baldwin Park
Bradbury, El Monte,
Hacienda Hts., Industry,
Irwindale, La Canada, La
Crescenta, La Puente,
Rosemead, Rowland Hts.
Valinda, Walnut

LA Co Animal Control
31044 Charlie Canyon Rd.
Castaic, CA
818 367-7696
Services: Agua Dulce,
Castaic
Newhall, San Fernando
Santa Clarita, Saugus,
Valencia, Acton

City Animal Regulation
3201 Lacy St.
Los Angeles, CA
213 222-7138
Services: Highland Park
Downtown LA Area
Echo Park,

City Animal Regulation
13131 Sherman Way
North Hollywood, CA
818 764-7061
Services:Arleta, Lakeview
Terrace, N. Hollywood
Pacoima,
City, Sunland,
Shadow Hills, Sun Valley
Sylmar, Van Nuys

LA Co Animal Control
5210 W. Avenue
Lancaster, CA
805 945-8378
Services:Green Valley,
Lake Hughes, Leona Vy
Littlerock, Llano,
Palmdale, Pearblossom,
Quartz Hill,
Lancaster

LA Co Animal Control
29525 W. Agoura
Agoura, CA
818 991-0071
Services: Agoura, Canyon Country,
Agoura Hills, Calabasas
Hidden Hills, Malibu
& Westlake Village

City Animal Regulation
735 Battery
San Pedro, CA
310 831-2414
Services: Harbor City
San Pedro, Wilmington

City Animal Regulation
20655 Plummer St.
Chatsworth, CA
818 882-8800
Services: Canoga Park
Chatsworth, Encino, Mission Hills,
Granada Hills, Reseda Panorama
Northridge, Sepulveda
Tarzana, Woodland Hill

169

Southeast Area Shelter
9777 Sesaca St.
Downey, CA
310 803-3301
Services: Bell Garden
Downey, Montebello,
Norwalk, Paramount,
Pico Rivera, Vernon,
Lynwood, S. El Monte
Santa Fe Springs

Long Beach Shelter
3001 E. Willow
Long Beach, CA
310 595-5449
Services: Long Beach
Cerritos, Lakewood

Santa Monica Shelter
1640 9th St.
Santa Monica, CA
310 458-8594
Services: Santa Monica

Burbank Animal Shelter
1150 N. Victory Place
Burbank, CA
818 953-9719
Services: Burbank

City Animal Control in LA Co.

Bellflower
310 804-1424

City Of Commerce
213 722--4805

Duarte
818 357-7931

Glendora
818 242-1128

Hermosa Beach
310 318-0209

Huntington Park
213 582-6161

La Habra
213 905-9772

Manhattan Beach
310 545-5621

San Bernardino County

San Bernardino County AC
800 472-5609

City of San Bernardino AC
909 384-5048
Services: City of San
Bernardino and Fontana

City of Redlands
909 798-7644
Services: Redlands &
Highland

Riverside Co Adoption & Shelter Agencies

Blythe AC
619 922-6111

Cathedral City AC
619 324-8388

Corona City AC
909 736-2309

Desert Hot Springs AC
619 329 8931

Hemet City AC
909 658-2202

Indio City AC
619 347-8522

La Quinta City AC
619 777-7050

Moreno Valley City AC
909 243-3790

Norco City AC
909 735-3900

Palm Springs City AC
619 323-8151

Perris City AC
909 682-1181

Riverside County AC
909 358-5083

Riverside County Health/AC
619 347-2319

Riverside Co AC Services
909 682-1181

Animal Welfare Groups

Humane Society of US
2100 L St.
Washington DC 20037
202 452-1100

Humane Society of US
West Coast Office
P O Box 417220
Sacramento, CA
916 344-1710

Am Soc Prevention of
Cruelty to Animals
441 E 92nd. St.
New York, NY 10128
212 876-7700

American Humane Assn
63 Inverness Dr. E
Englewood, CO 80112
303 792-9900
800 227-4645

San Diego Animal
Advocates
619 943-0330

San Diego Humane
Society & SPCA
1 800 98-ABUSE

Stop Taking Our Pets
(S.T.O.P.)
(Eliminate Pound Seizure)
619 755-1700

Orange Co. People for
Animals (OCPA)
714 751-OCPA

Orange Co Society for the
Prevention of Cruelty
to Animals (ASPCA)
8855 Atlanta # 164
Htngtn Bch, CA 92646
714 536-0050

Animal Assistance
League Of Orange Co.
P O Box 38
Midway City, CA 92655
714 978-7387

Actors and Others for Animals
5510 Cahuenga Blvd
North Hollywood, CA 91601
818 985-6263

Apartments for Pets

Pets OK
310 839-9760

Pet Friendly
619 687-5585

171

Dog Owners Guide

Artificial Insemination

North County Fertility
& Vet Clinic
Dr. Stockner
619 739-1091

Artists, Dog

Ruth Hyatt Maystead
20814 Horace St.
Chatsworth, CA 91313
818 882-9586

Animal Portraits in Pastel
217 S Fuller Ave.
Los Angeles, CA 90036
213 933-0937
Marilyn Cole-Shatz, Artist

Portraits by Janet
Janet Dierberger
714 979-1537

AVA Animal Portraits
140 S Birchwood St.
Anaheim, CA 92808
714 998-1537

Beau Bradford
Pet Masterpieces
310 652-4892

Attorney

Michael Rotsten, Esquire
16133 Ventura Blvd, 7th loor
Encino, CA 91436
818 789-0256
Specializing in animal rights

Backpack for Dogs

Wolf Pack
1742 Garnet Ave. Box 200 B
San Diego, CA 92109
619 581-2675

Behaviorists

Laura Christiansen
Canine Learning Centers
P O Box 2010
Carlsbad, CA 92009
619 931-1834

Dennis Fetko
619 485-7433

Patrick Melese, DVM
Veterinary Behavior
PO Box 99098
San Diego, CA 92169
619 273-4322

Mona Webb
310 559-2321

Edward Cohen
805 499-6959

Marla Quincy
909 672-4192

Bereavement Counseling

One of the drawbacks of dog ownership is the likelihood that we will outlive our beloved companions. Eight, ten, fifteen years down the line we are going to have to say goodbye.

Pet-Loss Counselors:

The Delta Society
PO Box 1080
Renton, WA 98057-1080
206 226-7357

San Diego Co Pet
Bereavement Program
619 275-0728

Lori Greene, PhD
619 275-0728

Pet Loss Support Hotline
School of Veterinary
Medicine, UC Davis
916 752-4200

Dr Sheila Frank
619 528-2399

Blood Banks for Dogs

This full service non-profit charitable blood bank ships canine blood products overnight to veterinarians anywhere in the United States that has a need. For more information call:

Hemopet Pet Life Line
Dr. W. Jean Dodds DVM
17672 Cowan #300
Irvine, CA 92714
714 252-8455

Also:
San Diego County Blood Bank
2317 Hotel Circle South
San Diego, CA 92108
619 299-7624
(Needs Dog blood donations)

Boarding Kennels

The American Boarding Kennel Association
4575 Galley Rd. Ste. 400-A
Colorado Springs, CO 80915
719 591-1113

American Pet Boarding Association
312 634-9447

173

Books, Dog

For all dog books:4-M Enterprises, Inc.
1280 Pacific St., Union City, CA 94587
800 487-9867

Dog Owner's
Home Veterinary Handbook
Delbert G. Carlson D.V.M.
James M. Giffin MD

Your Purebred Puppy
A Buyers Guide
by Michele Lowell

The Complete Dog Book
by The Am Kennel Club

The Right Dog for You
by Daniel Tortora Ph. D

How to Teach A
New Dog Old Tricks
by Ian Dunbar

How to Be Your Dogs
Best Friend
Monks Of New Skete

Playtraining Your Dog
by Patricia Burnham

Don't Shoot the Dog!
by Karen Pryor

Peak Performance
Coaching the Canine Athlete
M. Christine Zink DVM

How to Raise a Puppy
You Can Live With
by Rutherford & Neil

First Aid for Pets
by Robert W Kirk DVM
Sutton Books

Atlas of Dog Breeds of
the World
Chris & Bonnie Wilcox

Training Your Dog
J Volhard & G Fisher

Active Years for Your
Aging Dog by Hershhorn

Your Dog, Its Development,
Behavior and Training
by John Rogerson

Breeders Education

Educational Symposiums for Breeders, Aspiring Judges call:

Los Angeles Dog
Judges Educational Association
Mrs. Betty Claus
714 544-9372

Cemeteries, Pet

International Assoc.
of Pet Cemeteries
P O Box 1346
South Bend, IN 46624
219 277-1115

AA Sorrento Valley
Pet Cemetery &
Crematory
10801 Sorrento Vly Rd
San Diego, CA 92121
619 276-3361

San Diego Pet Memorial
8995 Crestmar Point
San Diego, CA
619 271-4242

Sea Breeze Pet Cemetery
19542 Beach Blvd.
Huntington Beach, CA
714 962-7111

Los Angeles Pet
Memorial Park
West San Fernando Vly
818 591-7037

Royal Pet Mortuary
310 841-2052

Cal Pet Crematory
213 875-0633

Chiropractic Care, Canine

American Veterinary Chiropractic Association
Dr. Sharon Willoughby
Port Byron, IL
309 523-3995

William Brennan DC
714 628-1137
Anaheim

Greg Ugarte DVM
714 628-1137
Chino

Kevin May DVM
619 444-9491
El Cajon

W C Wood DVM
800 285-3274
Escondido

Robert Smatt DVM
619 278-1575
San Diego

Anthony Gambucci
310 322-0912
El Sugundo

Complaints Against Veterinarians

The Board of Examiners in Veterinary Medicine regulates the
practice of veterinary medicine in California. Direct complaints to:

Board of Examiners in
Veterinary Medicine
1420 Howe Avenue #6
Sacramento, CA 95825
916 920-7662

Southern California
Veterinary Med. Assn.
8338 Rosemead Blvd.
Pico Rivera, CA 90660
714 523-0980

San Diego County:
Veterinary Medical Association
7590 El Cajon Blvd.
La Mesa, CA 92041
619 466-3400

Dog Owners Guide

Computer Bulletin Boards

Information bulletin boards on dog related subjects.

Compuserve
800 848-8199

Prodigy
800 776-3449

GEnie
800 638-9636

Delphi
800 695-4005

Computer Software

Screen saver software.

Screen Magic Dogs
800 655-6244

Pet records system for all AKC required records, vaccinations, medical, all show records, pedigrees, stud contracts, sales receipts, entry forms and more. Call:

STARLINE
7131 Kermore
Stanton, CA 90680
714 826-5218

TiedWay Software
PO Box 662
El Segundo, CA 90245
310 631-8337

Dead Animal Removal

San Diego Co.
619 390-0333

City of San Diego
Other Than Freeways
619 492-5055

Freeways
Cal Trans
619 688-6785 (SD Co)
714 724-2607 (Orange Co)
213 897-0383 (LA Co.)

LA Co. Call your nearest animal shelter or call the Dept of Sanitation

Den Trailing

Go to ground test for terriers and dachshunds.

Jim Tibbits
805 945-5874

Drink

Protect A Pet
Aloe Vera Drink for Pets
1 800 835-9899

County Emergencies

619 278-9760 (SD Co 24 hours)
714 935-7158 (In Orange Co)
In LA, call your local shelter

Education, Humane

Humane Education involves teaching children kindness and a caring attitude towards domestic pets and the humane treatment of all living creatures. Check with your local Humane Society.

Partners In Education
Training & Sharing (PETS)
Susan Daniels
RR # 6 Box 308 A
Tunkhannock, PA 18657
717 836-2753

San Diego Humane Society
619 299-7012

Orange Co Humane Society
714 536-8480

Helen Woodward Center
6461 El Apajo
Rancho Santa Fe, CA
619 756-4117

Western Humane
Education Assoc.
Micki Zeldes
Marin Humane Society
171 Bel Marin Keys Bl.
Novata, CA 94947

S D Co Animal Control
Sgt. Burke
619 595-4525

Orange Co An Shelter
714 935-7419

Los Angeles SPCA
5026 W. Jefferson Blvd
Los Angeles, CA 90016
213 730-5300

Emergency Hospitals

If there is an after hour emergency call your Veterinarian. If he or she is unavailable then contact:

San Diego County

All Creatures Hospital
3665 Via De La Valle
Del Mar, CA
619 481-7992

North County Emergency
1925 W Vista Way
Vista, CA 92083
619 724-7444

Emergency Animal
Hospital of San Diego
2317 Hotel Circle South
San Diego, CA
619 299-2400

So. County Emergency
3438 Bonita Rd
Chula Vista, 91910 CA
619 427-2881

Animal Emergency Clinic
13240 Eveing Creek Dr
Poway, CA 92128
619 748-7387

Pet Emergency Clinic of
East County
5232 Jackson Dr #105
La Mesa 91941
619 462-4800

Orange County

Costa Mesa AH
480 E 17th St
Costa Mesa 92627
714 548-3794

Newport-Mesa AH
1542 Newport Blvd.
Costa Mesa 92627
714 642-2100

Orange Co. Emergency Pet
12865 Garden Grove Blvd.
Garden Grove 92643
714 537-3032

S. Orange Co. Emergency Pet
28832 Camino Capistrano
San Juan Capistrano 92675
714 364-6228

Crown Valley AH
28892 Crown Valley Pk
South Laguna, 92677
714 495-1123

North Orange Co PC
1474 S. Harbor Blvd.
Fullerton, 92632
714 441-2925

Woodbridge Hospital
34 Creek Rd.
Irvine, CA 92714
714 786-0990

All Care Animal Referral
18440 Amistas St # E
Fountain Vly, CA 92708
714 963-0909

San Bernadino

Animal Emergency Clinic
12022 LaCrosse Ave
Colton, CA 92324
909 825-9350

Ventura

Pet Emergency Clinic
2301 S Victoria Ave
Ventura, CA 93003
805 642-8562

Los Angeles County

VCA West Los Angeles AH
1818 S. Sepulveda Blvd.
Westwood, CA 90025
310 473-2951

Riverside

Emergency Pet Clinic
27443 Jefferson Ave
Temecula, CA 92590
909 695-5044

Pet Emergency Clinic
2967 N Moorpark Rd
Thousand Oaks, 91360
805 492-2436

VCA Lakewood AH
17801 Lakewood Blvd
Bellflower, CA 90706
310 633-8126

Animal Emergency
Clinic of Pasadena
2695 E Foothill Bl
Pasadena
818 564-0704

Emergency Pet Clinic
of San Gabriel Valley
3254 Santa Anita Ave.
El Monte
818 579-4550

Emergency Pet Clinic
of South Bay
3225 Torrance Blvd.
Torrance
310 320-8300

No Bay Animal Emergency
1304 Wilshire Blvd
Santa Monica, CA 90403
310 451-8962

Eagle Rock Emergency
Pet Clinic
4252 Eagle Rock Bl
Los Angeles
213 254-7382

Animal Emergency
11470 Ventura Blvd
Studio City
818 760-3882

Animal Emergency
& Trauma Center
11057 Rosecrans
Norwalk, CA 90650
310 863-2522

Emergency Pet Clinic
10810 Alondra Blvd
Artesia, CA 90701
310 402-5898

Eye Care Registry

Canine Eye Registry Foundation (CERF)
317 494-8179

Eye Care Specialist

Dr. Alan MacMillan DVM
Dr. Darien Nelson DVM
Animal Eye Clinic of SD
2317 Hotel Circle So.
San Diego, CA 92108
619 293-7055

Dr. Douglas Slatter
1301 S. Beach Blvd.
310 943-3728

Financial Assistance

Financial aid for disabled or senior pet owners 65 and older on fixed incomes is available on a limited basis. Contact:

The American Health Foundation
338 Rosemead Blvd.
Pico Rivera, CA 90660
714 523-0980

Economic help for spay/neuter, veterinarian bills. Refer to adoption agencies, spay/neuter assistance.

Dog Owners Guide

Fencing, Invisible

This system is designed to contain pets in the yard using an electrical shock. An antenna is placed around the perimeter and a receiver is placed around the neck of the dog. When the dog approaches the boundary a warning is given. If they proceed, a shock is generated as a correction.

Invisible Fencing
1 800 538 DOGS National Hdq.

Field Trial & Hunting Test Clubs

Retrievers Field Trials
S C Retriever Club
3758 Alzada Road
Altadena, CA 91001
Dorothy Read

San Diego Retriever
Field Trial Club
584 Senda Lane
El Cajon, CA 92021
Dolores M Jenkins

North American Hunting
Retriever Assoc (NAHRA)
PO Box 6
Garrisonville, VA 22463
703 752-4000

American Kennel Club
5580 Centerview Dr
Raleigh,NC 27690-0636
919 233-9767

Antelope Vly Dachshund Club
805 943-3221

Hunting Test Clubs
San Diego Hunting &
Retrieving Club
619 689-2573 or
619 579-2376
Ron Gober

San Diego Sporting
Dog Club
619 583-8392

Inland Vly Retriever Club
Fran Young

United Kennel Club
100 E Kilgore Rd.
Kalamazoo, MI 49001
616 343-9020

Cal So Coast Retriever Cl
909 689-8668

Flea Exterminators

Flea-X
1(800) 773-5329
Southern California Area
1-year warranty

Flyball

North American Flyball Assoc
5325 W Hope Rd
Lansing, MI 48917
517 322-2221

Your local obedience club

French Ring Sport

Combines protection, agility and obedience.

Sage Working Dog Club
909 767-9163

Wild West Ring Club
619 767-5377

Frisbee Competition

To be put on a mailing list and receive event info:

FriskiesCanine Frisbee
Disc Championship
4060-D Peachtree Rd. #326
Atlanta, GA 30319
800 786-9240
(Free training Booklet)

In California write/call:
Box 725
Encino, CA 91426
1 800 423-3268
818 780-4913

Greeting Cards

Each of these photo cards showcases a different rescued animal and tells their story.

Home Free Greeting Cards (Sold by the dozen)
Hart To Hart Press
1180 Sidonia Ct.
Encinitas, CA 92024
619 633-4834

Greyhound Rescue

These groups work to save racing dogs that are scheduled to be killed.

Greyhound Pets of America
Darren Rigg
President & Founder
800 366-1472

Operation Greyhound
619 588-6611

Grooming, Dog

The National Dog Groomers Association of America sets standards and service guidelines for its members as well as conducts certification programs.

So. Cal. Professional
Groomers Assoc.
P O Box 143,
1822½ Newport Blvd.
Costa Mesa, CA 92627
714 631-9139

The National Dog
Groomers Association
of America
P O Box 101
Clark, PA 16113
412 962-2711

Groomers, Master

Rosemarie Lett
Preferred By Pets
San Diego, CA
619 223-9023

Guide Dogs for the Blind

Guide Dog of the Desert
P O Box 1692
Palm Springs, CA 92263
619 329-6257

4-H Club Guide Dog
Puppy Raisers
714 968-4385

Guide Dogs Of America
13445 Glenoaks Blvd.
Sylmar, CA 91342
818 362-5834

Guide Dogs For
The Blind
PO Box 1200
San Rafael, CA 94915
415 479-4000

Handlers, Professional

Professional Handlers Association
Kathleen Bowser, Secretary (No Joke)
15810 Mount Everest Lane
Silver Springs, MD 20906
301 924-0089

Hearing Tests

BAER Hearing Test for Dogs
Mark Wright DVM
310 928-2234

Hearing Dog Programs

American Humane Assoc.
Hearing Dog Program
9725 E. Hampden Ave.
Denver, Co 80231
303 695-0811

Riverside Humane Society
Animal Program for the Deaf
5791 Fremont Street
Riverside, CA 92504
909 688-4382

Dogs For The Deaf
10175 Wheeler Rd.
Central Point,OR 97502
503 826-9220

Paws With a Cause
1-800-253-PAWS

Herding

Jerome M Stewart
714 968-7051

Candy Kennedy
714 685-8696

American Herding Breed Association
Peggy Richter
619 377-5926

San Fernando Herding Assoc.
Janna & Ted Ondrak
818 343-1989

The Herdsman (AKC)
Rte 1, Box 52-A
Putman, Oklahoma 73659
405 661-2262

Terry Parrish
619 739-8673

Linda Merritt
619 442-7640

Mutton Punchers
Ken & Gayle Dugan
805 366-2437

Herding Breed Club of
San Diego
619 484-4377

Hiking with Your Dog

The American Dog Packing Assn
Dave Musikoff
2154 Woodlyn Rd
Pasadena, CA 91104
818 798-3912

Holistic Veterinarians

This approach to health involves the consideration of everything that affects the patient's well-being, including lifestyle, environment, diet and exercise. This approach treats the causes as well as the symptoms of the ailment.

Dog Owners Guide

American Holistic Veterinary
Medical Association
2214 Old Emmorton Rd.
Bel Air, MD 21014
410 569-0795

Dr. Stephen Blake DVM, CVA
9888 Carmel Mountain Rd.
San Diego, CA
619 484-3490

House Calls, Veterinarian

Dr. Gay Dorius
619 274-7005

Jane Meier
619 475-6237

Humane Societies

Provides the following services: shelter and adoption for homeless animals, investigates reports of animal cruelty, abuse and neglect, rescues animals whose lives are threatened or in danger, educates people about animal needs and offers pet visitations to many institutions.

San Diego County Humane Societies

San Diego County
Humane Society
887 Sherman St.
San Diego, CA 92110
619 299-7012
Fee: $48 & up (Seniors Free)

Rancho Coastal
Humane Society
389 Requeza
Encinitas, CA 92024
619 753-6413

North County Humane
Society & SPCA
2905 San Luis Rey Rd.
Oceanside, CA 92054
619 757-4357

Escondido Humane
Society
3000 Las Palmas Ave.
Escondido, CA 92029
619 745-4363 or
619 745-4362

Los Angeles County Humane Societies

Los Angeles SPCA
5026 W. Jefferson Blvd.
Los Angeles, CA
213 730-5338
Services: Beverly Hills,
Culver City,

So Cal Humane Society
12910 Yukon
Hawthorne, CA
310 676-2839
Services: El Segundo,
Palos Verdes Estates,
Lomita,Lawndale,
Hawthorne, Redondo Beach,
Rancho Palos Verdes
Rolling Hills,Torrance

Pasadena Humane Soc
361S. Raymond St.
Pasadena, CA
818 792-7151
Services: Pasadena, San
Marino, Sierra Madre,
S. Pasadena, Arcadia

Pomona Vly Humane Soc& SPCA
500 Humane Way
Pomona, CA 91766
909 623-9777
Services: Pomona,
Diamond Bar, Laverne, San
Dimas, Clairemont
Chino, Ontario, Montclair
Chino Hills

Golden State Humane Soc
555 Artisa
Long Beach, CA 90805
310 423-8406
Low cost spay & neuter and Vaccinations

San Gabriel Valley Humane Soc
851 E Grand
San Gabriel, CA
818 286-1159
Services: Azusa, Covina
Monrovia, San Gabriel,
W. Covina, Temple Cty

Glendale Humane Soc
717 W. Ivy St.
Glendale, CA
818 242-1128
Services: Glendale

Orange County Humane Societies

Orange County Humane Soc
21632 Newland Street
Huntington Beach, CA
714 536-8480

Golden State Humane Soc
11901 Gilbert
Garden Grove, CA
714 638-8111
Spay & Neuter
& Vaccinations ONLY!

San Bernardino County Humane Societies

Humane Soc of San Bernardino Vly
909 882-2934

Riverside County Humane Societies

Riverside Humane Soc & SPCA
5791 Freemont St.
Riverside 92504
909 688-4340

Humane Soc of the Desert
PO Box 44
Palm Springs, CA 92262
619 320-PETS

Private Shelters

Helen Woodward Animal Center
6461 El Apajo
Rancho Santa Fe, CA
619 756-4117

Animal Adoptions, Humane Education, Pet Encounter Therapy, Meals on Wheels Programs and Boarding. Accepts animals released by owners only. Maximum capacity 40 dogs, usually a waiting list.

Pet Adoptions & Home for Life Shelter

Living Free Animal Sanctuary
54250 Keen Camp Rd.
Mountain Center, CA 92561
909 659-4684

Adoptions, Low Cost Spay Neuter Clinic and Humane Education. Dogs available for adoption are rescued from Riverside Shelters. They do not accept private party animals. The public is invited to walk the dogs and play with the cats on their 140 acre mountain location.

Pet Adoptions and Vaccinations

West End Shelter for Animals
1010 East Mission Blvd.
Ontario, CA 91761
909 947-3519

Identification Suppliers

I D Tags

These companies will register your dog and issue special ID tags that allow them to put finders in touch with owners.

911-Pets Lost Service
1050 W 40th
Chicago, IL 60609
312 890-4911

Petfinders
368 High St.
Athol, NY 12810
800 666-LOST

Pet Find Inc.
P O Box 100
Gresham, OR 97030
800 243-2738

PeTag
800 PETAG-4U

TIP Use an O-ring rather than an S-hook to secure the tag to your pet's collar. There are a lot of dogs in the shelter with empty S-hooks hanging from their collars

ID-Microchip Services & Recovery

Microchip ID's are becoming increasingly common nationwide, but the method is only effective in an area where shelters are committed to using the scanner. Since there is more than one company marketing the method, a microchip might not be reliable if your shelter's scanner does not read the chip you purchased. Some animal organizations are waiting for standardization of scanners and chips before endorsing the method. An ID tag is still the best primary method, the pet is often returned before it gets to the shelter.

Avid Microchip
1 800 336-AVID

Identichip ID & recovery system
717 275-3166

InfoPet Identification System
612 890-2080

ID — Tattooing

Tattooing your dog for identification purposes won't do any good unless you register the tattoo with a national data bank.

National Dog Registry
Box 116
Woodstock, NY 12498
800 NDR-DOGS

U S Found
P O Box 521
Jarrettsville, MD 21084
410 557-7332

Local Dog Tatoo Services

Tattoo a Pet
1625 Emmons Ave.
Brooklyn, NY 11235
800 TATTOOS

ID Pet
Box 2244 Dept D
Norton Hgts,CT 06820

San Diego County

Angie Monteleon
619 443-8944

Ginger Noland
619 276-0564

Georgiann Schneider
619 274-7688

Los Angeles County

Michelle Fresener
818 753-1681

Leon Lewison
310 675-4403

Patricia Gesler
310 633-5766

Kerilyn Campbell
818 986-0654

John White
310 585-0783

Virginia Woodmaney
818 917-6000

Orange County

Lynn Whitehead
714 837-6408

Gloria Coleman
714 531-7650

Riverside County

Pam Jacobs
909 877-2580

Dog Owners Guide

Insurance for Dogs

One reason for getting pet insurance is that it reduces the chances of having to put a dollar value on the life of your pet. Compare each policy in the areas of age of dog, cost per year, coverage limits, deductible, amount paid by policy and look for things NOT covered.

Veterinary Pet Insurance Co.
400 N. Tustin Ave. Suite 375
Santa Ana, CA 92705
800 874-7387 CA

Veterinary Pet Insurance
800 345-6778

Judges

If you are interested in becoming a judge contact:

American Kennel Club
Judges' Department
51 Madison Ave.
New York, NY 10010

or write the parent club of the breed you want to judge

Licensing Info

All dog owners shall apply for and obtain a separate dog license for each dog they own after it is four months old. Fees vary from $10 to $30 per year depending on your locality. Fees are always cheaper for spay/neutered dogs.

In San Diego Co Call:
619 595-4555

In Orange Co Call
714 935-6300

Los Angeles County Call
213 730-5300

Lobby Groups

Responsible Dog Owners Assoc.
242 Chapman Rd.
Doylestown, PA 18901
215 249-1370

Cal Fed of Dog Clubs
Vern Johnson
714 731-6428

Lure Coursing

American Sighthound
Field Assoc.
2108 Tranon Ct.
Tallahassee, FL 32308
904 877-6795

AKC Lure Coursing
Director
1235 Pine Grove Rd.
Hanover, PA 17331
717 637-3011 (Day)
717 632-6806 (Night)

Irish Wolfhound Hunt Club
Chino, CA
Dixie Hirsch
714 649-2770

So Cal Whippet Assoc.
Riverside, CA
Cheryl Smith
909 699-0856

Cal Coursing Assoc
Pam Roberts
18481 Roberts Rd.
Woodcrest, CA 92508

Mo Aiken, Open Field
714 961-0413

Local Judges

Lyndell Ackerman
Riverside, CA
909 780-5872

George Martin
Garden Grove, CA
714 636-1798

Howard Lowell
Hesperia, CA
619 334-9354

Michael Hussey
Parris, CA
909 943-6908

Ann Billups
818 963-1038

Coleen Sayre
805 497-7305

Magazines

Ask your national or local breed club for a recommendation on pure
bred publications.

Dog Fancy
Subscription Dept
PO Box 53264
Boulder, CO 80323-3264

Front & Finish
The Dog Trainers News
P O Box 333
Galesburg, IL 61601

Gun Dog
P O Box 35098
Des Moines, IA 50315
515 243-2472

Hunting Retriever
United Kennel Club
Kalamazoo, MI 49001
212 696-8333

Hound Dog Magazine
P O Box 20
Holly Hill, FL 32117-0020
616 343-9020

The Gazette
American Kennel Club
51 Madison Ave.
New York, NY 10010

Dog Owners Guide

Schutzhund Magazine
DVG America
PO Drawer P
Stanford, FL 32772

Off-Lead
P O Box 307
Graves Road
Westmoreland, NY 13490

Dog Watch
11331 Ventura Blvd. #301
Studio City, CA 91604

Sighthound Review
PO Box 30430
Santa Barbara, CA
93130
805 966-7270

DogWorld
PO Box 6500
Chicago, IL 60680
800 247-8080

Memorials, Pet

Anderson Pet Memorials
207 Park Ave.
Carrollton, KY 41008
502 732-5860

Photo Pet Urns
909 627-3739

Pet Monuments
PO Box 995-A
Barre, VT 05641
802 454-1050

MLB International Urns
1 800 858-8767

Obedience Clubs

Obedience Club of San Diego
Dennis VanSikle
619 443-2827

All Breed OC San Diego
Esther Jones
619 287-2211

Valley Hills OC Conoga Pk
Loretta Greenberg
818 998-6644

Orange Empire DC Fontana
Gary Williamson
909 882-3119

Pasanita OC Pasadena
The Rayburns
818 797-7070

Santa Ana Valley KC
John & Maureen Tomlinson
714 897-2685

Hidden Valley OC
Mark Guinto, Pres.
619 259-5307

Southwest OC of LA
Mary Fry
310 923-7807

West Los Angeles OTC
Rex Mincheff
310 474-2649

Hollywood DOC LA
Daphne Bell
213 257-5127

LA Poodle OC
Doris A Schlicht
818 445-0323

K-9 OC
Linda Zapp
805 527-8327

De Anza DOC, Riverside
Margaret Paulin
714 688-0224

Downey OC, Downey
Margie Grissom
310 806-1277

High Desert OC, Lancaster
Bill Fisher
805 266-7097

Lakewood OC, Long Bch
Virginia Lee Dulin
310 421-1671

Lompoc OC, Santa Maria
Tom Freeman
805 925-3360

Los Padres OC, Snta Brba
Ray Gates
805 967-9390

Orthopedic

Orthopedic Foundation For Animals (OFA)
2300 Nifong Blvd
Columbia, MO 65201

Pedigree Service

Canine Pedigree Service
Rt 2, Box 168 Tally-Ho Rd.
Glyndon, MN 56547
218 498-2775

Pet Sitting

Look for a licensed, bonded and mature pet sitter who can provide references. Pets are generally happiest if they can stay at home, provided you can find someone responsible to take care of them. Professional services will come to your home and some will take care of your plants, mail, newspapers, as well as your pets.

Things They Should Know Before You Go
Where you can be reached in case of emergency
The name of your veterinarian

Payment arrangements in case of a medical emergency

Feeding, exercise and any medication instructions
What to do in case the pet becomes lost

National Association of
Professional Pet Sitters
1200 "G" St NW
Washington, DC 20005
800 296-PETS

Pet Sitters Assoc.
of Southern California
210 Marywood
Claremont, CA 91711
800 246-PETS

Good Buddies Home Pet Care
Clair Newick/ Lisa Bivens
619 453-6857 La Jolla Area
619 630-4301 North Co. Area

Critters Content
Mary Beth Gedeon
619 794-4086 Del Mar

Professional Pet Photography

Take photos of your dog in a three quarter pose facing the camera. Dark breeds should have a light background and light or parti-colored pets need a solid dark background. Make sure it looks its best. It may be a good idea to place a picture in with your veterinary medical records. And you may need a picture for flyers if your dog is lost

Photography by Karryn
1 800 7PET-PIX

Shirley Isaacs
714 838-3687

Harvey Branman
818 504-2684

Focus On Pet
619 967-9120

Easy To Spot
805 252-6303

Poison Control

National Animal Control
Poison Center
University of Illinois
24 hour Hotline ($30)
1 800 548-2423
1 900 680-0000 ($20 min)

Poison Control Hotline
1 800 876-4766 SD
1 800 544-4404 LA

Psychic for Pets

Sue Goodrich
1205 Bear Valley Parkway
Escondido, CA 92027
619 480-2474

Lydia Hiby
909 789-0330

Rabies Vaccination Clinics

San Diego County
Veterinary Medical Association
619 461-4523

Orange County
714 497-3552

Los Angeles County
310 948-2211

So Cal Vet Assoc
714 523-0980

Registries, Dog

American Kennel Club
51 Madison Avenue
New York, NY 10010
212 696-8200 Main,
919 233-9767 Registration
212 696-8245 Library
212 696-8226 Gazette Subscription
919 233-9767 Customer Services

Canadian Kennel Club
100-89 Skyway Ave.
Etobicoke, ONT
Canada, M9W 6R4

United Kennel Club.
100 E. Kilgore Rd.
Kalamazoo, MI 49001-
5592
616 343-9020

Federation Canofila
Mexicana AC
Apartado Postal 22-535
14000 Mexico DF
905 655-1600

Rare Breeds
American Rare Breed Assoc
P O Box 76426
Washington, DC 20011
202 722-1232

Mixed Breeds
The American Mixed Breed Obedience Registration
205 1st Street SW
New Prague,MN 56071
612 758-4598 or local Kristen Hurley 714 523-8202

Research

This organization helps coordinate and provide funding for researchers throughout the nation who are attempting to improve veterinary care for pets and wild animals.

Morris Animal Foundation
45 Inverness Dr.
Englewood, CO 80112-5480
303 790-2345

Rescue/ Adoption Referral Organizations

San Diego County

Abandon Animal Rescue Fndn
(AARF) 619 753-3091

Foundation for the Care of
Indigent Animals
619 466-0426 or 466-9137

Animal Rescue Team
(A-TEAM) 619 789-9659

Dog Owners Guide

Orange County

Animal Assist League of OC
714 978-7387 (Ref)

Animal Rescue Foundation
714 240-2899 (Dana Point Only)

Pet ProLife

Los Angeles County

Actors and Others for Animals
818 985-6263

Adopt A Pet
818 703-0903

Pet Orphans
818 901-0190

Amanda Foundation
310 472-1742

Pet Adoption Fund
818 340-1687 or
818 996-4049

St Anthony Canine Rescue
Arleen 310 830-8126 &
Jane 213 654-5848

CARE
818 347-1323

Friends For Pets
818 701-0674

Friends of Animals
310 396-2664

HART
805 524-4542

Pet Rescue Assoc
818 845-6222, 767-4400

Riverside County

Save-A-Pet
909 781-6319

Ventura County

Adopt A Pet
805 527-8238

National Rescue Groups

Project Breed
202 244-0065

Operation Greyhound
619 588-6611

Greyhound Pets of America
Darren Rigg
President & Founder
800 366-1472

Baja, Mexico

Friends of Bajas Animals
Ellen Tousley
619 291-9223

Runs, Dogs

American Fence Co.
1076 Grand Ave.
San Marcos, CA
619 744-4124

San Marino Pool & Patio
818 795-4386

Tamarack Custom Cage
P O Box 1086
Perris, CA 92370
909 657-6094

S / S Dog Runs
800 700-9152

Semen Bank

International Canine Semen Bank
2611 W Northern Ave.
Phoenix, AZ 85051
602 995-0460

North County Fertility &
Veterinary Clinic
Dr. Stockner
619 739-1091

Service Dogs

These are dogs that are trained to help the disabled. Support Teams for Independence and Canine Companions for Independence are local organizations that are always looking for puppy raisers. All these organizations rely on financial contributions. Call to see how you can help:

Canine Companions for
Independence
P O Box 446
Santa Rosa, CA 95401
707 528-0830
Rancho Santa Fe Site
619 756-1012

Paws with a Cause
1-800-253-PAWS

Support Teams for Independence
Perris, CA 92572
909 943-3972

Schutzhund

United Schutzhund
Club of America
3704 Lemoy Ferry Rd.
St. Louis, MO 63125
314 638-9686

Golden State Schutzhund
Chuck Buehler
714 633-8517

San Diego Schutzhund
John McKinney
619 789-4494

Landersverband DVG
America Inc.
Sandi Nethercutt
113 Vickie Dr
Del City, OK 73115
405 672-3947

San Diego Diensthund
Maurice Bullock
619 264-1796

West Hills WDA
June Lamb
818 246-6287

Big West
619 956-3647

Mildred & Leo Muller
Coast SC 909 350-8730

Sledding Clubs

Glenda Walling
7118 N Beehive Rd.
Pocatello, ID 83201
208 234-1608

Donna Hawley
P O Box 446
Norman, ID 83848-0446
208 443-3153

Spay/ Neuter (Low Cost) Directory

In 1991 California housed 493,000 dogs in 217 shelters. Of these:

296,000 or 60% were killed,
94,000 dogs or 19% were claimed by owner
103,000 or 21% of the dogs were adopted.
Call:

San Diego County

Pet Assistance Foundation
619 745-7986 North SD Co
619 697-PETS South SD Co

Spay Neuter Action Proj
619 748-3412 (SNAP)

Friends of Co Animal Shelter
619 454-4484 (FOCAS)

Mercy Crusade
619 278-1745

Orange County

Golden State Humane Soc
714 638-8111

United Humanitarians
714 894-4016

Animal Assistance League
of Orange County
714 978-7387 (Rep)

Los Angeles County

Pet Assistance Foundation
213 937-5204 LA City
818 709-0900 The SF Valley
818 330-1983 San Gabriel
310 372-9593 South Bay
310 920-1216 Long Beach
805 259-1578 Santa Clarita

Mercy Crusade
818 782-1495

Golden State Humane Soc
310 423-8406

New Hope for Animals
213 463-8572

Actors /Others for Animals
818 985-6263

Doris Day Foundation
818 352-8993

B A R C- Redlands
909 389-9552

Precious Life
818 348-6093

Friends of Long Beach AS
310 491-0280

San Bernardino/ Riverside

B A R C
909 797-2072

Pet Assistance
909 782-4742

Friendship For Animals
909 780-7711

Riverside Co Referrals
909 358-4495

Rancho Cucamonga
Friendship for Animals
909 980-7711

Ventura

Pet Assistance Foundation
805 583-6143

Spay/ Neuter Network
805 646-7849

Search & Rescue

Canine Search & Rescue (SAR) units are involved in using dogs to find lost people in various situations including wilderness, disaster, water, avalanche and urban situations. The different types of training are air-scenting, tracking/ trailing and water rescue work. National units such as the U. S. Disaster Dog Team are on ready status awaiting calls by local fire, police and emergency personnel.

Nat Assoc Search & Rescue
PO Box 3709
Fairfax, VA 22308

SAR Dog Alert
PO Box 39
Somerset, CA 95684

Orange Co Sheriff
Search & Rescue Reserve
Larry Harris
1807 Highland Dr.
Newport Beach,CA92660
714 665-1612

California Rescue Dog
Assoc.
Shirley Hammond
1062 Metro Circle
Palo Alto, CA 94303
415 856-9669

Sporting Equipment

For items like Jumps, Tunnels, Dog Walks, A Frames, Teeter Totters etc.

Action K-9 Sports Equipment Co.
707 F East 4th St.
Perris, CA 92570
714 657-0227

Stationery

Stationery or note pads with computerized scan of your pet's photo.
Personalized Products
1180 Sidonia Court
Encinitas, CA 92024
619 633-4834

Superintendents of Dog Shows

Jack Bradshaw
P O Box 7303
Los Angeles, CA 90022
213 727-0136
213 727-2949 (FAX)

Note: Entries close 3 weeks in advance of the event.

Temperament Testing

American Temperament Test Society
314 225-5346

Therapy Dogs

The following is a list of organizations that take pets to visit the
elderly in day care centers and nursing homes. These groups believe
that the well-being of the elderly and the disabled is enhanced by the
company of pets.

The Delta Society, through its pet partners program, offers accredita-
tion to volunteers and their pets in a national network of animal
visitation programs.

Delta Society
P O Box 1080
Renton, Washington 98057
206 226-7357

Therapy Dogs Inc.
Ann Butrick
2416 East Fox Farm Rd.
Cheyenne, WY 82007
307 638-3223

C. A. M. P.
714 896-0062

Therapy Dogs Int'l
91 Wiman Ave.
Staten Island,NY 10308
718 317-5804

Helen Woodward
Animal Center
6461 El Apajo
Rancho Santa Fe, CA
619 756-3791

Therapy Dog International
260 Fox Chase Rd
Chester, NJ 07930

Check with your local Humane Society or Animal Control agency
for other local organizations.

Tracking Tests

American Kennel Club
51 Madison Ave.
New York, NY 10010
212 696-8286

United Kennel Club
100 E Kilgore Rd.
Kalamazoo, MI 49001-
5592
616 343-9020

Gus Paul (San Diego)
619 453-0690
Nick Hammond
714 629-6374

Betty Regan
714 982-1238

Trainers Organizations

North America Dog
Obedience Instructors (NADOI)
Lonnie Morgan, President
810 655-4129

Trainers

Canine Learning Centers
619 931-1834
San Diego + North Co.

Connie Jankowski
Fountain Valley, CA
714 962-2699

Kimberly Flowers
818 339-8301

Sue Myles
714 272-1630

ABC Dog Training
Robert Penny
818 355-6191

Michele Sanfilippo
310 425-2681

Marla Quincy
909 672-4192

Roger Bortz
714 641-9280

Camp Canine
310 372-1980 Clark

The Tender Tudor
213 254-1520 Sandra

Julie Strauss
818 891-0175

Rainy Kemp
714 646 1163

Ron Berman
310 376-0620

Carole Schatz
619 460-3647

Daniel Tambourine
714 777-8246

Mona Webb
310 559-2321

Bob Burkhardt
619 748-7943

Dog Owners Guide

Travel

Hotel & Motel Guides

Send for:
Touring with Towser ($3)
Quaker Professional Services
585 Hawthorne Court
Galesburg, IL 61401

Vacationing W/ Your Pet
Pet-Friendly Pub ($14.95)
1 800 496-2665

Transportation Services

Some pet sitters provide transportation to and from the airport.

Pet Transfer
714 660-9390

World Wide Pet Shipping
818 448-6143

Travel Regulations for Pets

Prepared by ASPCA Send $4 to:

"Traveling with your Pet"
The American Society for the
Prevention of Cruelty to Animals
Education Dept.
441 East 92nd St.
New York, NY 10128

Travel Safety for Dogs

Do-It
Bud Brownhill
2147 Avon Circle
Anaheim, CA 92804
714 776-9970

Veterinary Assoc.& Referrals

American Animal
Hospital Assoc
P O Box 150899
Denver, CO 80215-0899
800 252-2242

American Veterinary
Medical Assoc
930 N Meacham Rd.
Schaumburg, IL 60196
1 800 248-2862

San Diego County
Veterinary Medical Assoc
7590 El Cajon Blvd.
La Mesa, CA 92041
619 466-3400

Southern California
Veterinary Medical
8338 Rosemead Blvd
Pico Rivera, CA 90660
310 948-4979

Video Tapes

Sirius Puppy Training
Dr. Ian Dunbar
Center for Applied Animal Behavior
2140 Shattuck Ave. #2406
Berkeley, CA 94704
510 658-8588

Volunteers

These non-profit organizations provide foster care and homes for pets; donate resources and supplies to help shelters run ads in local newspapers for found pets; assist the needy with impound fees and medical fees. Also, they assist at the shelters with fostering, animal care, pet-assisted therapy, mobile pet adoptions, humane education and fundraising projects. Some also have a thrift shop or antique shop that needs volunteers.

Contact your local Humane Society, Animal Control or:

SNAP
(Spay/Neuter Action Project)
619 748-3412

FOCAS (Friends of
County Animal Shelter)
619 454-4484 San Diego

Animal Assistance League
714 978-7387
714 760-6193

Save-A-Pet
909 781-6319

Friends of Mission Viejo Sltr
714 492-1617

Friends of San Clemente
714 348-2045

Washes, Do-It-Yourself

Poochies
619 541-2525

My Beautiful Dog-O-Matt
619 295-6140

Dog Beach Dog Wash
619 523-1700

Weight Pulling

International Weight Pull Assoc
310 364-1214

Wills

Pets' right to live declaration defines pet owners' specific wishes should something happen where you would be unable to provide care for your pet. To order the four copies of the document and guidelines, send a $12.50 donation to:

Muttmatchers
PO Box 920
Fillmore, CA 93016
805 524-4542

Index

A

accidental breeding 2-4, 12, 57

activity v, 2, 11, 19, 52, 60, 63, 66, 85-95

acupuncture 163

adoption
  adopting a dog from the shelter 49-51
    advantages 49
    disadvantages 49
  organizations 143-149
  seniors 164

Affenpinscher
  AKC popularity ranking 8
  breeders 97
  cautions 152
  club 97
  rescue 143

Afghan Hound 9, 93
  AKC popularity ranking 7
  breeders 97
  cautions 152
  club 97
  rescue 143

aggression 36, 43, 56, 67

agility 93
  clubs 164
  training 91

aging 19, 59, 61, 66, 85

aging dogs — see older dogs

AIDS/HIV assistance dogs 164

Airedale Terrier
  AKC popularity ranking 6
  breeders 98
  cautions 152
  club 98
  rescue 143

airline travel 81
  airline-approved crate 81

AKC (American Kennel Club)
  approved breeding standard 13
  early-age spay/neutering 4
  Good Citizenship Test 3, 75-76
  papers 13-15
  Popularity Ranking 1993 5-8

Akita
  AKC popularity ranking 6
  breeders 98
  cautions 152
  club 98
  rescue 143

Alaskan Malamute
  AKC popularity ranking 6
  breeders 99
  cautions 152
  club 99
  rescue 143

all-breed clubs 164-166

allergic reaction 1, 73

American Eskimo dogs
  AKC popularity ranking 6
  breeders 99
  cautions 152
  club 99
  rescue 143

American Foxhound
  AKC popularity ranking 8
  breeders 99
  cautions 156
  club 99
  rescue 145

American Kennel Club — See AKC

American Staffordshire Terrier
  AKC popularity ranking 7
  breeders 99
  cautions 152
  club 99
  rescue 143

American Veterinary Medical
  Association (AVMA) 4

American Water Spaniel
  AKC popularity ranking 7
  breeders 100
  cautions 152
  club 100
  rescue 143

Anatolian Shepherd
  breeders 100
  club 100
  rescue 143

animal abuse hotline 166

animal agent for film, TV & ads 166

animal control 19, 66, 76, 80, 166-171

animal welfare groups 171
animals in unattended vehicles law 78
apartments for pets 171
artificial insemination 172
artists, dog 172
Association of American Feed Control
    Officials (AAFCO) 61
attorney (animal rights) 78, 172
Australian Cattle Dog
    AKC popularity ranking 6
    breeders 100
    cautions 152
    club 100
    rescue 143
Australian Shepherds
    AKC popularity ranking 6
    breeders 100
    cautions 153
    club 100
    rescue 143
Australian Terrier
    AKC popularity ranking 7
    breeders 101
    cautions 153
    club 101
    rescue 143

B

backpack for dogs 172
backyard boredom 42, 47
barking 1, 36, 39, 44-45, 51, 52, 65, 75, 77
Basenji
    AKC popularity ranking 6
    breeders 101
    cautions 153
    club 101
    rescue 143
basic obedience classes 30, 35, 199
Basset Hound 9, 92
    AKC popularity ranking 5
    breeders 101
    cautions 153
    club 101
    rescue 143
bathing 57, 67, 72
beaches 64, 85-86
Beagle 9, 92
    AKC popularity ranking 5
    breeders 102
    cautions 153
    club 102
    rescue 143
Bearded Collie
    AKC popularity ranking 7
    breeders 102
    cautions 153
    club 102
    rescue 143
Beauceron
    breeders 102
    club 102
Bedlington Terrier
    AKC popularity ranking 8
    breeders 102
    cautions 153
    club 102
    rescue 144
bee stings 64
behavior problems 2, 3, 25, 32, 35-47, 49, 50
behaviorists 3, 33, 35-47, 52, 75, 172
Belgian Malinois
    AKC popularity ranking 7
    breeders 102
    cautions 153
    club 102
    rescue 144
Belgian Sheepdog
    AKC popularity ranking 7
    breeders 103
    cautions 153
    club 103
    rescue 144
Belgian Tervuren
    AKC popularity ranking 7
    breeders 103
    cautions 153
    club 103
    rescue 144
bereavement 67-68
    counseling 173
Bernese Mountain Dog
    AKC popularity ranking 7
    breeders 103
    cautions 153
    club 103
    rescue 144
Bichon Frise
    AKC popularity ranking 6
    breeders 103
    cautions 153
    club 103
    rescue 144
biological value 60
biting 20, 43, 65-66, 78
    dog bite laws 78
Black and Tan Coonhound
    AKC popularity ranking 8
    breeders 103
    cautions 153
    club 103
    rescue 144

Dog Owners Guide

rescue 146
Italian Greyhound
   AKC popularity ranking 6
   breeders 121
   cautions 157
   club 121
   rescue 146

J

Jack Russell Terrier
   AKC popularity ranking 8
   breeders 122
   cautions 157
   club 122
   rescue 146
Japanese Chin
   AKC popularity ranking 7
   breeders 122
   cautions 157
   club 122
   rescue 146
judges 88, 94, 174, 188
jumping up 45
junior showmanship 89

K

Keeshond
   AKC popularity ranking 6
   breeders 122
   cautions 157
   club 122
   rescue 146
Kerry Blue Terrier
   AKC popularity ranking 7
   breeders 123
   cautions 157
   club 123
   rescue 146
Komondor
   AKC popularity ranking 8
   breeders 123
   cautions 157
   club 123
   rescue 146
Kuvaszok
   AKC popularity ranking 7
   breeders 123
   cautions 158
   club 123
   rescue 146

L

Labrador Retriever
   AKC popularity ranking 5
   breeders 123
   cautions 158

club 123
rescue 146
Lakeland Terrier
   AKC popularity ranking 8
   breeders 124
   cautions 158
   club 124
   rescue 146
laws about dogs 76-78
leadership 23-24, 28, 29, 35, 36, 49
lemon law 76
Leonberger
   breeders 124
   club 124
leptospirosis 15, 20, 70
Lhasa Apso 5
   breeders 124
   cautions 158
   club 124
   rescue 146
liability insurance 78, 159
licensing 1, 76, 83, 188
   license required 76
life expectancy 66
limited registration 14
litter 3, 12-16, 23, 40, 56
lobby groups 188
lost & found 79-80
low-cost spay & neuter 3, 185, 186,
   196-197
lure 25-29
lure coursing 88, 89, 93-94, 189
lure/reward 25-29
Lyme disease 73

M

Maltese
   AKC popularity ranking 5
   breeders 124
   cautions 158
   club 124
   rescue 146
Manchester Terrier
   AKC popularity ranking 7
   breeders 125
   cautions 158
   club 125
   rescue 146
Mastiff
   AKC popularity ranking 6
   breeders 125
   cautions 158
   club 125
   rescue 146
Mastiff, Neopolitan

210

temperature 55, 62, 63, 78, 81-82
ten do's & don'ts for children's safety 20-21
ten items for the canine travel kit 83
ten questions you should ask a potential trainer 30-31
ten things a dog asks of its family v
ten things quality breeders do 13-14
ten things to do if your dog is lost 79-80
terriers 9, 57, 176
things to consider before deciding on a new dog 1-2
Tibetan Spaniel
  AKC popularity ranking 7
  breeders 139
  cautions 160
  club 139
  rescue 148
Tibetan Terrier
  AKC popularity ranking 7
  breeders 139
  cautions 160
  club 139
  rescue 148
tick removal 59
ticks 59, 69, 71, 73, 87
title terminology 89
tone of voice v, 24, 26, 29, 32, 54
Tosa, Japanese
  breeders 139
  club 139
  rescue 148
toy breeds 9
Toy Fox Terrier
  breeders 139
  club 139
  rescue 148
Toy Manchester Terrier
  AKC popularity ranking 7
  breeders 125
  cautions 158
  club 125
  rescue 146
tracking tests 88, 92, 199
trainers 3, 25, 30-31, 40, 52, 94, 199
training 1-4, 17, 23-33, 37-47, 51-54, 75, 86, 90, 91, 197, 199, 201
  tips 31-33
transportation 62
  airlines 81, 82
  law 77
  services 200
travel 81-83, 200
  car 63, 82
treats 25-29, 38, 43, 51, 52

types of breeders
  accidental breeder 12
  backyard breeder 12
  commercial kennel 12
  hobby breeder 12
  pet shop dealer 13
  puppy mill 12

U

unclaimed pets 80
unplanned litters 3, 14
urination, excitement/submissive 46
utility 88

V

vaccinations 2, 15, 19, 20, 25, 35, 50, 64, 66, 70, 73, 83, 86, 176, 185, 186, 192
veterinarian 25, 50, 51, 58, 62, 64, 69-74, 81, 82, 173, 191, 200
  complaints 175
  holistic 183
  house calls 184
vitamins for dogs 19, 60, 61
Vizsla
  AKC popularity ranking 6
  breeders 139
  cautions 160
  club 139
  rescue 148
voice, tone v, 24, 26, 29, 32, 54
von Willebrand disease (VWD) 13, 151

W

weight pulling 201
Weimaraner
  AKC popularity ranking 6
  breeders 139
  cautions 161
  club 139
  rescue 148
Welsh Springer Spaniel
  AKC popularity ranking 7
  breeders 138
  cautions 161
  club 138
West Highland White Terrier
  AKC popularity ranking 6
  breeders 140
  cautions 161
  club 140
  rescue 148
what you can do to solve pet overpopulation 2-4

FREE PUPPY EXAM

Directions:

1. Fill out Coupon
2. Call a participating veterinarian hospital and schedule an appointment
3. Present coupon at your scheduled appointment and receive a **FREE** physical exam

Name: _____

Address: _____

City, St, Zip: _____

Phone: _____

Veterinarian: _____

Hospital or Clinic
Stamp Here

Puppies no older than 16 weeks. This offer does not include fecal testing, deworming, vaccinations or any other laboratory testing.

For Veterinarian Office Only: Please stamp and mail coupon to address on other side of this form.

CANINE LEARNING CENTER PUBLISHING

Canine Learning Center
PO Box 2010
Carlsbad, CA 92018

FREE PUPPY EXAM
PARTICIPATING VETERINARY HOSPITAL LOCATIONS

SAN DIEGO COUNTY

Bonita
Bonita Pet Hospital
3438 Bonita Rd.
619 427-2233

Cardiff
Cardiff Animal Hospital
2159 San Elijo Ave.
619 436-3215

Carlsbad
El Camino Veterinary Hospital
2505 South Vista Way
619 729-3330

Carmel Mountain
Carmel Mountain Ranch
Veterinary Hospital
11925 Carmel Mountain Rd.
619 592-9779

Clairemont
Ark Animal Hospital
6171 Balboa Ave.
619 277-3665

Del Mar
All Creatures Hospital
3665 Via De La Valle
619 481-7992

El Cajon
Broadway Animal Hospital
380 Broadway
619 444-1166

Encinitas
North Coast Veterinary Group
285 N. El Camino Real #105
619 632-1072

Fallbrook
Avacado Veterinary Hospital
1111 E. Mission Rd.
619 728-5771

Imperial Beach
Imperial Beach Pet Hospital
538 12th St.
619 424-3961

Kearny Mesa
Animal Medical Clinic
5610 Kearny Mesa Rd. #A
619 278-1825

La Costa
La Costa Animal Hospital
7750-G El Camino Real
619 944-1266

La Jolla
The Animal Hospital of La Jolla
7601 Draper Ave.
619 459-2665

La Jolla
Nautilus Veterinary Clinic
6911 La Jolla Blvd.
619 454-0354

La Mesa
El Cerrito Veterinary Hospital
6911 University Ave.
619 466-0533

Lemon Grove
San Diego Pet Hospital
7368 Broadway #A
619 462-6600

Mira Mesa
Center Veterinary Clinic
8977 Mira Mesa Blvd.
619 271-1152

Oceanside
Mission Animal Hospital
3308 Mission Ave.
619 433-3763

FREE PUPPY EXAM
PARTICIPATING VETERINARY HOSPITAL LOCATIONS

Oceanside
Rancho Del Oro Veterinary
Hospital
4093 Oceanside Blvd.
619 945-0606

Pacific Beach
A B C Veterinary Hospital
2032 Hornblend
619 270-2368

Point Loma
Cabrillo Veterinary Hospital
4138 Voltaire St.
619 225-9684

Poway
Animal Medical Hospital of
Poway
14031 Poway Rd.
619 748-5989

Rancho Bernardo
Westwood Bernardo Veterinary
Clinic
11605 Duenda Rd. #D
619 485-7570

San Marcos
Family Pets Medical Center
997 W. San Marcos Blvd.
619 744-7559

Tierrasanta
Tierrasanta Veterinary Hospital
10799 Tierrasanta Blvd.
619 292-6116

University City
Governor Animal Clinic
3218 Governor Dr.
619 453-6312

LOS ANGELES COUNTY

Agoura Hills
VCA Agoura Meadows
Veterinary Clinic
5605 Kanan Rd.
818 889-0810

Alhambra
VCA Mission Animal Hospital
25 West Mission Rd.
818 289-3643

Bellflower
VCA Lakewood Animal Hospital
17801 Lakewood Blvd.
310 633-8126

Burbank
VCA Animal Hospital
2723 W. Olive Ave.
818 845-7246

Covina
Cypress Avenue Animal Hospital
1400 E. Cypress St.
818 331-0775

Culver City
Culver City Animal Hospital
5830 W. Washington Blvd.
310 836-4551

Encino
Encino Veterinary Clinic
17009 Ventura Blvd.
818 783-7387

Glendale
Arden Animal Hospital
407 West Arden Ave.
818 246-2478

Harbor City
Animal Clinic West
23820 S. Western Ave.
310 534-0315

Inglewood
Ber-Mar Pet Hospital
349 E. Florence Ave.
310 677-9187

FREE PUPPY EXAM
PARTICIPATING VETERINARY HOSPITAL LOCATIONS

Long Beach
Blue Cross Dog & Cat Hospital
2665 E. Pacific Coast Hwy
310 494-0975

Long Beach
Magnolia Animal Hospital
1749 Magnolia Ave.
310 435-6331

Los Angeles
VCA Animal Hospital West
2106 Sepulveda Blvd.
310 477-6735

Los Angeles
VCA West L.A. Animal Hospital
1818 S. Sepulveda Blvd.
310 473-2951

Manhattan Beach
Bay Animal Hospital
1801 Sepulveda Blvd.
310 545-6596

Monrovia
VCA Santa Anita Animal Hospital
245 W. Duarte Rd.
818 359-3281

Northridge
Porter Pet Hospital
18224 Parthenia St.
818 349-8387

Pacific Palisades
Blue Cross Pet Hospital
15239 La Cruz Dr.
310 454-2633

Pasadena
VCA Teresita Animal Hospital
2695 E. Foothill Blvd.
818 792-5143

Rancho Palos Verdes
Animal Clinic of Golden Cove ·
31236 Palos Verdes Dr. W.
310 377-7804

Rosemead
Community Animal Hospital
8338 Valley Blvd.
818 573-2650

San Gabriel
Temple City Animal Hospital
5406 N. Rosemead Blvd.
818 287-1173

San Pedro
Rolling Hills Animal Hospital
28916 S. Western Ave.
310 831-1209

Santa Fe Springs
La Mirada Animal Hospital
13914 E. Rosecrans Blvd.
310 921-3539

Sepulveda
Adler Veterinary Group Inc.
16911 Roscoe Blvd.
818 893-6366

Torrance
Clarmar Animal Hospital
20805 Hawthorne Blvd.
310 371-2474

Torrance
Country Hills Animal Hospital
2919 Rolling Hills Rd.
310 539-3851

Torrance
Crenshaw Animal Hospital
24260 Crenshaw
310 373-4190

West Hollywood
VCA Robertson Blvd. Animal
Hospital
656 N. Robertson Blvd.
310 659-2260

Whittier
Whittier Dog & Cat Hospital
12124 Philadelphia St.
310 698-0264

FREE PUPPY EXAM
PARTICIPATING VETERINARY HOSPITAL LOCATIONS

Woodland Hills

VCA Parkwood Animal Hospital
6330 Fallbrook Ave.
818 884-5506

ORANGE COUNTY

Anaheim
VCA Ana-Brook Animal Hospital
335 N. Brookhurst St.
714 772-8220

Corona Del Mar
Corona Del Mar Animal Hospital
2948 E. Coast Hwy
714 644-8160

Costa Mesa
Newport Harbor Animal Hospital
125 Mesa Drive
714 631-1030

Dana Point
Golden Lantern Animal Hospital
33282 St. Golden Lantern
714 248-1172

El Toro
Arroyo Pet Clinic
22421 El Toro Rd. #B
714 770-1808

Fountain Valley
Westhaven Veterinary Hospital
16161 Brookhurst St.
714 775-5544

Fullerton
Commonwealth Animal Hospital
1941 W. Commonwealth #A
714 525-2355

Garden Grove
Garden Grove Dog & Cat Hospital
10822 Garden Grove Blvd.
714 537-8800

Huntington Beach
Animal Hospital of Huntington
Beach
15021 Edwards St.
714 898-0568

Huntington Beach
Warner West Pet Clinic
6819 Warner Ave.
714 847-9617

Irvine
Northwood Animal Hospital
13925 Yale Ave. #115
714 559-1992

Irvine
Woodbridge Hospital for Animals
34 Creek Rd.
714 786-0990

Laguna Hills
Laguna Hills Animal Hospital
24271 El Toro Rd.
714 837-7333

Laguna Niguel
Aliso Viejo Animal Hospital
24038 Aliso Creek Rd.
714 643-0437

Los Alamitos
VCA Rossmoor - El Dorado
Animal Hospital
10832 Los Alamitos Blvd.
310 598-8621

Orange
Orange Pet Care Center
809-813 E. Katella Ave.
714 771-3870

Orange
Orange-Olive Veterinary Hospital
2187 N. Orange-Olive Rd.
714 998-1510

San Clemente
San Clemente Veterinary Hospital
1833 S. El Camino Real
714 492-5777

FREE PUPPY EXAM
PARTICIPATING VETERINARY HOSPITAL LOCATIONS

San Juan Capistrano
Capistrano Veterinary Clinic
31401 Camino Capistrano
714 496-3731

Santa Ana
Foothill Veterinary Hospital
2130 N. Tustin Ave.
714 541-6671

Santa Ana
Bristol Veterinary Clinic
3713 S. Bristol
714 979-3080

South Laguna Beach
South Laguna Village Animal
Hospital
31742 Pacific Coast Hwy
714 499-5378

OTHER SOUTHERN CALIFORNIA COUNTIES

Acton
Acton Veterinary Clinic
32033 Crown Valley Rd.
805 269-7060

Moorpark
Moorpark Veterinary Hospital
484 E. Los Angeles #104
805 529-7003

Ojai
Ojai Pet Hospital
1120 Maricopa Hwy
805 646-5555

Riverside
Victoria Animal Hospital
3400 Arlington Ave.
909 683-7133

Call 619 931-1820 for any late veterinary additions to the free puppy exam program.

ORDER & REORDER FORM

TO: **CANINE LEARNING CENTERS**
P.O. Box 2010
Carlsbad, California 92018
619 931-1820

Enclosed is a check for $_____ for _____ copy(ies) of *Southern California Dog Owners Guide.*

Ship to: _____

Address: _____

City/State/Zip: _____

Telephone: _____

_____ Copies @ $9.95 each (1-7 copies) $_____

_____ Copies @ $5.75 each (minimum 8) $_____

California residents please add 7.75% Sales Tax $_____

Shipping charge ($3.50 for 1-10 books; $5.00 for 11+) $_____

TOTAL $_____

SPECIAL OFFER FOR BREEDERS:
Help educate new puppy owners by offering a free book with each adoption. You save 40% and will provide your new owner with a Free Puppy Exam.

NEW & REVISED LISTINGS & SUGGESTIONS

We would like to receive your feedback on how to improve this publication. Anyone wishing to comment is invited to use this form to submit information or to request changes. Also, use this form if any other corrections are necessary. Please fill out the following and mail to:

CANINE LEARNING CENTERS
P.O. Box 2010
Carlsbad, California 92018

Name(s): _____

Old Address: _____

City/State/Zip: _____

Kennel Name: _____

New Address: _____

City/State/Zip: _____

New Telephone Number: _____

Other Comments or Suggestions: _____

_____

_____

_____

_____

_____

_____

IMPORTANT INFORMATION

DOG'S NAME: _____ Date of Birth: ___/___/___

Breed: _____ Sex: _____ Kennel: _____

Breeder's Name: _____ Phone: _____

Sire: _____ DAM: _____

Veterinary Hospital: _____

Veterinarian's Name: _____

Phone #: _____ Emergency Phone: _____

Address: _____

_____ Zip: _____

Insurance Policy No.: _____ Insurance Phone: _____

DATES:	TREATMENT / VACCINATION TYPE: